CREATING CARLETON

Creating Carleton

The Shaping of a University

H. BLAIR NEATBY

DON McEOWN

Published for
Carleton University by
McGill-Queen's University Press
Montreal & Kingston · London · Ithaca

Legal deposit third quarter 2002
Bibliothèque nationale du Québec

Printed in Canada on acid-free paper that is 100% ancient forest free
(100% post-consumer recycled), processed chlorine free.

McGill-Queen's University Press acknowledges the support of the
Canada Council for the Arts for our publishing program. We also
acknowledge the financial support of the Government of Canada
through the Book Publishing Industry Development Program (BPIDP)
for our publishing activities.

Illustrations, except where noted, are courtesy of the Carleton Archives.

National Library of Canada Cataloguing in Publication

Neatby, H. Blair, 1924–
    Creating Carleton: the shaping of a university / H. Blair Neatby,
Don McEown.
    Includes bibliographical references and index.
    ISBN 0-7735-2486-X
    1. Carleton University – History. I. McEown, Donald C. II. Carleton
University. III. Title.
LE3.C42N42 2002   378.713'84   C2002-902337-8

This book was typeset by Dynagram Inc. in 10/13 Sabon

Contents

Illustrations

Introduction

Carleton University in its early years was unique among Ontario universities. The older universities all trace their origins back to the initiative of some religious denomination in the nineteenth century, and those founded after Carleton were all financed in part by money from the provincial government. Carleton, which was founded in 1942, began as a nondenominational college, and it was a private college, financed largely by the students' fees, supplemented by small charitable donations from some of Ottawa's citizens. The Carleton University of today bears no resemblance to this early college. It is now one of some fifteen provincial universities in Ontario. It is a medium-sized institution by comparison with the other Ontario universities, and in many ways it resembles them: its admission requirements, academic programs, and academic standards differ only marginally, and its graduates compete on equal terms with the graduates of the other universities. But these similarities can be misleading. Each university in Ontario is different. Carleton fits into the broad pattern of Ontario universities but it is still unique.

What made Carleton a university and one that, for better or for worse, can be distinguished from other universities? The contributions of Henry Marshall Tory and A. Davidson Dunton were obviously important. Tory can be described as the founder of Carleton College, just as Dunton can be seen as the founder of Carleton University; their commitment, judgment, and energy led to decisions that shaped these institutions. But there are countless others who also have contributed to Carleton's development – as members of the Board of Governors and the Senate, as deans and departmental chairpersons, as members of committees, as teachers and scholars, and as students – so many that only a few are singled out in this story.

The contribution of these individuals, however, is only part of the story. The distinctive identity of Carleton as a college and then as a university has also been shaped by the broader community which supports it and which it serves. Carleton's location in Ottawa has had a formative influence. For many years it tried to take advantage of being close to Parliament Hill in a city of public servants. More recently it has forged links with the high-technology enterprises in the Ottawa region. Carleton did not establish faculties of law or medicine, because the University of Ottawa already had these faculties; but it did found schools of journalism, architecture, and Canadian studies, because there was an anticipated demand for them.

Carleton also serves a wider community than the city of Ottawa and the Ottawa Valley. It became a provincial university, taking advantage of the support offered by provincial governments and adapting to the shifting aims of these governments as they affected higher education. From an even broader perspective, Carleton has been shaped by a social revolution that has transformed postsecondary education in the Western world, with more and more students enrolling in university programs, and with these programs becoming more and more specialized.

The history of Carleton is thus the complex story of individuals making decisions against the backdrop of the pressure of a variety of communities. But it is more than a sequence of decisions. Every university is an institution with its own culture, a culture that to some degree will affect all who are part of the institution. Thus the story of Carleton is also a description of its evolving culture and what it was like to be a professor or a student when Carleton was a college and, later, when it became a university.

The following story begins with Carleton's origins. It then describes the college years, followed by the university years. In each part there are separate chapters dealing with the administrative history and the experience of the professors and students. The story takes Carleton through the dramatic social changes of the 1960s and concludes with an epilogue, which describes how Carleton tried to adapt to the changing social patterns in the decade that followed. So although this is a history of Carleton, it is at the same time a case study of the changes in higher education in Ontario in the postwar years.

CREATING CARLETON

Henry Marshall Tory (1864–1947), president of
Carleton College 1942–47 (Yousuf Karsh)

CHAPTER ONE

Founding a College

According to Henry Marshall Tory, Carleton College had its beginning when he met William Connor by chance on an Ottawa street corner in the fall of 1941. Connor was an Ottawa businessman who was active in many social agencies. The conversation, as Tory recalled it, "turned upon the question of the influx into the city of so many young people, many of whom had been practically forced by circumstances into war work. Could anything be done for them by way of assisting them to continue their education?" Connor mentioned that he had been a member of a YMCA committee that had considered this question just before the war. The two men were convinced that the war made a college even more necessary and agreed that something should be done. Tory suggested as a first step that he should meet with the former members of the committee to discuss what steps might be taken.[1]

Tory was not a modest man. His claim that this chance meeting marked the beginning of Carleton College ignored the earlier efforts of the YMCA committee to establish a college. The work of this committee would provide some guidance, and its members would bring their experience to a renewed project.[2] But there was some merit in Tory's claim. Without his involvement at this stage, the idea of a college would not have been revived. If we must assign a precise beginning to Carleton College, this chance meeting between Connor and Tory would be a good choice.

I

As Connor had mentioned, the committee of the Ottawa YMCA had already discussed the need for a college in the city. The members of the committee were senior civil servants and Ottawa businessmen who felt some personal responsibility for the less fortunate. In an earlier era, they might have been churchgoers undertaking charitable activities as members of a Christian community. In this more secular age, their charities were less sectarian. The members of the community were worried about the future of young men in Ottawa during the Depression, many of whom had ended their formal education and were trapped in jobs that required few skills and offered little hope of advancement. Hugh Keenleyside, a member of the Department of External Affairs and a member of the YMCA executive, suggested that the Y might offer university level courses in the evenings so that young men with ambition could better themselves.[3] It was not a radical suggestion. A number of YMCAs in the United States had been giving academic courses in the evenings for many years. Closer to home was Sir George Williams in Montreal – a YMCA college that had been running evening courses at the level of high school and first-year university; the program had been so successful that in 1934 it had been extended to make it possible for students to complete bachelor's degrees in arts, science, and commerce.

But why in Ottawa? Ottawa in the early 1940s was a city of 150,000 people, about 25 per cent of whom were French speaking. The federal government was the major employer, and those who did not work directly for the government usually provided services for the civil servants. With no mills or factories there was no great demand for manual labour, so economic opportunities for young people were closely linked to educational qualifications. Ottawa did have institutions of higher learning: the University of Ottawa, which was bilingual, serving the French-speaking community on both sides of the Ottawa River as well as offering degree programs in English; and St Patrick's College, which provided an undergraduate program in arts for English-speaking students. But both were Roman Catholic institutions, and this made them suspect on academic grounds, because among Protestants it was widely believed that Roman Catholic education was dogmatic, teaching students what to think rather than how to think. Even more serious was the requirement that all students take some religious instruction. For most Protestants, or even lapsed Protestants, this put these institutions beyond the pale, so the non-Catholic graduates of Ottawa high schools had to leave Ottawa to go to university. Queen's University in Kingston and McGill University in Montreal were the most common choices, but both involved the expense of living away from home. Thus there were religious and economic reasons for proposing a college in Ottawa.

How important was the religious motivation? The YMCA had been founded as a nonsectarian institution, but as the name suggests, it was not intended to be a secular institution. It had evangelical roots, and its purpose was to provide athletic and social activities in a suitable Protestant environment for young people in the growing cities of North America. Over the years, the evangelical focus had been broadened by secular pressures – some would say diluted – but the moral and ethical values of Protestantism had not disappeared. In Ottawa, the directors of the Y might not all be regular churchgoers, but they did come from Protestant backgrounds. Hugh Keenleyside, for example, had had an evangelical Protestant upbringing, and although he no longer attended church, his personal concern for the less fortunate was linked to this background.[4] Any college these men proposed would be nonsectarian, but it would certainly reflect Protestant values. The importance of religion was thus unstated but implicit. Some years later, when the Board of Governors had agreed on a motto for the new college, H.S. Southam – one of the early supporters of the college, and chairman of the board – expressed his approval of the board's decision but commented in an aside that the real motto of the college had always been "To hell with the Pope."[5] Not everybody would have agreed, but Southam's opinion is a reminder that in Ottawa in the 1940s the divisions between Protestants and Roman Catholics seemed as significant as those between rich and poor.

Whatever their motives, the members of the Board of Directors of the Ottawa YMCA were receptive to the idea of sponsoring college courses. Keenleyside and some other board members of the Y were further encouraged by a visit to Sir George Williams College in Montreal. The board then checked with Queen's University, which had offered some extension courses in Ottawa, and learned that it was not interested in collaborating with the Y to offer credit courses in Ottawa. In June 1939 the board appointed a committee, with Keenleyside as its chairman, to plan a college program.

The committee was side-tracked by the war. In the First World War the YMCA in Canada, in contrast to the Salvation Army, had played only a minor role in providing services for the armed forces, and it was determined not to make that mistake again. Arnold Ward, a member of the YMCA staff, had been expected to be a key figure in the planning and administration of any college, but the Y now preferred to focus its attention on such organizations as the Red Triangle, which became a popular servicemen's club in Ottawa.[6] Keenleyside was also less available because he became the Canadian secretary of the newly appointed Permanent Joint Board of Defence and then the assistant undersecretary of state for external affairs. The committee members still believed that an evening college was needed in Ottawa. If anything, the need was even greater because the expansion of the federal government brought many more young people to Ottawa who might benefit from more education. However, the project was shelved for the next two years. Then, late in 1941, came the chance meeting of Connor and Tory, and Tory's offer to get involved.

In 1941 Henry Marshall Tory was one of Canada's most eminent academics. His was the classic case of a farm boy whose mother expected her children to excel. Tory had left Guysborough County in Nova Scotia for McGill and had paid for his undergraduate education by teaching and by scholarships. He had been ordained as a Methodist minister but shifted to an academic career when McGill hired him as a mathematics instructor. He went on to complete his doctorate and become a professor of mathematics and physics. He was an efficient administrator as well as an excellent teacher, and in 1905 was sent by McGill to British Columbia to establish junior colleges in Vancouver and Victoria, which would be affiliated with McGill until they established their own identities as the University of British Columbia and Victoria College. Two years later, he left McGill to become the first president of the University of Alberta. In 1918 he took time off to organize Khaki College, in Great Britain, which gave college courses to Canadian soldiers waiting to return to Canada to be demobilized; its professors were academics serving in the Canadian forces. In 1928, at the age of sixty-five, Tory left Edmonton to become the full-time president of the National Research Council in Ottawa. He was bitterly disappointed seven years later when the government did not renew his appointment. He kept busy after his retirement – as chairman of a royal commission on anthracite coal and as president of the Royal Society of Canada – but in 1941 he had time on his hands.[7]

He was not idle for long. Shortly after his meeting with Connor he invited the former committee members to his home to discuss what could be done. The key figures, in addition to Keenleyside, were John Robbins from the Dominion Bureau of Statistics and William Connor, the Ottawa businessman who was chairman of the Council of Social Agencies in Ottawa. They agreed that a college for the non-Catholic youth in Ottawa was more urgent than ever and expressed a willingness to do what they could to establish one. But Tory was the key figure. He was the only one without a full-time job, and he had the energy and enthusiasm of a much younger man. Also, he had experience in establishing colleges, and his prestige as an academic and his contacts in the academic community would be of crucial importance. His guests were prepared to help, and the board of the YMCA also showed its continued interest. In November 1941 the board named a College Grade Education Committee, with Tory as chairman and Connor, Keenleyside, and Robbins as members. At the request of this committee, the board added a number of new members in January, including Frank Patten from the board of Ottawa Collegiate Institute; Clarence C. Gibson, a lawyer and the Y's solicitor; and Lloyd Shaw, the Y's general program secretary, who was to act as the committee's secretary. The committee members may have got more than they bargained for. Over the next few months the committee met almost every week, and between meetings many of the members were assigned specific tasks.[8] Tory was a hard taskmaster.

John Robbins, for example, was asked to survey the need for a junior college for non-Catholics in the Ottawa area. Robbins took it for granted that the Roman Cathholic institutions were irrelevant. As his biographer put it, the University of Ottawa "seemed simply too French, too Roman Catholic, and too identified with a cultural world drastically different from the English-speaking Protestant society of Ottawa."[9] Robbins's report assumed this cultural split and pointed out that the non-Catholics or Protestants (the distinction is never clear) had no institution of higher learning. This group, he noted, was larger than the population of many Canadian communities that already supported universities or junior colleges. He saw it as relevant that one-third of the graduates of Ottawa's collegiates went on to universities elsewhere, because the experience of other communities showed that many more would go to university if there was a local college. His conclusion was that the non-Catholic population in Ottawa could support what he called an "undenominational college." What this meant was not clear, but the implication was that the college would not be a secular institution; it would somehow be Protestant but with no denominational affiliation.[10] Robbins was also asked to propose the courses which a junior college should offer. The first-year courses would be at the senior matriculation level – grade 13 in Ontario. Robbins suggested a list of eight courses, five of which could be selected to meet the university admission requirements for most degree programs. He then suggested eleven courses at the second-year level, five of which could be chosen to meet the standard requirements for admission to second-year university programs elsewhere in arts, science, commerce, or engineering.[11]

Other decisions were made possible by generous support from the community. Frank Patten reported that the board of Ottawa Collegiate Institute would make school classrooms available after school hours and would even suspend the grade 13 courses that it gave in the evening as extension courses, thus eliminating any competition at that level for the proposed college. Ottawa Public Library was also very helpful. It offered to acquire three textbooks for each course and to make them and other reference books available to the college students in its reading room in the evenings.[12] Experienced teachers in the Ottawa high schools were ready to teach at the first-year level, and Tory was already collecting the names of academics doing wartime service in Ottawa who might be persuaded to teach the courses at the university level.

Even money did not seem to be an intimidating hurdle. The committee decided to set the fees at ten dollars for first-year and thirty dollars for the second-year courses, with an honorarium to the instructors of two dollars and fifty cents an hour. It was calculated that with a minimum enrolment of one hundred students, the fees would cover the payments to the instructors. Two or three thousand dollars more would be needed for janitorial services and administration. The YMCA might be able to provide the money, but this was complicated because the Y in turn depended on funding from the Community Chest, which did not have a mandate to fund educational services. In March the committee suggested an alternative. If the Y did not feel it could provide the money, the committee was prepared to sever its connection with the Y and solicit funds directly from private donors. The Board of Directors of the Y preferred this option, though it generously agreed to continue to provide office space and much of Lloyd Shaw's time until the college began operations.[13] By the end of April the committee was officially on its own.

This decision was possible only because by then the committee was confident that it had the support of the leading citizens in the community. Committee members had already been in touch with the publishers of the *Ottawa Citizen* and *Ottawa Journal* and with senior public servants and prominent businessmen, and they had been much encouraged by the response. Now they drew up a list of some sixty names and allocated individual committee members to solicit each of these potential donors for an annual donation for the next three years. The results were gratifying. Almost everybody who was approached agreed to contribute something. It is noteworthy that some of these donors were Roman Catholics. Religious divisions might still be important in the Ottawa of the 1940s, but even Roman Catholics recognized the need for educational opportunities for the non-Catholic youth and were prepared to support the college. The sums promised by the donors were not large, usually from $100 to $250 per year, but they came to a total of between $5,000 and $6,000.[14] The college would be able to pay its bills.

At this stage, however, the college had no legal existence. Tory was chairing a committee that now had no affiliation with the YMCA. How could it be held accountable for any funds collected? One possibility was to apply for a provincial charter that would authorize it to award university credits and even degrees. The difficulty was that the provincial government was not likely to respond quickly to such a request – no Ontario college charter had been issued in the twentieth century, and the government would worry about precedents. C.C. Gibson, the lawyer on the committee, suggested incorporation as a private company, to be known as the Ottawa Association for the Advancement of Learning. The primary purpose of the association would be "the organization and establishment of a non-sectarian college of higher learning in the City of Ottawa." The donors would be members of the association, which would meet annually.

The major responsibility of the association would be to elect a board of governors to manage the corporation.[15]

There was no time to waste. The committee approved the articles of association in May, and four weeks later, on the 18 June, the Ottawa Association for the Advancement of Learning had its first annual meeting at the Chateau Laurier. Thirty of the donors attended, listened to Tory explain the need for a college, adopted the articles of association, and elected the proposed slate of twenty-one to act as the board.[16] The slate was an expansion of the YMCA committee; the most important additions were P.D. Ross and Harry S. Southam, publishers of the *Ottawa Journal* and *Citizen*, respectively. H.M. Tory knew the importance of good public relations. Immediately after the Ottawa Association's meeting adjourned, the board met for the first time. One of its first acts was to nominate Tory as president of the college. "Dr. Tory explained that he had not intended to take on such responsibility but that under the circumstances he could not refuse. He wanted it understood, however, that he would not accept any compensation, and that any money spent in connection with the office would go to the securing of suitable secretarial assistance."[17] Tory hardly needed to explain "the circumstances." He was the only member of the committee with the time, energy, and prestige which the position required; but everybody knew that this was a stop-gap measure. Tory was seventy-eight years old, and he would be looking for a successor as soon as the college was launched.[18]

Incorporation would mean that the college could be operated as a business, accountable to the board and the association for its financial operations. But who would be accountable for its academic standards? The college might certify that students had successfully completed the equivalent of senior matriculation or first-year university, but would employers or other universities accept the credentials which the college provided? Universities are jealous guardians of their academic reputations and are properly reluctant to accept diplomas granted by a private college with no track record. But how could the college expect to attract students if there was no guarantee that its diplomas would be recognized by other universities or by prospective employers?

The dilemma was resolved because Henry Marshall Tory was now the college president. Tory simply wrote to the presidents of a number of Canadian universities and asked them to recognize in advance any credits which the new college would award. These men had been Tory's colleagues in the past, and it was difficult to refuse this favour. Queen's University, the University of Alberta, and some of the Maritime colleges agreed immediately. The University of Toronto was less cooperative. Canon Cody, the president, apologetically explained that he would have to get the approval of the

university's Senate and that this would take time. Tory made a trip to Toronto, where he managed to convert the executive committee of the Senate.
The Senate, however, was still dubious, and it would be December before
the executive committee could persuade the Senate to give Tory what he
wanted.[19] Tory was even more frustrated by delays at McGill, where he had
assumed that his long connection with the university would override any
objections. McGill did eventually agree to Tory's request, but final approval was delayed until the spring of 1943.[20] In the meantime, the committee found it wiser to make no reference to the problem of recognition by
other universities "but rather to take it for granted that all Canadian Colleges would recognize the first two years' work."[21]

The college would also need a name. There was no shortage of suggestions. It could, perhaps, commemorate a historical figure such as Philemon
Wright or Colonel By; it could use a geographical reference such as
Gatineau; or it could choose Confederation or Capital to emphasize its location in Canada's capital. The report in the *Ottawa Citizen* suggests that
Tory felt there were more important things to discuss than a name. "Carleton seemed appropriate because of the proximity of Carleton County and
in memory of Sir Guy Carleton", the newspaper reported. "The alliteration
attracted some: it would make an attractive crest, one said, for the athletic
teams. Besides, it rolled smoothly off the tongue. Dr. Tory said: 'Well, gen-
tlemen, unless someone has a better suggestion, we'll christen it Carleton
College.'"[22]

By August 1942 everything seemed to be in place. Tory was able to reassure the board that the number of inquiries about the evening courses to be
offered was very encouraging and that if more teachers were needed he had
a list of people on whom he could call. He was confident "that the matter
was now in hand, that all contingencies could be met."[23] But would the
students come? Four evenings were set aside in mid-September for registration. Hugh Keenleyside remembered the tense atmosphere of the first
evening when he and eight or ten other volunteers waited uncertainly,
afraid that nobody would show up. Some fifty students enrolled that
evening. Three days later the board members were jubilant: over seven hundred students had enrolled, more than four hundred of them in courses offering academic credits.[24]

There was no formal ceremony to mark the opening of the new college.
On the first night of classes President Tory told an "eager body of 500 students" in the auditorium of the High School of Commerce the he was not
"going to declare the College open. You're here and I'm here. And the
College is open."[25] Those who had classes that evening then left for their
classrooms.

Evening Citizen, 12 Sept. 1942

11

The opening of classes marked a significant change in the administration of the college. The active members of the committee and then of the board, had been involved in the planning and preparations of the college, but now the board would meet only once a month and its members would have little to do with the college's daily operations. After September, Henry Marshall Tory dominated the monthly meetings of the board; he told its members what had happened and what he planned to do. The board typically confirmed what he had done and authorized him to take whatever action seemed necessary. For the next two or three years, Carleton College was primarily Tory's responsibility.

During the school year, Tory drove almost every day to the High School of Commerce, where he had a long narrow office which he shared with one and then two secretaries. There were endless details to take care of. Instructors called Tory if they needed special equipment or had to miss classes. There was the problem of how students who worked during the day could find time to buy their textbooks. (Tory solved this problem by ordering the texts and then selling them to the students at cost.) There were countless financial matters to be dealt with. For instance, Tory had to re-reimburse students who decided to drop their courses for some reason, and he had to make sure that the continuing students paid the second instalment of their fees. As well, he had to ensure that the instructors were paid their honoraria each month. Some prospective donors had not made their promised donations, and Tory had to remind them. He also had to remind a number of donors when the second and third instalments of their donations were due. Meanwhile, he had to plan the courses and find the instructors for the next term. It was a lot to demand of an elderly volunteer, especially in wartime.

Fortunately for Tory, he could circumvent some of the restrictive wartime regulations. Although gasoline was rationed, he managed to get a special coupon book for his 1940 Packard. When his retreaded tires wore thin, he wrote a personal letter to the rubber controller and got new tires.[26] Even the mandatory examination at the age of eighty for his driver's licence was not a problem. Tory wrote a personal letter to the registrar of motor vehicles to tell him how important it was that he should be able to drive to work and to remind him that he was in good health and did not need to be tested. The registrar promptly assured him that the licence would be issued immediately without the formality of an examination.[27] The Canada of the 1940s was still not an egalitarian society.

Tory was soon looking for an assistant who would be able to succeed him as president when he decided to retire. The position was not easy to fill. His first assistant stayed for a year and then left for the security of a position as superintendent of schools on Prince Edward Island. After some searching, Tory offered the job to Maxwell MacOdrum, a Nova Scotian with a PHD in English from the University of Edinburgh. MacOdrum had been a Presbyterian minister and then had worked in industrial relations for the Dominion Coal and Steel Company in Sydney, Nova Scotia. He had come to Ottawa during the war to work with the National War Finance Committee selling war bonds, and by 1944 he was looking for something with a more secure future. MacOdrum was the kind of assistant Tory needed. He did not have Tory's contacts in the Ottawa establishment or in the academic world, but he had complementary talents. He could handle the administrative details efficiently, and he was an effective after-dinner speaker who could wax eloquent about the cultural and moral benefits of a college education. MacOdrum was conservative in dress and manners, devoted to his invalid wife, and would look to Tory and the board for leadership. Tory hired him as his executive as-

Maxwell MacOdrum, president 1947–55, at the entrance to the High School of Commerce (now Glebe Collegiate), where the first evening classes were held

sistant in 1944 with the understanding that "he wanted a man who could succeed him as head of the College at an early date."[28] Tory found the arrangement satisfactory, and the following year the board agreed to give MacOdrum the title of vice-president. For the next few years he taught a course in English and relieved Tory of much of the administration.

Carleton College in its first years accomplished what the founders had hoped. The students ranged widely in age and background, but most were civil servants between the ages of eighteen and twenty-five; most of them had come to Ottawa after attending high school elsewhere in Ontario or in other provinces; and the majority hoped eventually to complete a university degree. Not surprisingly, some of the students withdrew from their courses during the year, but most of them successfully completed the year. They seem to have been orderly and well behaved; certainly, there are no references to any discipline problems in the classrooms. When asked for his opinion about them, Tory replied that "broadly speaking the students were serious, hard-working, and measured up splendidly to a good average standard." [29] This was qualified praise, but it was probably a realistic assessment.

The student body did provide one surprise. The founders of the college had intended to give ambitious young men the opportunity to improve their education and so advance their careers – but it turned out that almost two-thirds of the students were women.[30] This was a reminder that the expanding government bureaucracy in wartime Ottawa depended heavily on the recruitment of young women. It was also an early indication that higher education would eventually become as important for women as for men.

The academic standards of the college seem to have been as good as could be expected. The students, with the exception of some married women, had full-time jobs and therefore limited time to read beyond the textbook. On the other hand, the instructors were all experienced teachers with an interest in teaching – it seems unlikely that the financial reward of $150 for the year's work was an adequate incentive. The instructors were also well qualified. Most of the teachers at the first-year level (grade 13 in Ontario) were experienced high school teachers who taught the same courses during the day in the regular high school system. For the second-year level, Tory was surprisingly successful in finding young scholars who had come to Ottawa for wartime service and persuading them to teach in the evening. At this level, over half of the instructors had doctorates and most of the others had an MA. The academic reputation of the college, however, was a matter of concern, not only to Tory and the board but also to the students. In the first year some of the students taking a course at the grade 13 level wrote the college examinaions and then took the precaution of writing the "departmental examinations" administered by the Department of Education for the same course. Tory was pleased to report to the board that the college and the departmental marks were comparable.[31]

In its first year, Carleton also offered courses that carried no grade 13 or university credits. There was a surprising demand for Russian, Chinese, and Japanese language courses, a reflection of the wartime interest in these languages in Ottawa.[32] Tory promptly responded to the demand and found the necessary instructors. In addition to these courses, the college offered a lecture course in child psychology, which was attended by some fifty house- wives and childcare workers, and another in labour relations, which drew men from personnel divisions in the public service and from trade unions.[33] These extension courses proved to be popular and four courses were of- fered in subsequent years, with Tory himself giving one on "The Evolution of Knowledge" in 1944.[34]

The first concern of Tory and the board was to present a program with sound academic content, but some of the founders of the college hoped to do more. As Hugh Keenleyside expressed it at the opening ceremony, "So- cial life is an integral part of a liberal education," and he hoped that the students would make some social contacts.[35] Munro Beattie, an English in- structor, shared this view and talked to his first class about the importance of extracurricular activity. With his encouragement, the students arranged to have each class choose a representative, and these representatives then met to elect a Students' Council. The council, with Tory's support, collected a one-dollar fee from each student and undertook a number of college ac- tivities. Some cross-country ski excursions were organized, other students met weekly for bowling and chess, and the Spanish students organized an active Latin-America Club for lectures and films. The most successful events that year were three college dances with Dr Tory, Dr Hugh and Katherine Keenleyside, and Munro and Mae Beattie as patrons. The dances may have been especially popular in wartime Ottawa because the Students' Council took the precaution of selling tickets in advance to men in the armed services "to ensure an equitable number of men."[36] The second year was better organized. This time the college collected the one-dollar fee from each student at the beginning of the year. It also arranged for a common room for Carleton students at the high school, to be furnished out of Stu- dents' Council funds. There were more academic activities, with a French Club to provide practice in the second language and a Current History Club to discuss international affairs. These activities may not have been an adequate substitute for the social and intellectual contacts of a college cam- pus, but they show the eagerness of some teachers and students for a fuller experience than evening classes could provide. Even so, it seems likely that for most students the Carleton College experience was limited to attending a weekly class at the High School of Commerce for thirty weeks.

While a sense of the college as a community may have been limited for most of the students, it was almost non-existent for the instructors; as senior high school teachers and civil servants, they were fully occupied else- where, and the college played only a minor part in their lives. Tory did in- vite them to his home in Rockcliffe each term to talk of common concerns, but these meetings were not enough to develop a sense of community. The

The college teachers on a Sunday afternoon in 1944 in front of President Tory's Rockcliffe home. Tory stands in the centre with his secretaries at his left.

first meeting, in November 1942, was typical. It was held on a Sunday because there was no other day available; civil servants worked on Saturday mornings in those days, and the college teaching was done on weekday evenings or Saturday afternoons. So on this Sunday in November they met for the first time as the faculty of Carleton College.

There was no formal agenda, though Dorothy Wardle – a recent graduate of Queen's and the first full-time employee of the college, with the title of "secretary in charge of records" – was there to take the minutes. According to her account, Tory began by asking his guests to comment on their progress. He went on to talk enthusiastically about the willingness of other Canadian universities to give credit for the university-level courses completed at Carleton. The Senate at the University of Toronto, he conceded, had expressed some concern about the academic standards of the new college, but Tory was sure that these would soon be resolved.

In the meantime, what guidance could be given to Carleton's instructors? The president did make the obvious suggestion that assignments should take into consideration the students' time and ability to cover the work. Coming to more specific advice, he proposed a marking system based on 150 marks, with 50 for the term work, 50 for the mid-term exam, and 50 for the final exam. In reply to a question from one of the guests, he said that mid-term exams were not compulsory but were strongly recom-

mended. There was apparently no discussion, on this occasion, of the examination format. A year later, however, at another faculty meeting, Tory
was asked about using "true-false" questions. Again, he did not impose a
rule, but he expressed a strong preference: "He preferred to force the student to put down in black and white his thoughts; they should learn to express themselves in English and say what they want to say and make the
meaning clear." The one definite decision made at the first faculty meeting
was that the mid-term examinations would be written during the third
week of January. There was no discussion of the broader aims and objectives of the college and no discussion of how the courses might be taught.
The instructors were largley on their own.

The meeting was then adjourned, and Mrs Moss, Tory's cook and house-
keeper, served tea with cookies and cakes. Years later, the guests remembered few details of the discussion at these meetings, but they fondly
remembered Mrs Moss's pastries at a time when sugar was rationed.[37]

III

Tory and the others associated with the new college had no blueprint for its
future. They were pleasantly surprised by the number of students who enrolled in the first year and were encouraged when the total enrolment went
up slightly over the next two years. By then, they were also confident that
the college was financially secure. The fees for the first year more than covered the payments to the instructors and office staff. William Connor, the
cautious treasurer, used the money from the subscriptions with some of the
surplus to buy a $5,000 government bond.[38] In the following years the sal-
ary for Tory's assistant increased the fixed costs – MacOdrum's initial salary was $5,000 – but raising the fees for the first-year courses from $10 to
$15 kept the budget in balance, with a small surplus. By the end of the
third year of operation, the college had accumulated a surplus of $17,000,
of which $10,000 could be attributed to donations.[39] The college was
clearly meeting a demand and meeting it successfully, and its future as a
night school seemed assured. For Tory and the other founders, however,
this was not enough. They hoped that some time in the future Carleton
would become a college like other colleges, with faculty and buildings and
full-time students. With its location in the nation's capital, it was even possible to dream that it might become a university, with a variety of programs
and even graduate students. In the meantime, the board would husband its
financial resources carefully and take advantage of whatever opportunity
presented itself.

The most distinctive advantage was the college's location. Ottawa was
the federal capital with an expanding public service. Almost from the

beginning, Tory and others hoped to capitalize on this fact. The proposed
articles of association, which C.C. Gibson had drawn up in May 1942,
even before the college existed, had referred not only to the organization of
a nonsectarian college but also to the organization of an Institute of Public
Administration.⁴⁰ It was not clear what this meant. In February 1943 Tory
invited some academics, who happened to be in Ottawa, to discuss the possibilities, and he admitted to them that the ideas concerning the institute
were "entirely tentative." It was clear by then that there was a demand
from prospective students for courses in accounting, economics, and labour
relations; it might be possible for Carleton to offer a professional degree in
public administration. However, Tory raised the possibility of a much more
ambitious project, suggesting that Carleton might become a research institute that would attract researchers and graduate students to study public
administration in Ottawa. The academics agreed that such a research institute might be useful and referred to the Brookings Institution in Washington as a possible model, but they had no helpful suggestions about how it
could be established.⁴¹ A meeting with some senior public servants a few
weeks later was more constructive. They expressed only a vague interest in
research seminars but showed an immediate interest in courses that would
be useful for young and ambitious civil servants.⁴²

Tory wasted no time. In April 1943 he suggested to the Board of Governors that "the work of the College was now on a sufficiently definite basis
to warrant starting the beginnings of the Institute." He suggested a pragmatic approach: "If in time the College becomes a full-fledged degree conferring body then the Institute would fall into place as a faculty of graduate
studies." In the meantime, he favoured offering "certain courses which
were demanded at the moment" and for which he could find qualified instructors. The board agreed.⁴³ When the courses were offered, they attracted some two hundred students, and Tory felt this justified the decision
to offer courses that "would be immediately helpful to the public service."⁴⁴ The next step came in the fall of 1944, when it was decided that
Carleton would offer a Bachelor of Public Administration to any students
who had completed the college's second year, or the equivalent, and who
then completed ten courses offered by the institute in subjects such as accounting, economics, political science, social policy, public finance, and
mathematics.⁴⁵ Carleton was now a degree-granting institution.

Yet it was still a night school, teaching its courses in high school classrooms; even the Institute of Public Administration had not changed that. In
January 1944, however, at the same meeting of the board that approved the
Bachelor of Public Administration, Tory mentioned a development that
might transform Carleton much more dramatically. The federal government was already looking forward to the end of the war and was planning

the re-entry of those in the armed forces into civilian life. A government official had asked Tory if Carleton would be able to offer a college education
to those who decided to return to Ottawa. "As this would be an important
departure from our present plans," Tory told the board, "it was one that
would require very careful consideration, as it would involve day classes
and the possibility of a certain number of permanent staff. In addition, this
would mean securing quarters suitable for daytime teaching purposes."[46]
Nothing had been decided, but Tory was obviously intrigued by the possibilities. Carleton College might become a full-time college much sooner
than anybody had imagined.

PART ONE

The College Years

After 1945 there were really two Carletons. The original Carleton College did not disappear. There were still evening courses offered for academic credit, taught by part-time lecturers and attended by part-time students, and there were still evening lecture series on topics of public interest, which offered no academic credits. This college continued to attract almost the same number of students as it had from the beginning, with an average of two hundred and fifty enrolled in academic courses and usually more than three hundred in the other lecture series. But after 1945 the original Carleton College was overshadowed by another college, which offered programs during the day and allowed full-time students to earn an undergraduate degree. The two colleges were not completely separate. After 1946 the evening and day programs were taught in the same building, and some of the evening courses were given by full-time professors who also taught during the day, and these courses might be attended by full-time as well as part-time students. But when the full-time professors and students talked of Carleton College, they were likely to ignore the evening college or to refer to it as an afterthought. For them, the real Carleton College was the new college that emerged after full-time professors were hired and full-time students were enrolled.

It was not clear what kind of college this new Carleton would become. There was no master plan, because for almost a decade it was not certain that the college had a future. Full-time enrolment hovered around five hundred students in these years. The student fees were not enough to pay the operating costs, and any major expenditures depended on donations from Ottawa citizens or on unpredictable government grants. But even though there were no plans, there were aspirations. The presidents and the active members of the Board of Governors seem to have shared an image of a small college that could provide a formative academic and social experience for young people from Ottawa and the Ottawa Valley who did not go to McGill or Queen's. Tory and some others also hoped that sometime in the remote future this new Carleton would be able to take advantage of its location in Ottawa and offer graduate programs in public administration and in the sciences and social sciences. In the meantime, the administrators of the college had to do the best they could with very limited resources.

The future of the new Carleton would not be decided by the administrators alone. The full-time professors shared common interests and common concerns. They too envisaged a traditional college that would foster both the academic and social development of its students. Their special concern, however, was that the new college should distance itself from the evening college by stressing high academic standards. The students were yet another group with their own image of what traditional college life should be. They too wanted to define the college, trying to duplicate this idealized college life as best they could.

The new college, it was clear, would not be a simple extension of the evening college. The evening courses would still be available for young people to raise themselves by their bootstraps, but the new college targeted a different group. It would downplay the practical and vocational and would emphasize the development of intellect and character. The three influential groups – the administration, faculty, and students – either shared or at least did not openly question this view of the purpose of the college. They differed only because they were linked to the college in different ways, and this affected their perspectives. The interplay between these three groups shaped the new college over the next decade. While Ottawa and the Canada of these postwar years provided the context, it was the interests and aspirations of the administration, the faculty, and the students that determined how the new Carleton College responded to its milieu.

CHAPTER TWO

The College Goes Full-Time

It was in January 1944 that the Board of Governors first heard of the federal government's interest in university places for veterans. The next two years were critical. The college of 1946 bore almost no resemblance to the college of 1944. By 1946 Carleton was still offering evening classes, but it now offered day classes as well, and it had its own building, with full-time professors and full-time students, and with many of the students enrolled in programs leading to university degrees. Special circumstances had made this possible, but Henry Marshall Tory deserves much of the credit. He saw the opportunity to transform the college, and his prestige made it possible for Carleton to take advantage of the circumstances.

It was nevertheless a gamble. The end of the war and the return of the veterans to civilian life had meant a sudden demand for university training. Carleton managed to provide classrooms and professors for some of the veterans in the Ottawa area, but would it be able to survive after these veterans graduated? Would it be able to compete successfully with other universities for high school graduates to replace the veterans? And even if the students came, would the college be financially viable? For years, the income from the fees, even with the federal grants for the veterans, did not cover the college's operating costs, while the acquisition of a college building meant shouldering what seemed a crippling debt of a quarter of a million dollars. The citizens of Ottawa were of little help. They might approve of the new college, but when asked for financial contributions they were far from generous. For some years the survival of the college was in doubt. Not until the 1950s, when governments began to provide annual grants, did Carleton emerge from the shadow of bankruptcy.

I

Tory had high hopes for Carleton College. As noted in the previous chapter, he believed that the federal capital offered unique advantages for a college, and he dreamed that Carleton might eventually become a full-fledged university with a wide range of faculties, offering programs at the graduate as well as the undergraduate level. But the first and most difficult step would be the transition from a college of part-time students to one with full-time students. Such a college would need, as a minimum, a building for its classes, with a library and laboratories, and some full-time professors. This would mean major financial commitments. Where would the money come from? Not from student fees. Such a college would be competing with established universities for students, and it would be many years before it could dream of attracting enough students – and collecting enough fees – to pay even the operating costs. It is not surprising that no new full-time university had been founded in Ontario over the last half-century. [1]

The end of the war created a unique opportunity, for the federal government was planning the transition from war to peace. Almost a million service men and women had to be reintegrated into civilian life at a time when wartime industries would be dismissing their workers. How could the government avoid the unemployment and labour unrest that had marked the years after the First World War? A program of university training was attractive because it would keep at least some veterans out of the labour market during the period of reconstruction while at the same time improving their skills and qualifications. This was such an attractive plan that the government was prepared to be generous. Veterans who enrolled at a university within fifteen months after demobilization would have their fees paid and would receive a monthly living allowance for as many months as they had spent in the armed forces. To win the cooperation of the universities, the government agreed to pay an additional hundred and fifty dollars directly to the university for every registered veteran. [2] But money could not solve everything. It was anticipated that 25,000 veterans would be applying to universities. Since Canadian universities had had a total enrolment of 60,000 students in 1944, they would not find it easy to accommodate this influx.

Realizing that the Department of Veterans Affairs would be looking for places and might be persuaded to include Carleton in its plans, Tory kept in touch with the department and was as helpful as possible. One of the department's concerns was that some veterans wanted crash courses to complete their junior matriculation so that they would be eligible to enter university in September 1945. Could Carleton help? [3] Indeed it could. Tory arranged for space at Glebe Collegiate for four-month courses from four

Veterans signing for their monthly cheques from the federal government (Bill and Jean Newton)

o'clock in the afternoon to ten in the evening for more than fifty veterans, and he found qualified teachers for them.[4] In September more veterans were trying to meet university entrance requirements, and some wanted to begin the first year of a degree in engineering. Again Tory was resourceful. In addition to more collegiate space, he found a room in a church that could be fitted up with blackboards and seats; in all, he was able to accommodate more than a hundred veterans.[5] As Tory apologetically explained to the Board of Governors in November, "he had been compelled to order some special equipment. He had secured 50 special chairs with large arms to fit up the room in St. James United Church and thought it would be necessary to have 100 more of the same kind."[6] By then the war was over, and the Department of Veterans Affairs was facing even more pressure, so Tory found and equipped rooms in two more churches. The department was convinced. If Tory offered degree programs for full-time students, it was prepared to include Carleton in its list of eligible universities. Clearly, it was time for Carleton time to find permanent accommodation.

Tory already had a building in mind. The Ottawa Ladies College had been a finishing school for young Protestant ladies before the war but it had come on hard times, and during the war its building had been taken over by the Department of National Defence. Now that the war was over, it might be available for Carleton. The property was in a residential part of Ottawa known as the Glebe, about a mile south of Parliament Hill. The

Carleton College under the elms on First Avenue (Malak)

four-storey red brick building would require considerable renovation, and
there was little space for playing fields, but it would provide the classrooms
that Carleton needed. In November 1945 Tory, with the consent of the
board, wrote to D.C. Abbott, the minister of national defence, describing
Carleton's eagerness to contribute to the education of the veterans and asking the government to make the building available.[7]

The government was slow to respond, and by the spring of 1946 Carleton was facing a crisis. The high schools now needed the classrooms and
laboratories that Carleton was using, and the college would have to look
elsewhere. If the Ladies College was not available, Carleton would have to
find or even build a temporary structure for the fall term. By June, Tory had
leased a former officers' mess at Lansdowne Park – also in the Glebe – and
had ordered some laboratory equipment. Meanwhile, a committee of the
Board of Governors was searching for other property that might be converted into temporary classrooms.

Then, in July, all these plans were jettisoned when it was learned that
C.D. Howe, minister of reconstruction, might be persuaded to accelerate a
decision on the Ladies College. Tory was back in Guysborough for the summer as usual, but H.S. Southam, an active member of the board, talked to

Howe and shortly thereafter the board was officially informed that the Ladies College had been declared surplus. By mid-August the Crown Assets Corporation offered Carleton immediate possession if the board would put up the purchase price of $125,000. Southam and William Connor personally guaranteed the amount. Carleton College, for the first time, had a physical identity. The laboratory equipment ordered for Lansdowne Park was installed in the Ladies College, and although the renovations were still underway, full-time teaching began in September.

The full-time programs offered by the college still depended on demand. For the students in arts and science, the college would add one academic year to its offerings each fall, with the first class graduating in 1949. But there were many veterans who were eager to get re-established in civilian life and wanted professional programs. A Bachelor of Commerce posed no serious difficulties. However, a degree in engineering was beyond the resources of the college. Tory's response was to offer the first two years and to persuade McGill, Queen's, and Toronto to admit the Carleton graduates to the final years of their engineering programs.

Some veterans also inquired about training in journalism. In 1945 no Canadian university offered a degree in this field, and the Department of Veterans Affairs was reluctant to pay for their training at universities in the United States. Tory had already seen this as an appropriate program for Carleton, given the presence of so many prominent journalists in the Parliamentary Press Gallery who could be called on to teach some of the courses. Indeed, he had already arranged for a popular extension course in journalism. In the fall of 1945 the college offered Canada's first degree course in journalism.[8] Like public administration, it was a two-year program for students who had already completed two years in arts. One of the students who enrolled that year recalls listening with fascination to practising journalists who could discuss their experience first-hand. He also recalled the class being moved from the Masonic Lodge to a church basement in the second week and finding Tory arranging the chairs and tables when the class arrived.[9] The president of Carleton College had many responsibilities.

In October 1946 the college held its first convocation. It was a remarkable affirmation of what had been accomplished – and, even more impressive, of what it expected to become. On a quiet evening thirty-three students, accompanied by their parents and friends, made their way along the elm-lined streets of a quiet residential district to attend a ceremony in a local school. When they had settled in their places in the school auditorium, a small procession filed onto the stage. The procession included businessmen and senior civil servants in their dark three-piece suits, conscious of the dignity of their high station as members of the Board of Governors at the first convocation of Carleton College. They were, in the words of the official program, "in the distinguished presence of His Excellency Field Marshal The Right Honourable the Viscount Alexander of Tunis, G.C.B., Governor-General of Canada," who was wearing a blue and grey academic gown specially designed for the occasion. The president and vice-president of Carleton College were also very much in evidence in colourful academic robes.

The program followed the well-established pattern of university convocations in North America. It began with a hymn, led on this occasion by the combined choirs of St James and Glebe United Church, with the congregation joining in after the first verse, promising a future when freedom and knowledge would bring man closer to God. Then came "God Save the King" played by the Ottawa Technical School Brass Quartette, followed by a prayer from the Reverend Frank Fisher. The medieval costumes and the formal ritual, with its religious overtones, might have seemed out of place in a community that had little wealth or sophistication and little interest in tradition, and in a country still recovering from a war, but for most of the participants this combination of pageantry and Christian dedication was important. How else would students know that this was a rite of passage?

The pomp and ceremony were all the more important on this occasion because it was obvious that Carleton College was not a firmly established institution of higher learning. After the prayer, Vice-President MacOdrum gave a report on the progress that had been made, but he could talk only of beginnings – that the college had now acquired its first building, had enrolled its first full-time students, and had hired its first full-time professors. Most of the graduates at this convocation had only completed one year of university work beyond senior matriculation, for which they were to be awarded diplomas as "Associates in Arts." Viscount Alexander, in his address, found little to say about a college that until then had been little more than a night school. He met his obligation as speaker by offering platitudes about the links between education and success, and talking of the duty of the graduates to contribute to the welfare of their country and, indeed, of all mankind.

President Tory, in his address, made it clear that the graduates were only incidental. Tory was still a striking figure, a white-haired gentleman in scarlet robes, with bright eyes and a firm voice and the optimism that belied his eighty-two years. For him, this was the celebration of an institution with a promising future. In addition to the diplomas, the college was awarding six bachelor's degrees – three Bachelors of Journalism and three Bachelors of Public Administration. Not only were these the first degrees that Carleton had ever awarded, but the degrees in journalism were the first to be awarded in Canada. And the college could look forward to more degrees, because it now had more than four hundred and fifty full-time students.

Carleton College's first convocation. Viscount Alexander at the podium, with (*left to right*) H.S. Southam of the *Citizen*, P.D. Ross of the *Journal*, and H.M. Tory. Not surprisingly, the convocation received good coverage in the local newspapers (T.V. Little).

This convocation, Tory concluded, was only the promise of better things. "The time is sure to come when we will have one hundred graduates instead of six," he told a receptive audience; the Ottawa community could now rest assured that Carleton had "a place in the future of education in Canada."[10]

Tory, as usual, exuded confidence, but both he and the members of the board knew that the young college still had major hurdles to clear. Space was only one of the challenges. Money was an even more intractable problem. The students' fees and the special federal grant for each veteran student could cover the salaries for the professors and support staff and pay for the equipment and supplies, but who would pay for the capital costs, the costs of the Ladies College and the renovations, and the costs of an adequate college library? The college had been careful with its funds. For three years it had retained its small surpluses and now had a nest egg of some $17,000; but this was not much in the face of a debt that amounted to almost a quarter of a million dollars. The answer seemed obvious.

Carleton would have to appeal to the public for funds. The minutes of the Board of Governors' meeting in November 1945 put the case directly:

Whereas the Board is convinced of the need and practicability of assuring to Carleton a permanent and even more useful place in the life of the community, and

Whereas the Board is of the opinion that the experimental stage of the College's existence is ended and its permanency assured and that the time has come when the administrators and well-wishers of the College must unite in a bold move forward,

Therefore Be It Resolved,

That a financial campaign be undertaken with the twofold object of meeting the immediate needs and anticipating in vigorous fashion the possible costs of future development and expansion. And further, that the money objective of this campaign be one million dollars.[11]

If Ottawa was to have a nondenominational college, the leading citizens of Ottawa would be asked to pay for it.

The campaign was slow to take off. It would be easier to ask for donations (and a bank loan) after the college had acquired a permanent home – not until August 1946 did the Ottawa Ladies College actually change hands. By then a campaign committee had been established, composed of prominent members of the board and prominent Ottawa citizens, of whom the most eminent and most wealthy was Senator Norman Paterson of the Paterson Steamship Lines. Tory could not find a suitable candidate to act as full-time chairman to organize the campaign, and in the end he decided to take on the responsibility himself, leaving the administration of the college to his assistant, Maxwell MacOdrum.[12] Age had not tempered his ambition. That same summer he was involved in plans for a hospital on his property in Guysborough, Nova Scotia.[13] But there were limits to what even Henry Marshall Tory could do. He died early in February 1947, at the age of eighty-three, with the campaign about to begin.

The board decided to proceed with the campaign in spite of Tory's death, possibly even hoping that his name would still be an asset. It was a low-key campaign. The objective had been reduced to half a million dollars, and the emphasis was on the benefits which Carleton, as a community college, would bring to Ottawa. The appeal was to prominent local citizens and to prospective parents who would benefit by being able to send their children to a local institution. The money, it was explained, would be used to provide more space and more equipment and to extend the existing programs to four years. Both the *Citizen* and the *Journal* published supporting editorials at the beginning of the campaign[14] and followed them up with news items relating to Carleton over the next few weeks, but the campaign was never first-page news; the coverage paled by comparison with the attention given to Barbara Ann Scott and her victory at the world's figure-skating championship at Oslo. The campaign consisted almost entirely of voluntary canvassers, including students, soliciting donations from individuals. It was all over in two weeks.

The results were disappointing. The three largest donors, H.S. Southam, Senator Paterson, and P.D. Ross of the *Journal* gave $25,000 each, but there were no other large gifts. The lists of smaller donors were published in the local newspapers, but even with this publicity and with an extension of the campaign, the results fell far short fo expectations.[15] Part of the explanation was that the campaign had been poorly organized. There seems to have been little effort by the members of the board or the associates to approach businessmen or prominent civil servants personally to solicit funds. The absence of Tory may have made a difference. But the results were also a reminder that Carleton College was not yet an Ottawa institution. It had no alumni and no community profile. Indeed, in Ottawa, it was difficult for any institution to have a significant community profile. Ottawa was a one-industry town and that industry – the federal government – encouraged a national perspective, which dwarfed municipal or community concerns. There was no evidence of any hostility to Carleton, but neither was there much evidence of interest or concern for its future. If the college was going to depend on the financial support of the local citizens, it would not be an affluent institution.

The board did not publicly admit that the campaign had not been a resounding success. A total of almost $400,000 was eventually subscribed, though three years later only about $300,000 had been collected.[16] However, the college had also received some gifts, which supplement the results of the campaign. Henry Marshall Tory had left the college the residue of his estate, which amounted to over $60,000. The college also benefited from the hundred $100,000 endowment fund of the Ottawa Ladies College when the donors of this fund were persuaded to transfer the money to Carleton. A more intriguing donation was made shortly after the campaign. Harry Southam, his brother Wilson, and Colonel C.M. Edwards, all members of the board, donated thirty-nine acres of land east of the Rideau Canal between Hartwell Locks and Dows Lake, valued at some $200,000. The donors were thinking of a possible move to a larger campus some day in the future, though in 1947 that day seemed remote.

For all its financial difficulties, Carleton College in 1947 was holding university classes, day and evening, in a building of its own. Tory's gamble had succeeded. It had succeeded because of the postwar demand for university places, but it had also succeeded because of Henry Marshall Tory. Tory's years at McGill, the University of Alberta, and the National

Research Council had established him as one of Canada's leading educators, and when he undertook to organize Carleton College and its evening courses, his name alone was enough to give the project academic respectability. When the Department of Veterans Affairs wanted university places for returning veterans, Tory saw the opportunity, collaborated with the department, and again gave the college the necessary credibility for degree programs. Tory also brought to the new institution an extraordinary energy. He found the teachers, found the classrooms, ordered the equipment, met the students, kept in touch with the board, and did all of this in what might have been expected to be his retirement years. In the five years after his street-corner meeting with William Connor, Henry Marshall Tory had accomplished a great deal.

II

The Board of Governors quickly appointed Maxwell MacOdrum as Tory's successor. There was nothing to suggest that MacOdrum would be a forceful or innovative president. As the new incumbent, he was still quite prepared to remain in Tory's shadow. It was a tragedy, MacOdrum told the associates in the summer of 1947, that Tory had not been spared to complete his work, but fortunately "his plans for the future of the College were in their general design made known to us before he left us." It would, said MacOdrum, be his responsibility to carry out these plans.

Maxwell MacOdrum was president of Carleton College for the next eight years. During these years, Carleton became established as a liberal arts college with a sound academic reputation. But MacOdrum's role in this development was never clear. Leadership in financial matters came from prominent members of the board, and leadership in academic matters came from some of the young professors. It is to MacOdrum's credit, however, that he maintained the confidence of the board. Most of the faculty saw him as a somewhat remote figure but one who listened to their complaints and tried to protect their interests. Even the students found him approachable. He was an isolated and lonely man, but he did avoid clashes and crises within the institution and did keep the college developing along the lines that Tory had envisaged. One example was the continued commitment to hiring highly qualified professors. As MacOdrum reminded the associates at the annual meeting in September 1948,

It is, I believe, an open secret among members of the Association that such success as Carleton has already achieved is owing chiefly to the quality of the instructors who have been employed. You will remember that the Governors of the College,

The Executive Committee of the Board of Governors in 1948. *Left to right*:
E.F. Sheffield, administrative officer; W.M. Connor, treasurer; Maxwell MacOdrum,
president; H.S. Southam, chairman; C.C. Gibson, secretary; F.G. Patten and John
Robbins, members (National Film Board)

from the beginning, have realized that good teachers must be offered reasonably
good salaries and working conditions if their services are to be secured and retained.
You will remember, specifically, that the Governors, following upon my assumption
of the presidency authorized a salary scale approximately that of the University of
Toronto. The result has been that as president of Carleton I have been able to go to
Toronto, Queen's, McGill and other universities here and abroad with offers sufficiently attractive to bring to Carleton College some of the best young graduates and
instructors.[17]

This did not mean that these young professors were well paid. A scholar
with a PHD or, more often, with the thesis not yet completed might be appointed at the level of assistant professor, with a salary of three thousand
dollars per year. Even at this rate, however, expenditure on salaries was a
major factor in producing annual deficits in the early years of the full-time
college.

The academic future of the college also depended on attracting students
from the Ottawa high schools. From the beginning, Tory had recognized
that when the veterans graduated the college's survival would depend on
competing successfully with other universities for the graduates of the Ottawa high schools. Since tuition fees were the college's major source of revenue, the fees were carefully set at $225 a year, which was slightly below

the fees of other Ontario universities.[18] Scholarships and bursaries were also needed in order to compete with universities that were already well endowed. Here the Southams provided an example by establishing an endowment for a total of six entrance scholarships for leading graduates from Ottawa high schools.[19] Under Tory it had also been decided to use the federal veterans' grant for scholarships and bursaries, but financial difficulties soon forced the college to use some of these funds to meet its deficits, though the funds were later built up again, in more prosperous times.

The harsh fact was that in the early years the cost of academic respectability always exceeded the revenue. In 1947–48, for example, with part-time enrolment holding steady and full-time enrolment over five hundred, the fees (which provided about 90 per cent of the college's annual income) amounted to just over $100,000. In that same year the administrative and faculty salaries alone amounted to $100,000. It is not surprising, therefore, that the college had an operating deficit of $17,000 for that year. The anticipated deficit of $60,000 for the next year was even more disturbing. In September 1948, MacOdrum admitted to the associates: "Where the money to offset this $60,000 is to be found we do not at this moment know." But, always upbeat, he reminded them of what had been accomplished and expressed his faith in the future. "We have launched our boat," he declared, "and we have got to row our way vigorously through the breakers until we reach the smooth expanse of ocean."[20] Unfortunately, the next few years saw a lot of hard rowing and not much smooth sailing. Fred Turner, a professor in economics who had become the bursar in 1948, was constantly juggling funds to pay the college's bills. For the next few years, he reported on the cash flow regularly to the Executive Committee of the Board of Governors because the college was always short of money. That summer the college negotiated an overdraft at the Bank of Nova Scotia and faced the prospect of another large deficit the next year.

It is to the credit of the Board of Governors that this financial stringency did not undermine its commitment to academic respectability. In the spring of 1949, as well as facing the prospect of an overdraft at the bank, the board had to decide what to do about the college library. Space had initially been allocated for the library on the fourth floor of the college building. The original collection consisted of textbooks and reference books and a heterogeneous assortment of other books from the Royal Canadian Legion and private donors. Students continued to rely on the good services of the Ottawa Public Library. A faculty Library Committee reported in the spring of 1949 that the library holdings had expanded to eight thousand volumes but that by the time the college reached an enrolment of eight hundred students, it would need twenty thousand books and more reading space for students.[21]

Top: This picture of the crowded library on the fourth floor of the college must have been taken at exam time (Malak). *Bottom:* The new library may not have been soundproof, but it was certainly more spacious.

The Executive Committee accepted the necessity for a major expansion of the library but concluded, quite logically, that there was not enough room on the fourth floor and that, in any case, the building was not designed to bear the weight of the books that would be needed. The only possible solution, it said, was a separate one-storey building on the southeast corner of the college property, with the possibility of adding two more storeys in the future.

Building the library would cost $65,000 and the furnishings would cost another $10,000. Nevertheless, the Executive Committee reluctantly concluded that the expenditures were "necessary to maintain the institution."[22] The board, not surprisingly, was worried about the financial commitment. It did not reject the advice, but it did ask the Executive Committee to give the matter more consideration. The Executive Committee was resolute. Library facilities, it argued, were second only in importance to good professors, and it told the board that it would be "impossible to significantly reduce expenditures if the College was to continue to improve, and that if it did not advance it must inevitably fall back."[23] The idea might have been expressed more felicitously, but the commitment to academic respectability was clear. The board was convinced, and in spite of the cost, the construction of the new building was approved.

By then, the board had also agreed to acquire other property. It was strongly committed to enhancing the students' college experience, and when a nearby house on First Avenue became available in 1948, the board agreed to purchase it for $18,000 to provide space for the Students' Council, the *Carleton,* and the student clubs.[24] A more significant development was associated with the purchase of another First Avenue house for a School of Public Administration. It was revealing that the initiative came from James Coyne, governor of the Bank of Canada and chairman of the Board of Governors. Coyne drew MacOdrum's attention to the possibility of a grant from the Atkinson Charitable Foundation, and he drafted the college's application. In 1952 the foundation agreed to give the college $200,000 to defray the expense of the building, the salary of the director, and the cost of some graduate scholarships.[25] Yet another house on First Avenue was acquired the following year to provide for needed space.[26] In spite of financial stringency, the college was expanding.

The revenue side of the balance sheet improved the next year. The provincial government was already making grants to the nondenominational universities of Toronto, Queen's, and Western Ontario. In 1949 the policy was extended to include Carleton College, and for 1949–50 Carleton received a grant of $65,000.[27] It was a significant amount, although it still left the college with an operating deficit of some $40,000. More significant was the recognition by the provincial government that Carleton College

The Students' Union on First Avenue (Capital Press Service)

was a legitimate institution of higher learning. The college could at least hope for larger grants in future.

The provincial assistance came none too soon. Student fees were still the major source of income, but student enrolment was declining. Full-time enrolment reached a peak in 1948–49, with 572 students, of whom 260 were veterans. Three years later, the veterans were gone and full-time enrolment was down to 442, with the possibility that enrolment would decline even further before the bottom was reached. Fees had been increased by 20 per cent, but this did not even compensate for the drop in enrolment, and any further increases might encourage parents to send their children elsewhere. The funds not specifically committed to the college endowment had been used to meet the deficits, and the college owed the bank $50,000. It was time for another fundraising campaign.

The 1951 campaign was better organized, being run by professional fundraisers. The campaign literature still stressed the benefits to Ottawa families, but there was more assurance about the academic standing of the

college and about its academic future. Carleton's "up-and-coming Arts college, with exceptional offerings in journalism and other studies," it was asserted, would be taking advantage of its location in Canada's capital and
within a few years would even be offering an MA degree in some departments. Reading between the lines, however, even a successful campaign
would not bring affluence. The objective was again half a million dollars,
of which $100,000 would cover the deficit, another $100,000 would go to
the library, and the rest would go to faculty appointments.[28]

Once again the campaign fell short of expectations. Individual donors
were expected to produce half of the objective because Ottawa had no major industries or corporations, but the citizens of Ottawa were not sufficiently generous. The total amount collected was less than $300,000, and
when the fundraisers' fees were deducted, the college received only half of
what it had hoped for. The blame could be laid on a fragile economy or
even on the shortcomings of the fundraisers, but these excuses were not
fully convincing. The board minutes probably touch on the basic reason
when they blame "a lack of a feeling of responsibility towards the College
on the part of the community."[29] In a city dominated by the federal government, Carleton College still attracted little attention.

Although the money from the campaign kept Carleton afloat, its future
was still in doubt. The revenue from student fees was declining, because although part-time enrolment in the evening classes remained fairly stable,
the college was not recruiting enough high school graduates to replace the
graduating veterans. Professors at Carleton remember the rumours at registration time and the anxious calculations at the end of each registration day
to see how enrolment was going. There were unavoidable economies. Hilda
Gifford, the librarian, recalled "the grim retrenching year of 1951–52 when
only 720 books were ordered for the Library."[30] Support for the athletic
program almost disappeared. In the spring of 1951 Maxwell MacOdrum,
in a speech to the professors, tried to put a positive spin on the situation.
The fundraising campaign, he assured them, even if it fell short of its objective, would cover the college's expenditures "for the period of the next
three years."[31] But the implication was that there was no guarantee that
after three years Carleton College would be able to pay their salaries.
MacOdrum was being frank, but he could not be reassuring.

Fortunately, in 1951 the fortunes of Carleton changed. In the fall of that
year full-time enrolment, which was expected to drop once again, levelled
off. The next year it rose sharply. Not until 1956–57 did full-time enrolment again reached the peak enrolment of the veterans' years, but by then
the baby boom was in sight and the problem was to plan for growth. The
shift in fortune was also the result of a major change in the pattern of university financing in Canada. In 1951 the federal government, concerned

about the financial difficulties of universities across the country after the
graduation of the veterans, initiated a program of annual federal grants to
universities. For Carleton this meant an unexpected windfall of $50,000
which, as MacOdrum told the faculty in the fall, made it possible "to make
plans for the retention of certain instructional services which in the spring it
seemed would have to be abandoned in 1952."[32] This was a euphemistic
way of telling the faculty that nobody would be fired.

This federal grant – plus the steadily increasing provincial operating
grant, which reached $100,000 for the 1951–52 year – marked a funda-
mental change in the college's finances. Five years earlier, Carleton had depended on student fees for 90 per cent of its annual income, whereas it now
received only 45 per cent from student fees and another 45 per cent from
government grants. In the spring of 1952 the provincial government added
a capital grant of $100,000 to meet the cost of the now-completed library
building.[33] Carleton College was still not affluent, but the combination of
rising enrolment and government grants meant that the college would survive. For a few years, it had been a near thing.

III

The problems of Carleton's early years were not only financial. Its status as
a degree-granting institution was also uncertain. When the Ottawa Association for the Advancement of Learning had been incorporated in 1943,
the letters patent had said nothing about granting degrees. This had not
prevented Carleton from awarding degrees and employers and other universities from accepting them as valid. But the college administration felt
uneasy. In 1948, after the decision had been made to offer Bachelor of Arts
programs, the Board of Governors had asked the provincial government to
pass legislation to give the college the necessary "powers and privileges" to
grant degrees, but the minister of education had procrastinated, assuring
MacOdrum that the letters patent were sufficient for the time being.[34] This
might be reassuring but it was not enough for a college that constantly
worried about what other academic institutions thought of it. It is revealing
that any sign of academic recognition was seen as important. In 1950, for
example, the president made a point of telling the associates that "employers had expressed satisfaction with the graduates of all divisions" and that
"graduates had been accepted for graduate work in many of the famous
universities of Canada and the United States."[35]

Carleton's legal status became more than a theoretical concern when in
1950 the Ontario College of Education refused to accept Carleton graduates. Recognition by OCE, as it was known, was vital because nobody could
become a teacher in Ontario without attending OCE, and the baby boom

meant that school enrolment was spiralling and many university graduates
were looking to teaching as a career. OCE insisted that it would not admit
Carleton's graduates until Carleton was specifically authorized to grant degrees, but the minister of education was not prepared to give this authority,
arguing that his department was not responsible for higher education and
had "never attempted to pass judgment on the merits of degrees of various
universities." An appeal to the University of Toronto, with which OCE was
affiliated, got nowhere; Toronto took the position that "to ask one university to pass such an opinion upon the degrees granted by another university
was not fair to either institution." The minister of education then suggested
that if the National Conference of Canadian Universities (NCCU) would admit Carleton College as a member, he would accept this as proof that Carleton had achieved the required academic status, and he would give it the
specific legal authority to award degrees.[36]

The NCCU did not know how to respond. It was a voluntary association of
institutions that had the legal authority to confer degrees, and it certainly had
no authority to give this power to Carleton. However, the NCCU did at least
try to be helpful. At MacOdrum's request it appointed a committee, chaired
by President Gilmour of McMaster, to investigate the credentials of the college. The committee reported favourably on Carleton and its academic program,[37] and on the basis of this report a frustrated MacOdrum was finally, in
1952, able to persuade the provincial government to give Carleton College a
charter, which specifically gave it the "power and authority to grant in all
branches of learning any and all university degrees and honorary degrees and
diplomas." The NCCU promptly admitted Carleton as a member. Then, and
only then, did the minister of education certify that Carleton students were
being awarded degrees "approved by the Minister," thereby ensuring that
Carleton graduates could attend the Ontario College of Education.[38]

As well as authorizing Carleton College to award university degrees, the
charter gave legal definition to the structures and objectives of the college.
In its major outlines, the charter established a traditional form of college
government. Although the Ottawa Association for the Advancement of
Learning survived, it was reduced to an advisory role. The Board of Governors was now clearly the legal authority for the college. The board was
distinctive because it was completely self-perpetuating. The YMCA had appointed four members to the previous board, but it now lost this privilege.
Nor did the provincial government claim the right to appoint members to
the board, as it later did for universities founded in the 1960s. Carleton
College was still seen as a private institution, even though it was now receiving government funding. In addition to appointing its own members,
the Board of Governors would be responsible for the appointment of the
chancellor, the president, the deans, professors, and all the other employees.[39] It would also levy the student fees and manage the college property.

ONTARIO

THE MINISTER OF EDUCATION

TO WHOM IT MAY CONCERN:

       re <u>Carleton College at Ottawa</u>

                               This is to state that Carleton

College at Ottawa, Ontario, is a member of the National Confer-

ence of Canadian Universities and, therefore, its graduates are

accorded recognition as graduates of a university "approved by

the Minister".

                                       Minister of Education.

November 4th, 1952.

Legitimate – finally!

The charter followed the traditional bicameral pattern, with a Senate that would be responsible for such academic matters as admissions and academic standards; but the Senate was not representative of the faculty. The president, the deans, and all full professors were automatically members, but additional members could be appointed by the Board of Governors. The board used its authority to appoint two senior associate professors to the Senate. It also took the opportunity to appoint such respected intellectuals from the Ottawa community as Kaye Lamb, the dominion archivist and national librarian, and Frank Underhill, an eminent historian who was curator at Laurier House.[40] This was in keeping with the image of the Senate as a group of senior scholars; there was no talk of professors controlling the Senate or even of electing some of their colleagues to this academic body.

The statement of "objects and purposes" also was traditional. In addition to "the advancement of learning" and "the dissemination of knowledge," the college was to be concerned with "the intellectual, social, moral

and physical development of its members, and the betterment of its community." Some of the original members of the board favoured the identifi-
cation of Carleton as a Christian institution, but the more secular majority
opted for "a non-sectarian college" as a less constraining definition.[41] In
1957 the charter was amended to change the name of the college to Carleton University, but the structures survived almost unchanged until the
1960s, when the traditional pattern no longer seemed appropriate.

By its tenth anniversary, then, Carleton College was an established liberal
arts college. Although the evening courses were still a distinctive aspect, the
focus had shifted to full-time studies, with degree programs in arts and sciences, public administration, and journalism, and with a two-year diploma
program in engineering. The college now occupied the main building, the
new library, and three renovated houses, it had forty-two professors and an
annual budget of almost $400,000. Its academic legitimacy was recognized
by a provincial charter. More important, its financial stability was assured
by annual grants from the federal and the provincial governments. In its
modest way, Carleton College was now one of the institutions providing
postsecondary education for the English-speaking community in Ottawa.

CHAPTER THREE

The Search for Academic Respectability

The professors who taught at Carleton College in the early years often looked back later with nostalgia, in spite of the cramped physical conditions and the limited financial resources. These were hard times for the college; the surviving anecdotes are often about the constraints of space and equipment, and the ingenuity with which people coped. But past poverty does not account for the positive memories. While the hardships are remembered, these were shared hardships, associated with a sense of community, a sense of having worked together for common goals and having surmounted the obstacles in spite of the odds. What remains is the memory of the collegiality, the shared hopes and ambitions, and making common cause. The nostalgia has created a myth of a golden age, with the frustrations and uncertainty fading into the background, but it rests on a proud sense of having built an institution.

The pride is justified. The administration and the Board of Governors had dealt with the problems of acquiring space, had managed the deficits, defined the academic status of the college, and obtained government funding. Yet these achievements, crucial as they were, did not determine what kind of college Carleton would become. Would it continue to emphasize the need to improve the economic prospects of the less privileged young people in the Ottawa community? Would the full-time college give more emphasis to the cultural experiences it could offer? Would it focus on character development? Would it concentrate on providing a challenging academic environment? The options would not be mutually exclusive – for each student, the college would offer a choice – but the personality of the new college would depend on the balance and emphasis. It was here that the professors would play a decisive role. The new members of the faculty, especially the younger members, did not see themselves as giving vocational training. Rather, they saw it as important for their students – and also for their own professional reputations – that the education at Carleton be recognized as rigorous and scholarly by potential employers and by other universities. Within a decade, this emphasis on scholarship would shape the character of the new college.

I

The concern for scholarship was a consequence of Tory's approach to recruiting staff. His insistence that Carleton professors should have the qualifications demanded by established universities meant that Carleton looked for academics with a doctoral degree. In the immediate postwar years, the demand for instructors with a PH D exceeded the supply, and universities compromised by appointing many instructors who had not yet completed their thesis, but there was an implicit understanding that they would have to complete their doctorate before they could expect job security.

This association of a teaching appointment with a research degree reflected the growing prestige of research as an academic activity. Small liberal colleges in the past had looked for teaching skills; the professors they appointed were well read and well informed in their fields without necessarily being committed to research. The young professors at Carleton would have a different focus. They would still be expected to teach three courses each term – which meant nine hours a week in the classroom and supplementary hours for discussion groups or laboratories – and most of them took these teaching responsibilities seriously. Research, however, was often more stimulating intellectually and was always more significant for their careers. This emphasis on research affected their teaching. For them, it was no longer enough to give their students a broad survey of the discipline. They believed that by the time the students graduated, they should have some specialization in their field and some introduction to the methodology of research. The best students, they assumed, should be qualified to pursue advanced research degrees at the best graduate schools. It was an assumption that significantly influenced the curriculum of the new college.

Where did Carleton's new instructors come from? The experienced professors who had come to Ottawa during the war were quickly welcomed back to the universities they had come from, where they helped cope with the influx of veterans. Some who already had roots in Ottawa, including H.H.J. ("Bert") Nesbitt, an entomologist at the Department of Agriculture, and Munro Beattie, an English teacher at the Technical High School, who had been recruited by Tory to teach evening classes, now seized the opportunity to become fully fledged academics. But Carleton had to rely mainly on younger scholars who were entering the profession. However, the recruitment of these professors was not efficiently organized. There was no marketplace or clearing house; information depended on informal networks. Graduate schools at major universities were asked if they had promising graduate students; the students themselves relied on news or rumours about possible openings. It was not an efficient system.

The appointment of John Porter as an instructor in political science in 1949 was unusual, but it illustrates how informal the system could be. Porter had been in the Canadian Army and had taken advantage of the veterans' benefits to complete an undergraduate degree in sociology at the London School of Economics. In the summer of 1949, with no job and no job prospects, he took advantage of his right as a veteran to get a one-way ticket to his former home in Vancouver. On his way he stopped in Ottawa to see some friends, including Paul Fox, a political scientist whom he had met at the London School of Economics.

Fox had been teaching for a year at Carleton while working on his PHD, but he had an urgent problem. Frank Mackinnon, the other political scientist at Carleton, had just resigned, leaving Fox with the responsibility of finding somebody to teach Mackinnon's courses. Over lunch, Fox persuaded Porter to stay in Ottawa and join him at Carleton. Porter's only formal academic qualification was that he had taken some undergraduate courses in political science, but Carleton had to have somebody and it was enough that Paul Fox, junior as he was, was confident that Porter could do the job. Carleton was not taking a serious risk, for it did not give Porter a formal contract and he had no job security.

Porter's experience over the next few years was by no means typical, but it does illustrate the demands made on the young Carleton professors. He had new courses to prepare, and although within a year or two he was teaching some courses in sociology, where he felt more at ease, he had little time during the term to do any research. His salary was barely enough to cover the expenses of a young family, and for two summers he supplemented his income by working as a researcher on the official history of the war.[1] Each year, Porter lived with the expectation that he would be fired by President MacOdrum because he was not acquiring the necessary credentials.[2] His fears had some foundation. He survived because his colleagues respected him as a scholar and rallied to his support. Even so, his advancement was slow. He had to wait until 1955 for his promotion from the rank of lecturer to that of assistant professor, and with it came the warning that he could not count on tenure after the usual three years unless he acquired the equivalent of a PHD.[3] Nevertheless, he was duly granted tenure and then further promotions, because increasing enrolment meant a shortage of professors – and also because by then Porter's early articles on class and power in Canadian society had established his scholarly reputation. But it was ten years before *The Vertical Mosaic* was published and the London School of Economics recognized his work with a doctoral degree. By then he was a full professor and probably Canada's most eminent sociologist.[4]

While Porter's experience was unusual, most of his young colleagues shared with him the stresses of beginning an academic career. They had new courses to design, the constant pressure of preparing yet another lecture for the next day, and, for most of them, the added pressure of having to find time to work on the as yet unfinished doctoral thesis. This was also often a formative period in their personal lives, with marriage, a mortgage, and children. It was an experience shared by young academics across the country in those years, but Carleton was exceptional because a higher proportion of its faculty was young.

Carleton was also exceptional because it was small. It was easier to develop a sense of community when some forty or fifty professors spent most of their time working in the same building, shared an office with one or even two colleagues, passed each other in the corridors on their way to classes, and met in the basement canteen for lunch at noon or for coffee at any hour. As teachers, they had the advantage of being able to discuss with their colleagues the personalities and problems of individual students; even gossip could have pedagogical benefits. Only in a small college could the faculty meet at the end of the year to consult about the grades of the graduating class. For these young scholars it was also an interdisciplinary experience. With so few colleagues in their own discipline, they discussed their research with professors in other disciplines and benefited greatly from these exchanges.

Carleton's sense of community was further strengthened by its limited resources, for it was poor as well as small. The professors had in common the frustrations of an inadequate library and rudimentary laboratories – and, in the early years, of having a single stenographer who shared an office with the president's secretary.[5] Scott Gordon, an economist, was one of the more fortunate, because a contract with the Department of Fisheries provided him with a telephone. He generously shared it with the others in his office and even with the historians in the neighbouring office (through an opening in the wall).[6] Professors became ingenious at making do with very little. Bert Nesbitt in biology solved the problem of providing rabbits for dissection by buying some live rabbits at a bargain price and asking Charles Hulse – a member of the board who was also an undertaker – to help him embalm them. Nesbitt is also remembered by many of his colleagues for a week of foul air in the college when he decided to boil a fox in order to have a skeleton for his class.[7] While the shortage of teaching aids was not amusing at the time, there was the pride of making do with very little.

The basement cafeteria, with its dingy walls and exposed pipes, did not impress visitors, but it was the central meeting place for everybody in the college (Newton).

These shared academic experiences were reinforced by social links. These were the years of the postwar baby boom, and many of the younger professors had a similar experience of babies, crowded accommodation, and second-hand cars, complicated by the difficulty of finding time and money to continue their research. Social activities were low key and inexpensive. One small group gathered for Scottish dancing on Saturday evenings. Hilda Gifford, the librarian, was the initiator, and the early sessions were held in the new college library until the students complained that the library could be opened on Saturday nights for the faculty but not for them. From then on, the group usually met in Gifford's apartment, where they went through the figures and then had refreshments. The membership of the group fluctuated, but the Scottish dancing continued long after Carleton's pioneering days and only came to an end after some thirty years, when the muscles and bones of the loyal members protested.[8] A more important social event was the annual Christmas party. Initially, James Gibson and his wife entertained the faculty in their home. Later, as the college expanded, the party shifted to the college auditorium and involved children as well as adults, complete with a Santa Claus and gifts for each child. Common interests led another group to acquire property jointly at Lake Constan, north of Ottawa, and to build summer cottages there. It was noteworthy that the group included representatives of different disciplines and even one administrator.[9]

The close social contacts within the Carleton community were in part a response to the isolation from the wider Ottawa community. In these early years, many Ottawa citizens may not even have been aware that Carleton existed. The story is told of a student coming to Ottawa in 1947 to enrol at Carleton and hailing a cab at the train station, only to discover that the cab driver had never heard of the college.[10] Ottawa was a city of federal public servants, and college professors had no easy access to this hierarchical world. Nor did the college have a place on the agenda of civic politicians. City politics in Ottawa was dominated in those years by the problems of expanding services to meet the needs of a burgeoning federal government, and it was the battleground of the feisty Charlotte Whitton on one side and the developers on the other. Neither side had any reason to court Carleton. The isolation of the college was all the more complete because there were no prominent college alumni to defend its interests. Those associated with Carleton were left largely to themselves.

Although Carleton was an isolated community, it could not be described as radical. The young academics were too busy with their students, their careers, and their families to have much energy left for political activism. To be sure, many of them had working-class backgrounds, but their choice of career does not suggest a rejection of the established institutions. The experience of the Depression and the war often meant approval of a welfare state at home and of internationalism abroad, but in Canada in the 1950s this was not radical. In any case, there was no established pattern of active political involvement by Canadian academics. While Carleton professors might be keenly interested in current events, they were not political activists.

The attitude to women is consistent with this social orthodoxy. Carleton had been coeducational from the beginning, and the importance of attracting students in these years ensured that women students would be welcomed. Once at Carleton, women faced the same academic hurdles as the men. Was there discrimination? It would be surprising if these women did not somehow experience in the classroom what would now be called gender harassment from some of the male professors. We can only say that there is no evidence to suggest that it went beyond the acceptable norms of the time; it was not an era when women voiced their objections publicly. It is also likely that some of the professors were more interested in the academic development of their male students, because training for a career seemed more important for men than for women. But, again, there is no public record, because the students, male or female, did not publicly challenge this attitude.

We can also assume that when appointments were made, a woman would get little consideration if there was an eligible man available. By 1952, of the forty-two full-time members of faculty, only four were women (three in English and one in philosophy); of the fifty sessional lecturers, only seven were women.[11] Even after a woman was hired there was discrimination. Pauline Jewett, for example, had a doctorate from Harvard and was hired in 1955 as a lecturer. She shared an office with Kenneth McRae, another political scientist, who had been hired in the same year as an assistant professor at a higher salary. The two concluded that their qualifications were comparable; although McRae had not yet completed his Harvard doctorate, he had two years' teaching experience at Toronto. The difference in rank and salary could only be attributed to gender discrimination. McRae protested to the president, and Jewett was promoted the next year, though her salary continued to lag behind. This may have been an exceptional case, but it is consistent with the experience of female academics at other institutions; women regularly fell behind their male colleagues in salaries and promotions. This incident is also consistent with the experience of other women, in that once they had been appointed, they found that most of their male professors accepted them as legitimate colleagues. It was not even unusual for a woman to be chosen by a majority of her male colleagues as departmental chair. Pauline Jewett, for example, became chair of her department in 1960.[12]

II

The curriculum and the requirements for the degrees to be offered by the young college provoked considerable debate. The Board of Governors, led largely by businessmen in the Ottawa community, found the financial problems of the college enough to occupy them and left such academic matters to the faculty. President MacOdrum appears to have had no strong views on curriculum matters and relied on faculty committees to deal with such details. Curriculum planning was needed because the college introduced a number of BA programs in 1946 and added some honours programs two years later. Linked to this curriculum planning were crucial questions about the goals of the college. By the early 1950s, a series of curriculum decisions had gone far to define these goals.

Carleton continued to offer evening courses after the war, and these were still a distinctive feature of the college. The total evening registration, of between six and seven hundred, remained fairly stable over the next decade, with approximately two hundred and fifty formally registered in degree programs. Nobody questioned the importance of these evening classes. They brought in much-needed revenue, and they also provided the opportunity for ambitious young people to better themselves. Some of the new professors were concerned, however, that these financial and social goals might undermine the academic goals that were so important to them.

Their concern was that Carleton would become another community college in the pattern of Sir George Wiliams College in Montreal. [13] Sir George Williams proudly served the working-class population of Montreal, but to many Carleton professors its faculty were primarily teachers, not scholars, and its degrees were academically suspect. The social scientists at Carleton were the most vigorous exponents of this concern, possibly because in this postwar period the social sciences across North America were affirming their academic importance. The humanities could be left to discuss the age-old verities, but the social sciences aspired to create new knowledge and solve social problems. Carleton's location in Ottawa might also be part of the explanation. In these years the federal government dominated the political scene in Canada; not only did foreign policy and defence have a high priority during the Cold War, but this was the Keynesian era when fiscal and monetary policies were dominant and the federal government was taking initiatives in social policy. The social scientists at Carleton saw themselves as ideally placed for the study of Canadian politics, Canadian economics, and Canadian society in general. But this role for Carleton would only develop if the college established a high academic reputation.

The danger of becoming a college along the lines of Sir George Williams seemed serious at the time. Enrolment was a major concern and there were subtle pressures to retain the borderline students by giving them passing grades. There was also some sympathy for the social goals of a community college. The young social scientists who sensed the danger quickly identified Edward Sheffield as the most dangerous exponent of this point of view within Carleton. Sheffield, who had been registrar at Sir George Williams before the war, had come to Carleton in 1947 to fill the same position and had quickly become MacOdrum's closest adviser. Sheffield certainly believed that extending the educational opportunities to the less privileged was a worthy goal, though he was probably more favourable to high academic standards than his opponents admitted. In any case, his presence at Carleton strengthened their resolve to maintain these standards. [14]

How could the young professors ensure high academic standards in the credit courses taught in the evenings? Here the evening school heritage of Carleton and the academic concerns of the young faculty merged easily. From the beginning, the full-time faculty knew that one of their three courses might be offered in the evening. It was a pattern that lasted until the sweeping full-time enrolment increases of the 1960s dwarfed the evening enrolment. Until then, there were few objections from professors about evening teaching, because it was an aspect of Carleton's identity; and, possibly more significant, because it ensured that the credit courses, whether offered daytime or evening, would have the same academic standards.

H.E. English, Economics

D.M.L. Farr, History

M. Frumhartz, Sociology

S. Gordon, Economics

Pauline Jewett,
Political Science

John Porter, Sociology

These young professors completed their graduate studies after the war. They saw both teaching and research as integral to an academic career and fought for high academic standards at the new college (*Raven 60*).

The combination of courses required for an arts degree required more compromises. During the war the programs followed by students had been determined by the program requirements of other universities. After 1946, Carleton could establish its own requirements. Nobody questioned the traditional pattern for a degree of five courses per year for three years. But which courses? For a Bachelor of Arts some specialization would be needed, but at Carleton there could be very little specialization because there were only one or two professors in most disciplines. The pragmatic solution was to require students to complete at least three courses in each of three disciplines. While this did not meet the increasing academic pressure for more concentration, it was defended at the time by arguments in favour of a broad liberal education. The four-year honours degrees, introduced in 1947, were also unusually broad. The general honours degree in arts required at least four courses in each of three subjects. An honours degree in a specific discipline required a major and a minor field, though here the major fields were limited to history, political science, and public administration because the other disciplines offered too few courses. For those who associated academic respectability with a specialized introduction to an academic discipline, these programs were seen as a temporary compromise.

In 1949 the college sought guidance from a Faculty Board Committee on Curriculum, chaired by the president, which conducted an ambitious study on "Goals in Education for Carleton College." The committee paid careful attention to the debate going on in the United States, which had been provoked by the apparent success of communist ideas in Europe and Asia and the need to respond to it by ensuring that American students would acquire a faith in democracy. The committee was not impressed by the American emphasis on education for citizenship, but it did agree that Carleton should not offer an easy or uncoordinated degree. Unfortunately, the committee was less clear about what should be done, and it ended up with high-sounding platitudes. Carleton, it concluded, should ensure that its students should be able to acquire "powers of rational analysis and mature judgment, and the ability to express themselves; and that they will have a chance to exercise their faculties, moral, spiritual, aesthetic and emotional." Not surprisingly, the committee's report was of little help in the planning of a revised curriculum. The Faculty Board sensibly asked the committee to come back with more specific curriculum decisions.[15]

A year later the committee still had no helpful recommendations. Instead, it asked the Faculty Board to give it some guidance. "Should Carleton College." it asked, "contemplate a uniformly high standard of instruction and research activities with increasingly high standards required for admission into the second year (i.e. the year after senior matriculation); OR should Carleton College cater to a variety of 'popular' needs as a 'community centred' institution?" The Faculty Board was not prepared to answer such a loaded question. It accepted the first option as the college's primary purpose but saw the second option as an "ancillary" goal and asked the committee to try once again.[16] At this stage the committee, probably wisely, gave up.[17]

The problem, as the Faculty Board's reaction suggested, was that Carleton's goals in education could not be simply defined. President MacOdrum, for example, was acutely aware of the importance of the adult education courses and the continued enrolment of the less gifted students, because they brought in needed revenue and could be used to justify fundraising appeals. As he told the Faculty Board during the discussion of the second report of the Committee on Curriculum, "One of the biggest challenges facing the College was that of providing services to the business community and the civil service."[18] The reformers within the faculty, on the other hand, were not narrow-minded specialists. They were in favour of a liberal education, in which students would receive a broad introduction to science, the humanities, and the social sciences, if it could be combined with a thorough grounding in a selected discipline. The choice was not between breadth or specialization but the proper balance between the two.

The solution adopted in 1952 was a "common first year" after senior matriculation, followed by two years of more focused study. For a degree in arts or social sciences, the common year included three courses – in English, philosophy, and a social science – and two other courses, chosen from three subject groups: a second language, a science, and mathematics. The common year in science was more specialized; it required three science courses, a course in mathematics, and one course from English, philosophy, or classical civilization. The two years that followed were even more specialized; a major required a minimum of five courses in a discipline, and a combined major required three courses in each of two disciplines. It should be noted that these were minimum requirements; students could choose to follow an even more specialized program if they wished.

The Carleton undergraduate program now more closely resembled the pattern in other Ontario universities, thus helping to ensure academic respectability. The options suggest that support for a broad liberal education – at Carleton as elsewhere – was already on the wane. Arts students might never take a course in science; science students might never be exposed to a social science. In the balance between breadth and specialization, the common first year was a compromise that exposed the students to some diversity but required a significant degree of specialization in the following years.

The inclusion of classical civilization as one of the options for science students in the first year deserves special comment. In 1950 President MacOdrum had initiated Spring Conference, a weekend reunion of the faculty at the end of term to discuss college affairs. At the Spring Conference in 1951, MacOdrum had outlined the serious financial difficulties of the college and had explained that if enrolment continued to decline, major economies would be necessary. As an example, he pointed out that enrolment in courses in the classics was limited and that it might be necessary to replace the full-time classics professor by part-time lecturers who could offer some of the courses in the evenings. H.H.J. Nesbitt, a senior science professor, had a traditional view of what constituted a respectable academic college, and for him this included a respect for the classics. His solution was to include the course in classical civilization as one of the science

Taking a break at the 1957 Spring Conference. *Left to right:* R.O. Macfar-
lane (*background*), David Farr, Tom Brewis, Bert Nesbitt, Wilf Kesterton,
and Hilda Gifford

options in the science students' common first year. It worked. Enrolment in
classical civilization went up that fall, the classics professor's job was secured, and Carleton could satisfy one of the traditional criteria of academic
respectability.

The debates over the programs in public administration were even more
revealing. Evening courses in public administration had been some of the
most popular among young civil servants. A Bachelor of Public Administration could be earned by taking the equivalent of three years of university
work after senior matriculation. Some of the younger faculty members,
however, were concerned about the academic requirements for this degree;
they believed that many of the courses offered were little better than vocational training and that a legitimate program required a more solid
foundation, based on courses in economics and political science. A Public
Administration Committee of the Faculty Board, chaired by Frank Mackinnon, a political scientist, with Scott Gordon, an economist, Paul Fox, a political scientist, and Walter Duffet, the dominion statistician, proposed
sweeping changes. Part-time students would be offered a ten-course program for a Certificate in Public Administration. In place of the bachelor's

degree in public administration, the college would offer a Bachelor of Arts with honours in public administration, with a program heavily weighted towards courses in the social sciences.

For the committee, these curriculum changes were not enough. Its report included a direct challenge to the academic validity of academic degrees based on evening courses. According to the report, the committee

looks forward to the day when the night school of the College will be clearly separated from the day activities and relegated to the subordinate position of extension work, to accommodate the [certificate] course and other such developments. This Committee is aware that its views and efforts are shared by many other Departments in the College, and has designed its courses to fit with the general plan.[19]

This disparaging view of the evening courses was too radical to win majority support of the faculty Board, and these provocative comments were eventually withdrawn. But the committee accomplished its immediate goal; the recommended changes in the public administration programs were adopted.[20] Subsequent changes followed a similar pattern. In 1952 the certificate program was further downgraded by being reduced to six courses. At the other end of the spectrum, the college added a graduate Diploma in Public Administration based on five courses beyond an undergraduate degree, to be followed two years later by a two-year MA in public administration. The shift towards more demanding academic standards was unmistakable.

Some professors also believed that the Bachelor of Commerce program, instituted in 1946, was more vocational than professional. Here the key figure was the economist Scott Gordon, who became the acknowledged leader in the quest for academic respectability after Mackinnon's departure. Gordon chaired the Committee on Commerce Studies, which in 1951 recommended a reduction of the number of accounting courses and an increase in the number of economics courses required for the BA in commerce. As he explained to the Faculty Board when presenting the committee's recommendations, the proposed program avoided "specialized training in the techniques of business management and administration," which the committee considered to be too vocational.[21] Once again the Faculty Board accepted the committee's recommendations.

The concern for respectability went beyond curriculum revision. The reformers did not ask for higher admission requirements, because although the idea of first-year classes limited to brighter students was academically attractive, a combination of practical and philosophical constraints made it unacceptable. Carleton needed higher enrolment for financial reasons, and the tradition of offering the opportunity of higher education to the less privileged was still attractive. The relatively low admission standards, however, strengthened the determination of the reformers to demand high standards from students after their admission. Even though it might be easy to get into Carleton, the reformers saw it as their duty to make sure that it was not easy to graduate. Scott Gordon spoke for this group when he boasted to the faculty that the commerce degree, though only a three-year program, was almost the equivalent of an honours degree.[22] His committee later noted that academic standards were higher in commerce than in arts courses, but it offered no apologies; its recommendation was that the academic standards in arts should be raised.[23]

The quest for academic legitimacy had its costs; for example, President MacOdrum expressed some concern about complaints that only a small number of the students enrolled in commerce made it to the final year.[24] It was also true that first-class marks were rare. Douglas Hartle, one of the first graduates in economics, went on to Harvard with a B-plus average, and he concluded, on the basis of comparison with the other graduate students there, that he would have been an A student at other institutions. As Hartle wryly commented years later, this might have seemed more important if, because of his marks, he had not been admitted to Harvard's graduate school.[25]

It is revealing that there were no major confrontations between the faculty and the administration over academic standards. In part this was because neither the president nor the members of the board were prepared to interfere with the professors' right to make academic decisions. The professors assigned the work in class, set the examinations, and assigned the marks.[26] The also recommended to the president the composition of the various Faculty Board committees,[27] and these committees in turn played a decisive role in academic matters. But why did neither the president nor the Board of Governors intervene? The implication is that to some extent they shared the perspective of the faculty. They too hoped that Carleton would become more than an undergraduate college serving the Ottawa community.

Disagreement between the faculty and the Board of Governors was more likely to occur over salaries. Professors all across Canada felt underpaid by the early 1950s. This stemmed partly from the pressure of the postwar years, when overcrowded classrooms and heavy teaching loads had been accepted as a patriotic response to the return of the veterans. A few years later, after the veterans had graduated and enrolments showed no dramatic decline, professors across the country felt less inclined to accept the heavy demands on their time as normal. They also argued that their salaries had not kept up with those of other professions or even with the wages of tradesmen after the war. Over the past twenty-five years, it was calculated,

Honorary degrees were linked to the quest for academic legitimacy. Dag Hammarskjöld, secretary general of the United
Nations, was awarded Carleton's first honorary degree. Here
he signs the register under the watchful eye of Ted Sheffield,
the registrar (Capital Press Service).

the real income of university professors had remained almost unchanged,
while other groups had significantly increased their purchasing power.[28] It
was not just a matter of money; the professors saw their salary levels as an
unfavourable commentary on their status and prestige, as well as affecting
their living standards. The response was to form a national organization,
the Canadian Association of University Teachers (CAUT), to work for improved salaries and benefits.

James Gibson was Carleton's first contact with this organization. Gibson
was an historian, a graduate of Oxford, who had been a foreign service officer in External Affairs and was attached to Mackenzie King's office during the war; he was among the more senior of the early appointments to the
Carleton faculty. Late in 1950 he received a circular letter from F.A. Knox,
an economist at Queen's, suggesting a meeting of university representatives

the following spring to form an association of Canadian professors in order
to exchange information on such matters as salary scales and promotions.
Gibson expressed his interest and that of some of his colleagues. At the first
meeting an executive committee was formed, with representatives from fifteen universities, to draft a constitution. Gibson was named as Carleton's
representative, but in 1952 Carleton established a separate Faculty of Arts
and Sciences with Gibson as the dean. At that time, CAUT had not decided
whether professors holding administrative positions could belong, but Gibson – always punctilious about such matters – refused a nomination to the
executive. It says something about the collegiality of the teaching staff at
Carleton that none of them seems to have objected to having a dean as their
representative. However, they were clearly interested in the status that came
with being a member of this national association. They formed the Carleton College Academic Staff Association (CCASA), with thirty of the forty-
two full-time professors signed up as members. In 1953 CCASA submitted
its dues to CAUT and so became one of the nine original charter members.[29]

The formation of CCASA and its membership in CAUT may reveal more
interest in participating in a national organization than a concern about
salary levels. Certainly, the professors at Carleton were not militant. While
they did send an annual brief on salaries to the Board of Governors, they
did not ask that the board receive a delegation. At the president's request, a
faculty committee met with him on at least one occasion to discuss salaries,
but there the matter ended. The faculty members apparently assumed that
the president and the board understood and sympathized with their point
of view and would give them whatever salary increases the college could
afford.[30]

The faculty showed a similar restraint where other benefits were concerned. It was noted at one CCASA meeting that its members had no formal
protection against arbitrary dismissal at Carleton. There seemed no reason
to suspect the intentions of the administration, however, and the association
decided to leave well enough alone.[31] On another occasion, it was pointed
out that the professors at Carleton had no formal right to sabbaticals,
though the administration did encourage them to take time off to complete
their doctorates by granting them leave of absence on half salary. Since this
was as generous as at most Canadian universities, the association again saw
no reason "to press for a definite statement of policy at Carleton."[32]

For some of the professors at Carleton, academic legitimacy encom-
passed more than academic standards and remuneration; James Gibson
was one who believed that form and ritual were also important. As chairman of the Committee on Symbols and Ceremonials he tried to make sure
that Carleton acquired the academic trappings of older institutions. One requirement was a crest. The initial crest, proposed by H.M. Tory, was an

"Other duties as required." Here (*left to right*) Kibby Coates,
Bev Moore, and an unidentified member of the staff hang out
the laundered hoods and mortar boards on the roof of the
college before convocation (Marvin Flatt Photography).

open book on a maple leaf, with the Latin phrase *Quaecumque vera* (which
can be translated as "Whatsoever things are true").[33] Unfortunately, the
University of Alberta protested because Tory had borrowed this phrase
from the University of Alberta crest. Gibson eventually proposed the addition of a phoenix above the shield. As a motto he chose "We take up the
task eternal," drawn from Walt Whitman's *Leaves of Grass*, which was
duly translated into *Opera nobis aeterna* to give it a proper academic tone.
When this version reached the board, some of the governors objected that
Latin was too pretentious for a college with egalitarian goals. The board finally adopted a retranslation of the Latin motto, which emerged as "Ours
the Task Eternal."[34]

Some of the younger professors found this concern for ceremonies and
symbols almost laughably pretentious.[35] This was unfair. Their endeavour

to achieve higher academic standards at Carleton College meant adopting the academic requirements of well-established universities. Similarly Gibson, with his emphasis on form and pageantry, was in his own way imitating the pattern of established institutions. Both approaches contributed to the shift in emphasis from a community college with a focus on less privileged students to a college that emphasized academic respectability.

CHAPTER FOUR

Student Life at Carleton College

When classes began on First Avenue in the fall of 1946, the war was over but it was not forgotten. For the students, the past had a weight that was felt, even if it could never be measured. The young people who came to Carleton over the next decade were from families that had in various ways been marked by the Depression and knew that economic security could not be taken for granted. Although the war had ended the Depression, it had contributed to the sense of instability, for men and women had been uprooted; they now wanted a more settled and predictable life for themselves and their children. Yet even the end of the war had not meant the end of insecurity; the Cold War was now dividing the world regionally and ideologically, and the atomic bomb had added a new and ominous dimension to international diplomacy. College students could not help but be affected by the uncertainties of the postwar world.

A special category of students felt the postwar pressures more directly. They were older than the usual high school graduate and were often distinguished by their dress; most of them wore boots or items of clothing that marked them as veterans. They were a significant proportion of the student body – in the peak year, 1948, almost half of the students at Carleton were veterans - and their influence was even more pervasive than the numbers would suggest. Most of them took their work and their leisure seriously, because their life had been disrupted by the war and they were eager to reestablish themselves as civilians. At other universities, and even more in a new college that had no prewar precedents, they set the tone for student life.

The veterans left as quickly as they came. By 1950 nearly all of them had graduated, and most of Carleton's full-time students were men and women who had come directly from high school. These new students were younger, farther removed from the Depression and the war, and less concerned about catching up for lost time. But there was no sudden transition. While the outside world was of concern for many of them, they had an image of what life on a college campus should be like, and they tried to replicate that life at Carleton. In their own way, they sought respectability by imitating student life at older institutions.

This did not mean challenging or defying the established authorities. The campus experience they wanted can be seen as a transition from the life of a child to that of an adult, best described in the time-worn phrase *in statu pupillari*. As students, they conceded that the university authorities would direct their academic development. They also took it for granted that the same authorities would make and enforce rules of behaviour. As adolescents, they would be given more freedom – and more responsibility – in organizing their studies and leisure time, but they recognized that the university authorities had a duty to intervene if students behaved irresponsibly. Growing up meant learning what lines could or could not be crossed.

I

The veterans at Carleton, as elsewhere, fitted into academic life with surprising ease. Many of the soldiers returning from the First World War had been scarred by their experience and had found it difficult to adapt to civilian life, and it was widely believed that the veterans of the Second World War would face similar difficulties. Most of these fears proved to be groundless. The trench warfare of the previous war seems to have had more impact. Most of the veterans coming to Carleton seem to have regarded their time in the armed forces as an interruption in their life. Certainly, they adapted easily to student life, without making any claims for special consideration based on military service or military rank. For the most part, they were a disciplined group, interested in their course work and in good marks, and respectful of professors as long as they seemed competent.

It is difficult to assess the influence of the veterans at Carleton, because they did not act as a group in the classroom or in the extra-curricular activities associated with the college. Their presence, however, certainly helped set the tone. Within the classroom, at Carleton as elsewhere, the veterans are remembered by their professors as almost model students. There is nothing to suggest that they were more gifted than other students, but they had characteristics which any professor would appreciate. They were, on average, a few years older than the other students and were eager to complete their education and begin their careers; this made them more attentive

The Model Parliament was one of the extracurricular activities intended to prepare
young people for the responsibilities of citizenship. The Union Jack makes clear
that this is a serious occasion (Newton).

and more disciplined. Most of them attended classes regularly, did the readings, completed their assignments, and accepted the grades they were assigned. Small wonder that in spite of the crowded classrooms and the
shortage of equipment, the professors had such fond memories of the era of
the veterans!

Yet college life, even for the veterans, was not all work. They showed an
active interest in politics and world affairs, and here too they set the pattern. One student who arrived at Carleton as a seventeen year old recalled:
"Being thrown in with the veterans of World War Two was an experience
I'll never forget. Their maturity, ironic outlook on life, and concern about
the real world made us youngsters grow up in a hurry."[1] College life in
those years offered membership in a variety of political and cultural clubs
as well as participation in a number of social and athletic activities. The administration and many of the professors encouraged the students in these
activities, convinced that the college experience should be more than formal
classwork. Given the handicaps of limited recreational space in the college
buildings and the absence of playing fields on the college grounds, it is remarkable how much extracurricular activity there was.

The Spring Prom at the Chateau Laurier, 1956. The year explains why no wine is
in evidence.

The Students' Council had the major responsibility for organizing the social activities and the clubs. The importance of the council is illustrated by
the way the student body supported the regular increases in its annual fees,
which rose from one dollar per student in 1945–46 to two dollars and fifty
cents the next year, eight dollars in 1947–48, and thirteen dollars in 1949–
50. The major social events organized by the council were the Christmas
Dance and the more formal Spring Prom, complete with corsages. Less formal dances were sponsored by college clubs. By the end of the decade, with
a larger nonveteran enrolment, the Freshman Dance, the Sadie Hawkins
Dance, and the Valentine Dance emerged as important secondary events.
The dances were held in the Assembly Hall, on the third floor, which was
used as a lecture room for the large first-years courses during the day but
was cleared for the evening, with the chairs stacked at the back of the hall.
The president and some professors were guests on these occasions, though
it was not always clear to the students or their guests whether they were
there as chaperones or just to give a more formal status to the evening.
Sometimes the students aspired to something more prestigious than the Assembly Hall. In 1949 the social convener scheduled the Spring Prom at the
Chateau Laurier, which elicited the approving comment by the president of
the council: "It's taken a long time but we've finally arrived."[2] The stu-

dents, like the administration and the professors, were constantly looking for signs that the new college had indeed arrived.

The student newspaper, the *Carleton*, was an important contribution to the collective identity of the full-time students in the early years. It began as a monthly late in 1945 and became a weekly publication two years later. Much of the information it provided was oriented towards college activities, with an emphasis on the work of the Students' Council and of various clubs. Columns entitled "Campus Personalities" and "Meet the Faculty" were clearly intended to foster the sense of community. Campus sports, especially football, basketball, and hockey, were given wide coverage, despite the often disappointing scores, while articles on student conferences in Canada and abroad made the *Carleton* less parochial. The newspaper subscribed to the Canadian University Press wire service as soon as it was eligible, and could then include news items about students across the country. By the end of the decade, it was also responding to a wider range of student interests by including some short stories and poems. The *Carleton* remained self-centered. Even the editorials on off-campus topics never lost an opportunity to draw attention to any evidence that Carleton was achieving a respectable status as a college.

One of the characteristics of these years was the continuing interest in international affairs. Each year some Carleton students participated in the International Students Services seminars abroad and wrote long articles for the *Carleton* on their return. The articles were not on the work of the United Nations or on Canadian foreign policy, but on the tragic experiences and fragile hopes of young people in Europe and the Third World – the underlying message being that Carleton students should be sympathetic and generous. The idealism of these articles is not surprising, but it is intriguing that so little attention was paid to the preponderant influence of communists in many of the international student associations. The explanation may be that Carleton students were so pleased to be accepted as delegates to these associations that they were less concerned than students from other Canadian universities about the risks of belonging to communist-dominated organizations. At any rate, the sympathy expressed in these articles for less fortunate students outside Canada was widely shared on the Carleton campus. On a per capita basis, Carleton College regularly ranked as one of the most generous in the annual campaigns for funds for the International Students Services. As might be expected, the *Carleton* boasted of this tangible sign of international commitment, though the coherence of the small student body probably helped account for the success of the fundraisers at Carleton.

The annual Mock Parliaments, beginning in 1946, also suggest a serious approach to the responsibilities of citizenship. The political clubs devoted a good deal of time and energy to the election campaigns, with their political platforms adapted from the respective federal parties. The two-day parliaments, however, which received full coverage in the *Carleton*, were less notable for their exposition of national policies than for the efforts to score partisan points and win tactical victories against the other parties. They survived only because a managing board, under the guiding hand of Paul Fox, took over control of the topics and the schedule of the debates. From then on, the sessions were more orderly but also were less of a game and more like a supervised laboratory for political science students.

For most colleges, life outside the classroom had long been associated with team sports and competition against other colleges. It was not surprising, therefore, that some Carleton students felt the need for such competition as a confirmation that life at Carleton was indeed a valid college experience. But this was not easily arranged. The college had almost no athletic facilities. As an early report on athletics put it, "Carleton's athletic programme is difficult to expand because of the lack of training and playing facilities. There is no gymnasium, no playing fields, no swimming pool and few facilities for storing sports equipment. The athletic budget is sagging under the expense of renting someone else's ice, water and turf."[3] Both Tory and MacOdrum agreed that life at Carleton should include college and intercollege athletics, and in 1947, despite financial difficulties, MacOdrum allocated one thousand dollars to sports. In 1949, at the request of the Students' Council, the administration took over direct control of the athletic program, appointed a director of athletics, and increased the budget to four thousand dollars.

Even if the college had found more money for sports, there would still have been major hurdles. Intercollege competition was not easy because the established universities did not believe that Carleton was prestigious enough or that its teams were good enough to be admitted to their league. In the early years, Carleton did have some individuals successes in intercollegiate competitions in skiing, swimming, and golf, but these attracted only the fleeting attention of the student body. Basketball received more coverage in the *Carleton*, and the men's and women's basketball teams won their share of games but their handicap was that they were competing in city leagues. The ambiance which some associated with college life depended on participation in a league with other colleges, with students as enthusiastic spectators, cheering on their team. In North America this meant football.

The importance of football, to some students at least, was shown by the sustained efforts to field a team in spite of the difficulties. In 1945 some of the first engineering students decided over a few beers at the Bytown Inn to organize a team.[4] They found a coach and some cast-off equipment from local teams and played their first exhibition game a few weeks later at

Ste-Anne-de-Bellevue against Macdonald College. Not surprisingly, they lost, but they soon improved enough to win two subsequent games. The cost for the first year was one thousand dollars, which they paid mainly by raffling bottles of rye. Years later one player recalled that the remaining deficit of one hundred dollars was covered by a donation from President Tory.[5]

By 1949 Carleton had become a member of the newly formed Ottawa–St Lawrence Conference, which included teams from the University of Ottawa, the Royal Military College, Bishop's and Macdonald colleges, and intermediate teams from Queen's and McGill. It was not a prestigious league, but Carleton students participated enthusiastically. For home games they held a pre-game rally at the college and then marched the half-mile to Lansdowne Park to cheer their team, with the encouragement of cheerleaders to add to the college atmosphere. Unfortunately, the football program was short-lived. As the coach of the previous year had explained to President MacOdrum, the Carleton teams were seriously handicapped. "First and foremost," he wrote, "was the lack of an adequate practice field. We held our practices on a small, poorly-lighted grounds at the rear of the college. Due to its size we were unable to practice kicking, passing or pass defence … Our every move, both defensively and offensively, reflected cramped football."[6] An added problem was the decline in enrolment with the graduation of the veterans, which meant that there were fewer eligible players to choose from. Carleton's teams had losing records for the next two years. Even more serious was the impact of enrolment on the college's finances. In 1951 the college cancelled its $4,000 grant for athletics. In that year Carleton withdrew from the league, and only interfaculty football games were played. Football might be important at other colleges, but at Carleton in these early years there were no football stars, and the game was not the focus of campus life.

Yet the importance of spectator sports can be exaggerated. Carleton College in these years clearly had a sense of community which older and better-endowed institutions could only envy. The small enrolment and limited space meant that students knew many of their classmates. When the student leaders found a cause that seemed to touch on serious social issues, they could mobilize the student body in a way that students at larger institutions could not hope for. The collegiality is strikingly illustrated by what became known as the Tim Buck affair.

In the spring of 1949 the Labour-Progressive Club, the campus communist club, asked permission from the Students' Council to invite Tim Buck, the general secretary of the Communist Party of Canada, to speak on the campus. It was not an outrageous request. Tim Buck has spoken on other Canadian campuses. The Labour-Progressive Club had only two members

The college grounds could look attractive in the evening
shadows, but the football coach was not impressed
(*Raven 56*).

at the time, but it was a recognized club and other political clubs regularly
invited the leaders of their parties to Carleton. It was nonetheless a touchy
issue at a time when the Soviet veto had hamstrung the United Nations and
when the threat of Soviet expansion in Europe had provoked the negotiations that would lead to the North Atlantic Treaty Organization. Douglas
Hartle, the president of the Students' Council, was not a veteran but he
shared the interest in public affairs. On this occasion he favoured granting
permission on the grounds of freedom of speech: the students should be allowed to listen to Buck's ideas and judge for themselves. But Hartle felt that
the decision was too important to be made by students. He went to Presi-

dent MacOdrum, who then asked Hartle to present his case before the Executive Committee of the Board of Governors. The Executive Committee was convinced and left it to the students to make the final decision.[7] The Students' Council then gave its permission and the Labour-Progressive Club duly invited Tim Buck to speak at Carleton on the following Monday.

The incident would probably have passed unnoticed if the *Ottawa Journal*, in its Saturday edition, had not printed a provocative editorial to warn its readers that "the unspeakable Tim Buck, Canadian Communist leader, is to address the students of Carleton." The editorial conceded that the students should know about communism, but to invite Buck to speak to "an impressionable body of young people" was surely unacceptable. More disturbing, according to the editorial, was that the invitation had come from the Students' Council, with the approval of the president and the Executive Committee of the Board of Governors. This, it suggested, "will surprise and, we think, shock many persons in Ottawa who have given this institution financial and moral support," and it concluded that Carleton was inviting trouble "if it opens its doors to Red agitators and their well-organized propaganda."[8] At least one person in Ottawa was shocked by the news. Frank Ahearn, a prominent businessman, announced that he was cancelling his pledge of $3,000 to Carleton College.

The Students' Council was quick to react. It called for an open meeting on Sunday, relying on telephone calls and word of mouth to alert the students. Almost two hundred students showed up. At the meeting, the council proposed that the students should attend the Tim Buck meeting next day, but instead of being disorderly, they should maintain absolute silence during the speech and the question period and then walk out in protest. At the same time, the Students' Council proposed a two-dollar contribution from each full-time and part-time student to replace the money which Ahearn had pledged to the college. The students supported both proposals with enthusiasm and agreed to spread the word to those who were not there.[9] The strategy was politically impeccable. It would demonstrate the students' maturity, their respect for freedom of speech, their abhorrence of communism, and their willingness to pay the price of their high principles. It was a response that only a small and close-knit student body could orchestrate. Tim Buck was certainly impressed; he decided not to come.

The students could not let it end there. They held the meeting on Monday, with Tim Buck present in effigy. Speakers made the point that Carleton did not have what the provincial premier had allegedly described as the "Red Rash." The Students' Council agreed to finance an extra edition of the *Carleton* to denounce the *Ottawa Journal*'s editorial, printing enough copies to permit distribution in downtown Ottawa. That same day the lead editorial in the *Journal* apologized for any suggestion that the college authorities or the students might be sympathetic to the "reds" and reversed its position by concluding that "Ottawa people have taken great pride in this institution and there is no reason why they should not support it wholeheartedly."[10] But the students had made their plans and no apology would stop them.

On Tuesday many of those who should have been in class were on downtown street corners passing out copies of the *Carleton*, with its denunciation of the bigotry of the *Journal's* Saturday edition.[11] Ironically, the *Journal*, on that same Tuesday, had yet another conciliatory editorial, commenting: "Carleton College comes out of the incident with its head high."[12] Fortunately the *Journal* did not retaliate. Two days later the *Journal*, in a final editorial on the topic entitled "We Are Lambasted," noted with some amusement that the *Carleton* had done "a spirited job on us." It had no objection: "In fact, we find much to admire about this copy of the college paper: the vigor of the writing, the fierceness of the editor in defending a cause in which they believe, and this proof that although Carleton College is young in years it commands in its student body affection, pride and respect. We are seeing the development of a Carleton tradition."[13]

There the incident ended, in part because the special edition had almost exhausted the *Carleton's* budget. The next and last issue of the term came out in April when the students had more pressing concerns. It made some references to the Tim Buck affair; it reported that the Three Grand Club had almost reached its $3,000 objective, and the editorial quoted the flattering reference in the *Journal* to the emerging Carleton tradition. There was also a discreet apology on the front page for not having given credit to the *Ottawa Journal* for some of the photographs which the *Carleton* had printed.[14] Life was getting back to normal.

II

By the 1950s, with most of the veterans gone, the day students on the First Avenue campus were, for the most part, graduates of high schools in the Ottawa area. The change, gradual as it was, meant a heightened interest in public displays of student spirit. Successive presidents of the Students' Council wanted more students to get involved in college-wide activities, and editorial writers the *Carleton* were quick to deplore student apathy when students did not respond with the desired enthusiasm. At the same time there was plenty of evidence that Carleton students were not apathetic. Two hundred couples regularly attended the Spring Prom in the 1950s, complete with formal wear and corsages. The *Carleton* could denounce the students' lack of interest in the meetings of the Students' Council, but an impressive 75 per cent of the day students regularly voted in

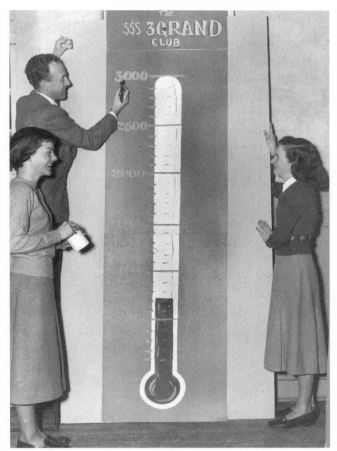

The Three Grand Club begins its campaign (Bill and Jean Newton).

student elections. Also, Carleton students were prepared to give financial support to the college; they contributed to three funding drives during the decade, and in 1957 they doubled the $5,000 target assigned to them.[15] The clubs at Carleton also continued to be active, with an average of twenty-five clubs or associations each year.

For the student leaders, however, college spirit clearly meant something more. They did occasionally boast of the advantages of belonging to a small and cohesive community, but more often their emphasis was on college-wide events in which the numbers involved and the enthusiasm displayed would impress the students themselves and, possibly more important, might even attract the favourable attention of students from other colleges or of reporters from the Ottawa newspapers. Theirs was often a traditional, almost nostalgic, view of adolescent enthusiasm and hijinks. Not all students shared this view – hence the editorials on student apathy – but no alternative was suggested. The student leaders recognized the limited facilities for student activities at Carleton and later in the decade frequently referred to the prospect of a new campus. In the meantime, students were supposed to experience at least an approximation to college life and to show the proper college spirit.

Initiation for first-year students was seen as part of the desired experience. In the first years of the college there had been no initiations; there were no precedents at the new institution and, in any case, the first-year veterans would have ignored any humiliating initiation requirements. But by 1948 there were hardly any veterans among the first-year students, and a debate developed, with some members of the Students' Council arguing that initiation exercises would create college spirit and also make Ottawa more "Carleton conscious." The editor of the *Carleton* was more circumspect and warned that any publicity would almost certainly be bad publicity. The council nevertheless decided to go ahead, "providing that the initiations and punishment for infringement cause no financial or bodily harm to anyone."[16]

Within a year or two the pattern was established for the next decade. It included a sports afternoon at the Dominion Experimental Farm across the canal, and an evening pyjama parade from the college to the downtown war memorial, followed by a scavenger hunt. There was also a frosh revue, for which tickets had to be sold, and a frosh dance to mark the end of the week. In the pattern of most college initiations, there were regulations to make the first-year students conscious of their junior status, including a voluntary dress code, which included short pants or bloomers and unmatched shoes. Over the years the dress code became more exaggerated. In 1956 the acting president, James Gibson, objected that some students might find it too expensive to conform to the regulations that year, and the joint Student-Faculty Committee, to which the matter was referred, asked that the code be revised. The Students' Council was cooperative and, eager not to go too far, it obtained Gibson's consent before adopting the revised regulations.[17]

The frosh court was more controversial. The court first appeared in 1950, complete with judge, counsels, and jury, to impose sentences on first-year students who broke the dress code, failed to stand in the presence of seniors, refused to sing the college song when requested, or were accused of some other breach of regulations. The accused were "guilty until found guilty" and were then required to display their guilt by performing some humiliating task, such as brushing the teeth on the lions at the Sparks Street post office or removing a manhole cover to fish in the sewer. The frosh court grew rowdier as the years went by, with tomatoes, flour, water pistols and then pails of water to disrupt the court. Not to be outdone, students in 1955 pushed a hose through a broken window to dampen the ardour of the spectators. On this occasion there was a journalist present, and a photograph of the incident was distributed across the country by the Canadian Press. According to the *Carleton*, the college was made to "appear indeed like a very young and immature university."[18] The next year, with city reporters now looking for excitement, some less inhibited students interrupted the frosh court with a phial of tear gas.[19] At this stage the administration intervened, and the following year the frosh court was banned from the Assembly Hall. The Students Council made a show of independence and held it in the Students' Union building. However, the council agreed that matters had been getting out of hand, and that same year it reduced frosh week to three days and took steps to make it more orderly.

The reluctance of the college administration to suppress such student activities entirely was not unique to Carleton. The presidents of most Canadian universities believed that a college education should be more than the academic experience of classroom and laboratories, essays and exams. Participation in clubs and student societies was seen as an important part of college life. By planning and administering extracurricular activities, the students would also acquire experience that would be useful in adult life after the ivory tower. There were risks involved, of course. If students broke the unwritten moral code of the community too brazenly, or if their rowdiness led to accidents or property damage, the reputation of the college might suffer. University administrators were ready to intervene for the sake of the college, but like wise parents they preferred not to interfere and did so reluctantly.

It was significant that Carleton students took special pride in their autonomy in extracurricular affairs and came to believe that they had more freedom in these areas than students at most other institutions. As the president of the Students' Council expressed it in the *Students' Handbook* in 1955, "Thanks to the broadminded policy of the late Dr. MacOdrum and his colleagues, the Students' Council has enjoyed a practically interference-free history. In very few other Canadian universities will you find the students in such complete control of their activities."[20] There is no way of proving whether this claim was justified, but Carleton's special circumstances in these years probably did foster the confidence of administrators in the maturity of Carleton's students. In an earlier *Students' Handbook* the president of the Students' Council had given the students the usual warning against "the growing apathy towards student affairs and student responsibilities," but it is significant that he then went on to warn against "the marked tendency towards highschoolism which should be offset by a more mature behaviour."[21] It was not always easy to maintain a balance between

Awards contributed to college spirit. Bill Boyd (*third from left*) shows his trophy for outstanding athlete of 1953 to Norman Fenn. Dr Jim Holmes of Chemistry (*far left*), a longtime member of the Athletics Board, looks on with John Metras, the guest speaker for the evening (*Raven 53*).

high spirits and mature behaviour, but clearly the student leaders shared the administration's concern for the reputation of the new college. With Carleton's small and cohesive student body, the restraining influence of the student leaders may have been more effective than at other universities.

Another factor of some importance was the presence of Norman Fenn. Fenn was a Quaker who had served with an American ambulance service in Burma and had done relief work in India and Pakistan after the war. He had master's degrees in physical education and guidance, and came to Carleton in 1952 as director of athletics. Fenn stood out on the campus – a tall man with a military bearing, usually accompanied by York, a large black dog. Under Fenn the college basketball teams competed with some success in the city league. More important than athletic success was Fenn's conviction that the social and moral benefits of participation far outweighed the development of athletic skills. Under him, athletics became part of the orientation week, with a field day at the Experimental Farm, including three-legged races, a tug-of-war across the canal, and a wiener roast at the end of the day. He also persuaded the students to sponsor Mountain Day (which by the end of the decade drew close to a hundred students for a day of hiking, baseball, and football in the Gatineau Hills) and a Winter Weekend of skating and skiing. Fenn also encouraged intramural competition in a wide range of minor sports. Fenn associated participation with character formation; he insisted that the students organize and supervise their activities. For him, the college's role in developing character was even more important than developing intellect; maturity would come with responsibility.

A relatively minor incident with the football team illustrates Fenn's approach. Football had returned to Carleton in 1952 after a year's absence, and three years later the tradition of a homecoming game against the University of Ottawa was established. The game that year was memorable for two reasons. Pedro the Panda was the idea of a student leader at the University of Ottawa, who bought the panda, had it displayed at a Sparks Street jewellers, and then had it kidnapped to attract publicity. Pedro reappeared when he was parachuted from the roof of Lansdowne stadium at half-time. The other memorable feature was that Carleton won the game and Pedro as well. In the years that followed, the adventures of Pedro often attract more publicity than the football games. In 1957 Carleton gained some recognition by becoming a member of the Ontario Intercollegiate Football League, with Ottawa, Royal Military College, McMaster, Waterloo, and Guelph.[22] Over the next three years Carleton won only two games, but at least it was in the same league as some other Ontario universities.

For Fenn this kind of recognition was less significant than the development of leadership and responsibility. In 1955, for example, when some Carleton students went to Kingston on a Booster Club excursion and behaved rowdily, Fenn took no action but did announce that he considered this behaviour was "a smear to the name of Carleton College." The Students' Council decided not to intervene on the grounds that the incident had taken place off campus. Fenn expressed his disappointment but did nothing more because, as he explained to the *Carleton*, it was up to the student leaders to deal with the situation.[23] Even if the students had not acted responsibly, he assumed that they would learn something from the experience.

This incident, like almost any incident in the 1950s that related in some way to student spirit or student autonomy, was likely to be linked with the consumption of alcohol. The drinking age in Ontario was twenty-one, which meant that many students could not drink legally. Even at the age of twenty-one it was legal to consume alcoholic beverages only in licensed premises or private homes, which meant that it was against the law for anyone to drink or have liquor in college buildings or at football games. Students knew the rules and did not formally contest them – they did not demonstrate or petition to have the laws changed. But for students at Carleton, as elsewhere, drinking was associated with most social occasions. Not all students drank, but liquor was readily accessible and was consumed at college dances and football games with only token efforts at concealment.

College officials were partly to blame. Social attitudes were changing, and although members of the administration and the faculty did not encourage student drinking, they condoned it. Those who chaperoned the dances or attended the football games ignored students who went to the washrooms or drank openly from a bottle. They were only concerned if the flouting of the law or rowdy and destructive behaviour threatened to attract unfavourable publicity for the college. Character building, it could be argued, meant teaching students to hold their liquor.

The student leaders were even less likely to criticize students who broke the law. Flippant comments in the *Carleton* about councillors who were "stewed" or had "tied one on" and about dances that "practically floated," or the claim that "today a case of beer or a bottle is bought for a football game before the ticket" reflect a tacit acceptance, an amused tolerance, and even a certain pride in the students' behaviour. Given the widespread acceptance of this illegal behaviour, what could be done? As one student put it, "Unless the people are noticeably unruly, it's hard for us to snoop around in the women's lounge and look into people's coke bottles for something other than coke."[24] Those who drank may have been "little children who wanted to show maturity by flaunting [sic] authority," as one editorial suggested,[25] but getting drunk was seen by many as part of the process of growing up.

The Students' Council did occasionally intervene but not to defend a legal or moral code. If college authorities and the police were prepared to look the other way, so were the student leaders. Student intervention was justified only to forestall action by the college administration. As an editorial in the *Carleton* put it in 1955, "Carleton students are proud of their autonomous position. The privilege of holding this position must be safeguarded by the students, through their representatives on the Council. It seems obvious that someone must be responsible for the actions of students, when such actions reflect on the college. *The Carleton* would like to see Council assume this responsibility rather than have the college authorities forced to a position where they must take precautions to protect Carleton's name."[26] The editorial was provoked by a rowdy incident in the Students' Union. After a complaint by the janitor, the Students' Council charged four students with unbecoming conduct, breaking house rules, and damaging Students' Union property. The four admitted that they had been drinking in the building and pleaded guilty to breaking the rules. The Judicial Committee, a body appointed by the Students' Council, gave them a "severe reprimand" and put them on probation for a month but carefully avoided mentioning their names in the committee report "to relieve their embarrassment." The name of one of the students did appear in the *Carleton*, but only because he was a member of the Students' Council and had submitted his resignation after the incident. The council apparently felt that the reprimand was punishment enough; it refused to accept his resignation.[27]

THE CARLETON   Thursday, January 20, 1955

Third Section At Work In Union

The *Carleton* makes light of the complaints about drinking in the Students' Union. The editorial accompanying the cartoon asks, "Why all the fuss?" (*Carleton*, 20 Jan. 1955)

This ambivalence towards student drinking meant that drinking continued on college property and at college functions and that no effective measures were taken to stop it or punish the drinkers. Decisions of the students' Judicial Committee could be appealed to the Joint Commission on Student Affairs, composed of three students and three members of the faculty. The infractions of the ban on campus led the Senate to establish a disciplinary committee, composed of the president and senior faculty members, as the final court of appeal.[28] These quasijudicial structures, however, were irrelevant. They were never called on to pass judgment, because no charges were laid over the next few years. The student leaders and the administration preferred to ignore the breaches of the law. It was probably a combination of student civility and good luck that there were no incidents involving major property damage or serious injury in the 1950s.

The emphasis of the student leaders on high spirits and student autonomy was largely irrelevant for some students. Readers of the *Carleton* might easily forget that the student body still included part-time students enrolled in evening courses. The part-time students, some six or seven hunded each year, were still an important source of revenue for the administration, but their relative importance declined as full-time enrolment rose.

They could vote in student elections and participate in extracurricular activities, but for most of them college life was limited to attending classes. For the full-time students trying to foster a wider college experience, the efforts to incorporate the evening students were rare and ineffective.

Among the day students a more intriguing minority were the female students, who in the 1950s formed about one-third of the student body. Women were almost as numerous as men in the arts programs, but elsewhere (as in engineering) there were only a few hardy pioneers. In some ways these women fitted into the traditional social pattern of having a special status, distinct from the men and presumably more in keeping with a supportive and nurturing role. They were automatically members of the Hleodor Club, which hosted a "freshette tea" during orientation and more teas at Christmas and graduation. The Hleodor Club also took on such feminine responsibilities as serving donuts and coffee at the Students' Union open house, running the Red Feather campaign, and even occasionally supplying blind dates for delegates when student conferences were hosted by Carleton.[29]

This special status also meant limited participation in college athletics. There were women's college teams in basketball and swimming, though the *Carleton* gave them very little coverage. In football they provided the cheerleaders while the men competed. Women were also less likely to participate in interfaculty sports. Norman Fenn, to his credit, encouraged women to participate in athletic activities during orientation and at the student outings on Mountain Day and Winter Weekend, and he arranged to include a woman from the Hleodor Club on the Athletic Board and expressed a willingness to organize more interfaculty competition for women if they were interested.[30] Fenn's reluctance to impose his authority directly, however, meant that any initiative for fuller athletic participation had to come from the women students, and in the 1950s it never came.

In other aspects of student affairs, however, there were some signs of change. The Sadie Hawkins dance did not have the status of the formal proms, but it did at least give women the initiative for this one evening to select their escort. The beauty contests – a feature of the decade at the faculty as well as university level – certainly implied a special status for women, but it was perhaps a sign of the changing times when in 1956 the Sadie Hawkins dance included the election of the most popular man on the campus.

There was one area of student activity at Carleton in which women had a status of equality with men that was unusual in this decade. The standard pattern for student associations at other universities was still one of male dominance. Most students' councils were restricted to men only or had only recently arranged for some form of special representation for women on the council.[31] The Carleton structure, which dated back to the night-school years when women were in the majority, had never made any distinction between men and women as voters or as candidates for the Students' Council. The same procedures were adopted without debate when the day students arrived; the candidature of women was never challenged. Women regularly presented themselves as candidates and were regularly elected to positions on the Students' Council. On two occasions in the 1950s, they successfully ran for the office of president, and for one year the editor of the *Carleton* was a woman. Equal status for women in the direction of student affairs came more easily for a small student body with no outmoded traditions.

Nevertheless, the Carleton students in the 1950s continued to suffer from a sense of inferiority. Some had chosen to come to Carleton because of its special programs in public administration and journalism. For many, however, convenience and financial factors seem to have been important. Most of them came directly from high school and were still living at home.[32] One president of the Students' Council bluntly greeted the incoming freshmen by commenting, "Many of you came to Carleton as a last resort."[33] But he went on to promise them that with time and a willingness to participate they would enjoy their stay. There is some evidence that he was right. Carleton may have lacked the prestige and facilities of older institutions, but there were compensations. In a survey conducted many years later, the students of those years remembered the classrooms as being inadequate, but they had almost no complaints about the professors or the library. Two out of three remembered attending intercollegiate sports events, and an even larger proportion recalled participating in student clubs. Looking back some thirty years later, they thought of their college days as having been happy and satisfying.[34] Carleton may not have been well endowed as a college, but the intimate surroundings of a small college had some academic and social advantages.

CHAPTER FIVE

The Decision to Move

In 1957 Carleton officially became a university. The designation by the provincial government made little legal difference, but the prestige of the new title came at an appropriate time because it coincided with the move to a new campus. The decision to move, unlike the name, changed the institution significantly. Carleton University would be very different from the college on First Avenue.

The college could have stayed at its First Avenue location, expanding slowly by buying and adapting more adjoining houses, but it would have continued to be a small institution with cramped facilities and limited space for extracurricular activities. On the other hand, there were serious risks involved in any move. In the early 1950s it was still not clear that the college would attract enough high school graduates from the Ottawa area to secure its future; in any case, the college had no money to pay for land or buildings. President MacOdrum counselled caution. The initiative would come, not from the president but from the chairman of the Board of Governors. In retrospect, the decision to move was a wise one. Many more young people wanted to go to university in the 1960s, and the provincial governments was encouraging universities to meet the demand. By then, Carleton had a new site, and public funds were available for further expansion. In the 1950s, however, the advantages of a move were not so obvious, and there were some unexpected roadblocks. Even the acquisition of the new site would provoke opposition.

Carleton College officially became Carleton University in
1957, but it would take more than a change of name to change
the institution (Capital Press Service).

I

It will be recalled that in 1947, Harry and Wilson Southam and Colonel
C.M. Edwards had donated thirty-nine acres south of Dow's Lake "as a
site for a future College campus."[1] The land was part of a triangular area
of some two hundred acres bounded by the Rideau Canal on the west,
Bronson Avenue to the east, and the Rideau River to the south. At the time
it was an isolated area, with no buildings except for a few squatters' summer cottages. To the west, across the canal, was the Dominion Experimental Farm; to the south, across the river, was more federal property, which
was reserved for driveways and parkland; to the east, along Bronson Avenue, there were some houses and, towards the river, some land set aside for
a municipal park. However, move to this location seemed far in the future.
As President MacOdrum told the Board of Governors the next year,

It is the belief of your President that for the next five years or more, the above mentioned programmes (now offered at Carleton) can best be developed in the Glebe area, centred about the present College building; neighbouring houses to be bought and adopted to college uses as the programme of study expands.

Certainly it would seem that no move of teaching units to a site beyond the city limits can be recommended until the rate and volume of influx from the city high schools and other points outside the city can be estimated with a greater accuracy than is at present possible.

As to the long range view – any time beyond five years – your President believes that the interests of the College will best be served by the continuing exercise of alertness to the community's needs, opportunities and resources on the part of the administrative leaders and individual members of the Board.[2]

The board apparently agreed with the president, and over the next year or two, with the consent of the donors, it even considered selling the land if the price was right.[3] By 1951, however, the number of potential purchasers was limited because the Federal District Commission had designated the area for recreational use and proposed a national sports centre and a zoological garden.[4] In that year the commission offered to buy the land at a thousand dollars an acre, but the Board of Governors asked for three thousand an acre.[5] There the matter rested, but an ominous resolution by the commission to acquire all the land in the area by expropriation if necessary was not encouraging.

The situation changed dramatically in December 1952 when Harry Southam offered to sell the college two adjoining properties, of thirty-seven and sixty acres, respectively. He asked for $133,900, the amount which the Federal District Commission had offered him. James Coyne, as chairman of the board, quickly agreed. Coyne, the governor of the Bank of Canada, was a "mandarin" and one of the small group of federal public servants who had won respect at home and abroad for their administrative competence during the war and postwar years. He was a confident and even stubborn man, as his clash with John Diefenbaker would show some years later, but he was not a gambler. The sudden decision to buy the land seems out of character. He may have consulted leading members of the board, but there was no formal consultation and the offer to buy the land was made without the board's prior approval. However, Coyne had hedged his bet. What on the face of it seemed to be "speculative recklessness"[6] actually involved very little risk. As Coyne explained to the board early in January, "both parcels of land could be sold back to the previous owners if the Board did not approve of the purchase."[7]

But even if there was no financial risk, why had Coyne acted so precipitately? The future of the college was still uncertain. Enrolment statistics were discouraging. By 1949 enrolment had risen to more than 572 full-time students but it had declined in the years that followed, as the veterans graduated. In 1952, when Coyne purchased the land, the number was down to 442. Unless this trend was reversed, the college would have no future. However, Coyne was not intimidated by these statistics. As he explained to the members of the board in a memorandum distributed before their January meeting, he did not expect Carleton to become a big university: "The nucleus of the university will, we hope, always be a relatively small, high-quality liberal arts college," with some specialized work in public administration and graduate studies. But he argued that the college was sure to grow beyond its present size. It was already established as a community institution, and the census returns showed that "the number of youth reaching university age in Ottawa ten or fifteen years" would double. As the community grew, so would Carleton. Coyne's estimate, which he described as conservative, was that the "total full-time enrolment at Carleton College in 1960 will be double what it is today, and by 1970 will be triple what it is today." Clearly, the college would need a new campus.

Coyne's conclusion was coloured by his image of what a small college should be like. Instead of a cluster of crowded buildings in an urban community, his ideal was a parkland setting where young people would be insulated from the pressures of city life. As he explained in his memorandum, Carleton would need "a large block of land capable of supporting a substantial number of buildings, while maintaining the character of a university campus with some open spaces, including lawns, walks and playing fields. Some degree of rustic scenery would certainly be desirable." At the same time, the site should be easily accessible for the part-time students and those enrolled in extension courses. Developers, Coyne pointed out, were quickly acquiring the available land in areas that might be suitable, so although it was not necessary to build the new campus immediately, an early decision on the site could not be delayed. Coyne wanted to plan for the future. "We have felt," he said in the memorandum, "we must if at all possible provide room for development over a period of at least a hundred years ahead," and he argued that the site south of Dow's Lake matched these requirements. The location was ideal. Based on the federal government's National Capital Plan, the city was expected to grow to the south and west, and "the area in which we are thinking of building ... will be just about in the centre of the Ottawa of the future." The college would not need all of its land for many years, but in the meantime the surplus could be used for recreation.[8]

The board was not completely unprepared for the question because it was already facing problems with its science courses. The college's accommodation for science had always been rudimentary, with rooms that had

The site of the new campus, bounded by the Rideau River in the foreground and the canal on the left, with the railway running through it. In the background the Peace Tower can be seen silhouetted against the Ottawa skyline.

never been designed for laboratories and with makeshift equipment, much of it salvaged from government laboratories. Expropriating another house in the neighbourhood would provide more space, but even with costly renovations it would be less than satisfactory. It would be preferable to build a new science building. The question was where. To squeeze it behind the main college building would eliminate what little space there was, and if the college eventually moved, the investment would be lost. If there was to be a new campus, it made more sense to make the decision immediately and build the science building on the new site. Coyne made his presentation to the Board of Governors in mid-January 1953. The minutes record that Dr MacOdrum supported the proposal, stating that "in his view the present holdings of 130 acres would be adequate for at least the next hundred years." The board then gave its unanimous approval of the motion to purchase the two additional lots.[9]

Carleton still had to persuade the Federal District Commission to modify its plans for the area, but Coyne did not expect any problem. He told the board he was sure that "Carleton College can put up a reasonable case that the establishment of a well-planned university in that area will not detract from but will be of real benefit to the general scheme for the beautification and improvement of the National Capital." Indeed, he stated that "some preliminary indications" of Carleton's plans had already been given to the Federal District Commission and to its planning agency, the National Capital Planning Committee. The next step after the land was acquired would be to have an architect survey the property and suggest plans for the possible location of buildings and the landscaping arrangements. The college could then submit these plans for approval to the Federal District Commission and its National Capital Planning Committee.[10]

The architect Watson Balharrie, who had been the architect for the library building, faced some serious problems with the site. A major inconvenience was the Canadian Pacific Railway line, which bisected the property into eastern and western sections, with only a narrow underpass near the Rideau River to link the two. It was assumed that the railway line would eventually be removed, but for the time being Balharrie resolved the difficulty by proposing to locate all the university buildings in the western section, between the railway and the canal. This western section was itself divided by a bywash – or overflow – running from the Hartwell Locks on the canal to the river. This problem would disappear when it was decided that the bywash was not needed. Meanwhile, Balharrie proposed transforming it into a decorative pond. There was concern also about the land towards Dow's Lake, which was low and subject to flooding. Fortunately the height of land in the southwest corner was an attractive site and had the advantage of a solid rock foundation. Balharrie suggested that most of the buildings needed to serve Carleton in its first phase as a college of one thousand students – and even in its second phase of two thousand students – could be built here.

Coyne assumed that Carleton's plans would receive prompt approval from the Federal District Commission. Jacques Gréber, who had prepared the initial plan for the development of the national capital, was apparently open to the idea of a college on the Dow's Lake site, so the chairman of the National Capital Planning Committee supported Coyne's proposal. Nor did the chairman of the Federal District Commission have any objection. The agenda for the June meeting of the commission included a motion to rescind its earlier decision to expropriate the Dow's Lake property. One member of the commission, however, was not persuaded. The motion came late in the day and Charlotte Whitton, the feisty mayor of Ottawa, objected so strongly that a majority voted against any change in policy.

Charlotte Whitton was a penny-saving administrator who was already feuding with developers and seemed to object, almost on principle, to any expenditures.[11] Her motives, however, were not always clear. In this case the chairman of the National Planning Commission suspected that she was "getting back ... at Mr. Southam, against whom her animus is well known."[12] A more logical objection, from her point of view, was that the previous plans for the area would have brought the city a federal grant in lieu of taxes, whereas the college would be exempt from municipal taxes. However, her stated objection was that the college would find that the cost of sewer and water mains on this site would be prohibitively expensive; she recommended that the college look elsewhere to find a suitable site. Coyne and MacOdrum appeared in person at the next meeting of the commission in November to argue that the estimated costs for sewer and water mains were reasonable and quite feasible for the college, but Whitton was still not convinced. At her suggestion, the commission postponed any decision until its staff had checked the college's cost estimates.[13]

The commission staff agreed with Carleton's estimates, and in January 1954, one year after Carleton had acquired the land, the Federal District Commission agreed to allow Carleton to use the Dow's Lake site to build a university. Even then, Charlotte Whitton did not give up. Instead of following the usual pattern of extending the city's water mains and sewers to the edge of the university property, she insisted that Carleton would have to pay for the construction of the links from its property to the closest city mains and for the pumping station that would also be required. Three more years passed before the city and the college could agree on the costs for this construction; Carleton's sewer and water mains were not connected until 1957. As a sequel, two years later, when the city was extending Bronson Avenue over the Rideau River and needed a narrow strip of college land, including the pumping station, it discovered to its chagrin that it could not expropriate university property.[14] In the negotiations that followed, Carleton agreed to cede the land if the city would reimburse it for the expenses incurred for the pumping station and the sewer line built under city property. Carleton received $65,000 – but did not endear itself to Charlotte Whitton in the process.

II

The acquisition of the new site was timely. In 1953, when the purchase of additional land was confirmed by the Board of Governors, the full-time enrolment was fewer than five hundred students. Over the next few years each fall registration showed an increase. By 1955 full-time enrolment exceeded the peak enrolment during the veterans' years, and by 1959, when classes began on the new campus, it exceeded nine hundred. By then it was clear that the gamble of founding a college had paid off, that enough students would enrol to ensure a viable institution, and that the college could look forward to steady expansion in the future. Even the dubious were convinced that Carleton needed a new campus, though it was still not clear how the new campus should be developed or how the development could be paid for.

The rising enrolment was not the only factor that precipitated the move to the Dow's Lake property. The inadequacy of the science facilities in the First Avenue building was made even more glaring by the decision to extend the engineering program to four years. Canada's economic growth in the 1950s had increased the demand for engineers but, paradoxically, this had created difficulties for Carleton's two-year program. Engineering faculties elsewhere were turning applicants away and were less willing to provide places in mid-program for Carleton's graduates. The administration of the Carleton program was also complicated by the need to meet the course requirements of these other institutions. When Queen's revised its program in 1954, Carleton students faced the loss of a full year when they transferred. The logical solution was to offer a four-year degree in engineering at Carleton.

This decision was facilitated by the appointment of a new chancellor in 1954. Carleton's first chancellor, H.S. Southam, the publisher of the *Ottawa Citizen*, had had firm roots on the Ottawa community and been a generous patron of the fledgling college. C.J. Mackenzie, his successor, reflected the evolving identity of the college. Mackenzie was a prominent public servant who brought to Carleton a broader national outlook. He was an engineer, a former dean of engineering at the university of Saskatchewan, and had come to Ottawa as president of the National Research Council, where until his retirement he played an important role as unofficial scientific adviser to the federal government. As chancellor, Mackenzie was actively involved in university affairs for the next fourteen years, not only in his formal role but as a trusted adviser of university administrators on many issues.

Mackenzie played an important role in the development of the engineering program. Carleton planned to offer four branches of engineering: civil, electrical, mechanical, and engineering physics. The trend in engineering faculties in North America was towards increasing specialization, but Mackenzie was critical of this pattern because he was convinced that the best preparation for engineers was a broad education which stressed the fundamental sciences, especially physics, and which would also be enriched "by devoting a reasonable amount of time to the humanities."[15] Such a program had a special attraction for Carleton, because it would permit a common program for the first three years and, as James Gibson explained to the Ottawa Association for the Advancement of Learning, would therefore require "only a fraction of the outlay" of a more specialized program.[16] Mackenzie's prestige within the profession was enough to reassure the timid that the Association of Professional Engineers would give the proposed program the necessary accreditation. Quarters would be narrowly cramped, however, until classrooms and laboratories were available on the new campus.

The School of Engineering did not have an auspicious beginning. The first year of the new program began in 1957, and the program was to be extended one year at a time, with the first graduates scheduled for 1961. The professors and first students faced inadequate equipment and frustrating overcrowding, but found some satisfaction in coping with adversity, buoyed by the prospect of moving soon to a modern building on the new campus. The new director, however, resigned in protest after only a year, frustrated by not getting full assurance of all the laboratory equipment he wanted in the new building. He added to the college's embarrassment by informing the press of his reasons.[17] A turning point for the School of Engineering came in 1959 with the appointment of John Ruptash as its director. Ruptash was strongly committed to the broad-based approach to the training of engineers. Possibly more important, he was a forceful and decisive administrator, and had an energy and enthusiasm which he devoted to the School of Engineering and the university for the next fifteen years.

The sudden death of Maxwell MacOdrum in the summer of 1955 delayed any planning for the new campus or for raising the funds that would be needed. James Gibson, the dean of arts, became the acting president until a successor could be found. The Board of Governors was legally responsible for finding a successor, but the decision was left to C.J. Mackenzie, the chancellor, and James Coyne, the chairman of the board. Both men were confident that the college now had a secure future, based on the increasing enrolment and on demographic forecasts predicting that "the university population in Canada will probably double in the next twenty years."[18]. The two men also agreed on the suitable qualifications for a new president. The man they were looking for – they never thought of a woman – was not to be primarily an academic administrator. His role would be to convince governments and the public generally that Carleton College was a respectable academic institution and deserved their support. As Mackenzie explained to the president of Dalhousie when asking for suggestions:

They [the Board of Governors] feel, and I agree, that the academic pattern of Carleton has been pretty well established and that the Deans and senior staff will carry out our ideals of a strong liberal arts college and in particular a liberally conceived public administration course. We feel that the principal duties of the new President in the immediate future will be of a public relations nature using the term in its best sense. We therefore are thinking in terms of someone trained in the humanities or social sciences and preferably one who has a knowledge of Governmental activities and who would have a standing not only academically but for his wise knowledge of broad public relations.[19]

Mackenzie recognized that the new president would need academic qualification that would "carry the respect of his staff"[20] but thought that his influence outside the college was more important.

Claude Bissell, vice-president of the University of Toronto, had the qualifications which Mackenzie and Coyne were looking for. He was recommended to them by Sidney Smith, the president of the University of Toronto, and other senior academics warmly agreed.[21] Bissell was a professor of English with a PH D and was also a veteran, so he was doubly respectable. By his own account, he had become an administrator almost by accident,[22] but it probably weighed heavily with Mackenzie and Coyne that he had, as Bissell put it, "walked the thoroughfares of provincial bureaucracy"[23] and was well known at Queen's Park in Toronto. Bissell, in turn, was attracted by the freedom of action he would have as president and by the chance of shaping a new institution. His appointment was announced in the spring of 1956.

The professors at Carleton had not been consulted. Donald Rowat, a political scientist, had already prepared a report for the Canadian Association of University Teachers in which he had argued that in Canadian universities, influenced more by American that British patterns, the faculty were regarded by boards of governors as nothing more than employees and were not involved in management.[24] At Carleton, Rowat argued for more consultation with the professoriate on the grounds that "the ability of the faculty to come forward with good ideas and proposals should not be overlooked."[25] Under his chairmanship, a faculty committee "concluded that there is a need at Carleton College for continuing machinery to provide for consultation with the Faculty on matters of organization and administration affecting the academic development of the College."[26] It was not a call to man the barricades, but it was a claim to an enhanced status for the professors within the college.

The faculty were right to see the appointment of a new president as an important academic decision, but the Board of Governors, presumably confident that it knew what was needed, showed no interest in their opinions. At the last minute, James Coyne did accept an invitation from some professors for the search committee to come to dinner and discuss the qualifications the new president should have. The discussion was a waste of time. When Coyne announced Bissell's appointment the next day, it was clear that the search committee had already made up its mind. The faculty had no objection to Bissell as the choice, but they were infuriated by the board's high-handed behaviour.[27]

Claude Bissell fitted almost everybody's criteria for a university president. He had the appropriate academic credentials and an obvious commitment to scholarship. He was a cultivated man, interested in ideas and in their felicitous expression, but at the same time he recognized that universities could not survive as ivory towers. He built no barriers of dignity or pretension to keep others at a distance, and adapted easily to the small-town atmosphere of Ottawa and to college life, speaking at clubs and regularly inviting students and faculty to the president's house, which Carleton provided. Bissell also accepted the role of fundraiser that was envisaged for him by the board.

Money was certainly needed. For a projected enrolment of one thousand students it was estimated that the construction costs for a new campus would be $5 million. The provincial government had announced a capital grant to Carleton of $1 million in the spring of 1956, before Bissell's arrival, but private funds would be needed to supplement this amount and to give weight to the argument that governments should do even more. In the fundraising campaign of that year the Ottawa community was still important, and Brooke Claxton, a recent appointment to the board, effectively organized the campaign within the federal civil service. It was a sign of the wider perspective of the board that this time the campaign literature put more emphasis on Ottawa as the nation's capital, and that chartered banks and national foundations were seen as potential donors. The key figure in this part of the campaign was Senator Norman Paterson of the Paterson Steamship Lines, who opened doors on St James and Bay streets. Bissell remembered the "cheerfully amateurish" way in which he and the senator and C.J. Mackenzie set off for Montreal in the senator's Rolls-Royce to see the magnates of St James Street. Amateurish or not, Senator Paterson's contacts and his generous personal donation of half a million dollars went far to account for the total collection of over one million dollars.[28]

Bissell recalls an incident that underlines the unsophisticated approach of universities to public relations in those days. To make the most of Paterson's gift it was decided to have a public rally in Ottawa, at which the donation would be announced. The senator was in Florida, but it was arranged that Bissell would proudly tell the audience that the campaign was going well, with over half a million dollars collected, and at that moment the telephone would ring and the senator's amplified voice would announce that Bissell was mistaken – he was going to make that a million dollars! All went according to the script, except that after Bissell's statement the telephone link to Florida was interrupted, leaving him desperately wondering how to save the situation. Fortunately, Paterson's voice finally came through and all was well.[29]

Bissell was not content to be only a fundraiser. He had an agenda of his own for the young college. One of his ambitions was to make Carleton "a

President Bissell speaks at the beginning of the 1957 fundraising campaign (Capital Press Service).

cultural and intellectual centre for the community."[30] He initiated a series of chamber music concerts, the annual Plaunt Lectures on Canadian issues, and also a series of evening lectures on eminent Canadians, later published in a series entitled *Our Living Tradition*. In the days when television was still in its infancy and the citizens of Ottawa were looking elsewhere for their entertainment, these events drew large town and gown audiences – so large that the college library was sometimes unable to accommodate the crowd.

The new president also wanted Carleton to take advantage of its location in the national capital and become a centre of graduate studies and research. For this, the academic qualifications of the faculty would be more important than buildings. Bissell was quick to appreciate that the new enrolment predictions would mean competition among Canadian universities for qualified professors. In 1957 he persuaded the Board of Governors to raise faculty salaries dramatically, with increases of close to 25 per cent. In his annual report for that year he announced: "It is a matter of pride that Carleton University now has one of the best salary scales in Canada, one of the best, indeed, on the continent."[31] Other universities soon followed suit, and although the salaries at Carleton did not keep up with those at Toronto, the gap was narrow enough that over the next few years money was not considered a major factor when professors were deciding to come to or stay at Carleton.

Bissell was impatient to develop graduate studies. Carleton already had a number of professors with established academic reputations, and some departments did offer graduate seminars. But no individual department was large enough to support a graduate program, and it would be some years before strong disciplinary programs could be established. Bissell's solution was the Institute of Canadian Studies, which would allow students to follow an interdisciplinary program for a master's degree by selecting graduate seminars from a number of departments.

The creation of the institute ruffled a few feathers. Bissell – in what he ruefully described later as acting "in the spirit of the old monarchical presidency" – had recommended that Robert McDougall, who would be joining the English Department the following year, should be appointed director of the institute.[32] Some faculty members resented not being consulted about the appointment, though most of them limited their criticism in public to reservations about the academic respectability of an interdisciplinary program that would not have the coherence or rigour of a program based on a single discipline.[33] The Senate, however, accepted Bissell's recommendation, and McDougall's commitment to high academic standards soon reassured the critics. The Institute of Canadian Studies was exceptional at the time because it was the first area studies program with Canada as the focus. It benefited from the emerging interest – and pride – in Canadian identity associated in the 1950s with the Massey Commission and the Canada Council. The institute was well placed to take advantage of its location in Ottawa and of the flowering Canadian nationalism of the next decade.

Meanwhile, plans for the new campus had advanced slowly. As early as November 1953, when Coyne and MacOdrum had appeared before the Federal District Commission, they had talked of a "planned university campus, with buildings of character and dignity and with generous open spaces."[34] A planning document in the summer of 1954 stressed the aim to "create an impression of substance and dignity."[35] An early news release from the Board of Governors avoided details but promised an integrated plan for the development of the new site, with the location and design of each building fitting into this master plan: "Buildings will be related to each other in a formal development based on the natural features of the site. A formal approach which uses and masters the contours, waterways and trees, will give a sense of order and cohesion to the whole, while maintaining the interest of the varied topography."[36] This architectural jargon is not very helpful as a description of the proposed college, but again it underlines the importance given to a planned campus. A faculty poll in the same period was more specific; the professors wanted the plans to include a faculty common room and, above all, a separate office for each of them. In spite of the different emphasis, the board and the faculty agreed on one

Rob McDougall (*centre*), director of the Institute of Canadian Studies, makes a
point with Jack McClelland (*left*), of McClelland and Stewart, at the launching
of the Carleton Library series in 1963. The series made an important contribution to Canadian studies by publishing more than one hundred out-of-print
books, as well as documentary collections and special monographs on Canadian topics (Capital Press Service).

thing – the new campus was to be the antithesis of the cramped and makeshift First Avenue campus.

The responsibility for transforming these expectations into reality was
entrusted to the Architectural Associates for Carleton University, to be
chaired by Watson Balharrie and to include eminent architects from Montreal and Toronto.[37] In 1956 the architects announced that the campus
would be developed in three stages. The first stage, to be completed by
1960, would serve an estimated thousand students and would "include a
central group of buildings, including a science building, the first phases of a
library and arts building, a students' union and an administrative building," all grouped on the height of land at the south end of the property. It
was an attractive site, with a sharp drop to the Rideau River, but the architects made no effort to take advantage of the view. Instead, the buildings
were to form a closed courtyard; if they faced in any direction it would be
to the north along the canal towards the Parliament Buildings. Student residences to the north and a fieldhouse and playing fields on the other side of
the railway tracks would complete the first phase. Some twenty years later,
by which time enrolment was expected to have doubled to two thousand

James Gibson, the acting president (*right*), and Fred Turner, the bursar (*left*), planting trees on the new campus to hide the railway tracks (Capital Press Service)

students, additional floors would be added to the library, and an extension to the arts building would complete the main court, A group of science buildings would create a science court, and an assembly hall would be built. The third stage, planned for early in the next century and a projected enrolment of six thousand students, would have additional buildings for the social sciences, fine arts, graduate studies, and engineering.[38]

The integration of this planned campus was to be achieved by a distinctive architectural style. There would be no vine-covered towers in university gothic. Carleton University was to be new and forward looking, with modern designs and modern materials. As a student handbook put it, there would be "architecture and landscaping of the latest contemporary design, in keeping with Carleton's lively spirit and progressive outlook."[39] Unfortunately, this was a period when architectural design had little distinction and when many of the modern materials proved to be unsatisfactory. In the spring of 1956, however, when this master plan was unveiled, new was still beautiful, and James Coyne could describe the proposed campus as "one of the most exciting university developments in the history of higher education in Canada."[40]

The future might be exciting, but the planning for the first building was an architect's nightmare. This was the science building which was to be named, appropriately, after Henry Marshall Tory, the college's first president. The building was so urgently needed that it was decided to build it on the new site while the arts students continued to use the First Avenue buildings. The problem was that initially the new building would have to accommodate both science and engineering students, with differing requirements for laboratories and classrooms, yet the design would have to be flexible enough for the building to be adapted as the student body grew and some programs were moved to other locations. Compromises were also necessary in the face of the initial demands of optimistic professors. To compound the architects' difficulties, Carleton, like most North American universities, divided the responsibilities for academic and financial decisions between the Senate and the Board of Governors. Every decision on space or equipment in the new building had both academic and financial consequences. The architects would find it difficult enough to outline the many possible compromises between objectives and costs; university government seemed almost designed to ensure that the decisions required by the architects would never be made.

The solution at Carleton was the Building Advisory Committee. This was initially a users' committee, which was intended to outline the requirements of the proposed occupants of the building. It was then expected to report to the Building Committee of the Board of Governors, which would decide what the university could afford and would give the appropriate instructions to the architect. But there were so many options and so many possible compromises that the board's Building Committee did not have the time or knowledge to decide on possible changes and negotiate the costs. So the chairman of the Building Advisory Committee developed the habit of dealing directly with the architect and informing the board's Building Committee at regular intervals.

The Building Advisory Committee soon became responsible for planning the new campus. For example, it concluded from enrolment forecasts that all the space in the projected science building would be needed for offices, classrooms, and laboratories, with no room for a proposed science library. This would mean that science students would have classes and laboratory work on the new campus while still depending on the library on the First Avenue campus. The committee suggested a radical solution. If the projected new library could be built at the same time, there would be enough office and classroom space to move the entire university to the new campus, and the chaos and confusion of a divided campus would be avoided. The committee therefore recommended that the two buildings be constructed at the same time. Although money was not yet available, the attitude of the provincial government was encouraging and the move would permit the sale of the First Avenue buildings. The Board of Governors' Building Committee was convinced, and it in turn convinced the board.

If the library was to be built at the same time it would have to be planned quickly. Ross Love, the physics professor who chaired the Building Advisory Committee, had impressed the board and the architect by his ingenuity, his clear exposition of the requirements of the users, his respect for the financial constraints of the board, and his tactful negotiation of disputes. He was now persuaded to take over the planning of the library. It was a significant decision. In fact, he planned and directed the building program of the university for the next decade; he largely determined the physical form of the university.

The new library, named after Maxwell MacOdrum, was planned in stages. The library on the First Avenue campus had been built for 40,000 books. The first stage of the Rideau River library was to be a two-story building that could house 100,000 books and could serve an enrolment of a thousand students. In twenty years, with an expected enrolment of two thousand, three additional floors would be added. It was an attractive building, with tall narrow windows separated by almost classical fins of charcoal grey fibreglass, which protected the interior from much of the direct sunlight.[41] It was planned as an undergraduate library with open stacks and accessible study areas. The major concern of the Library Committee was to avoid the faults of the earlier library; soundproofing and carpets were high priority.[42] The architects, in close cooperation with the Building Advisory Committee, quickly produced a design which the board approved.

When tenders for the new building were opened in the summer of 1957, the board faced a difficult decision. The lowest tender was over $1 million, substantially more than had been expected.[43] The university had accumulated almost $2 million, and the province of Ontario had provided half a million for capital expenditures, with a promise of a million more. But Carleton had already committed over $3 million to prepare the site and construct the science building. The board was naturally concerned, and James Coyne seriously considered postponing construction for a year.[44] Bissell cut short his summer holiday to make the case that the university could not wait. Full-time enrolment had reached 600 in 1956–57, and an even larger increase was predicted for the fall of 1957, so the new buildings would soon be needed. Even cutting costs on the new library would be a false economy; the extras such as soundproofing and carpets were essential. The board was persuaded and the contract was awarded.[45]

The board's financial problems were only beginning. In September 1957 enrolment rose more sharply than expected, with over 700 full-time stu-

The central quadrangle, with the Tory Building, Paterson Hall, and the
MacOdrum Library (Capital Press Service)

dents, an increase of almost 20 per cent. Even the two new buildings would
not meet the expected demand. Bissell now argued for a third building,
pointing out to the board that the library would be eligible for a federal
grant of $400,000 from a capital fund to be administered by the Canada
Council for the humanities, and that "sources close to the Provincial Government" had given assurances of more generous provincial grants.[46] The
Building Advisory Committee was already planning an arts building. It
now recommended a less satisfactory design "on the grounds of economy
and the speed of construction," which the board accepted.[47] Any student
who has had to sit behind the pillars in some of the lecture rooms in Paterson Hall knows the consequences of this decision. Even so, the building
would not be cheap. Once again, the lowest tender was more than expected, exceeding a million dollars.[48] Once again the board took its cour-
age in its hands and authorized construction. With the addition of the
fieldhouse for athletics on the other side of the railway tracks, the board
had committed itself to capital expenditures of close to $6 million by 1958,
without being sure where the money would come from.

The college moved to its new campus in the summer of 1959. The President's Report for 1958–59 describes the move:

In the still of post-examination time in May, Carleton University moved to its new
campus on the Rideau River. With the precision of a well-planned military operation,
over 40,000 volumes disappeared from the old building and were marshalled on
their allotted shelves in the new Maxwell MacOdrum Library. The administration

The students see the new campus as the Promised Land
(*Carleton*, 13 Mar. 1958)

offices closed at the end of one working day on First Avenue and opened the next on
the new campus. Science professors who for some months had been dividing their
time between the two locations moved their last equipment to the Henry Marshall
Tory Science Building. At the beginning of June, all summer courses opened at the
new site. Only arts professors had to work from their old offices as they prayed with
the rest of the University that the new Norman Paterson Hall would not be delayed
beyond indicated completion dates, and would be at least partially ready for the
opening of classes in September.[49]

By then Claude Bissell had gone, because Sidney Smith had become secretary of state for external affairs, and the University of Toronto needed a
new president. Bissell had been offered the job, and although he may have
felt some reluctance, he could not resist the siren charms of what he
thought of as "the great good place."[50] But he left a new campus that had
already taken shape:

When we left Ottawa in the late May of 1958 and drove slowly past the Rideau River
site, I could see the basic quadrangle of the new university. On one side stood the
Henry Marshall Tory Building ... almost completed, on the other the MacOdrum Library rising in formal elegance, and between them, the Norman Paterson Hall for the

Humanities and Social Sciences ... If there was cause for regrets and some self-accusation, there was also cause for satisfaction.[51]

For many students and professors there would be nostalgic memories of the First Avenue campus. Bissell had described the spirit of the old college shortly after his arrival, nicely capturing its positive qualities. What, he had asked, were the college's distinctive features? "First of all, a sense of a close community life that at the same time does not smother individual expression. Second, an amateur zest in work and play, combined with professional thoroughness in what is important. Finally, and above all, a belief in the centrality of human values in studies, in sport and in social life."[52] To be sure, the old campus had always had its drawbacks, with its cramped offices and crowded classrooms and non-existent playing fields. The former Ladies College had been "a homely, even tawdry building, certainly a far cry from the spaciousness of the new buildings on the Rideau River campus." But there had been "a feeling of intimacy and community that would be difficult to recapture."[53] For most of those associated with Carleton, however, the mood was one of relief and optimism. The president of the Students' Council certainly expressed no regrets. "Our university," he boasted, "will be a beauty spot in Ottawa, as well as an intellectual and cultural centre. It will be the most modern in Canada and to the eye will present an intellectual unity, quite aptly described by President Bissell as "Brave New World without the gothic."[54] The new campus promised a new and hopeful beginning.

PART TWO

The University Years

The Carleton University that moved to the new campus was an institution in transition. Within a decade it would bear little resemblance to the college on First Avenue, and indeed it developed in ways that few would have predicted. When it arrived on the new campus, it had already moved some distance from its night school beginnings and could be broadly described as a liberal arts college, mainly serving the Ottawa community. While the college did offer professional training, most of its students were enrolled in arts programs, and even those in journalism and engineering found that their programs included a strong emphasis on arts and social sciences courses in the first years. By the end of the 1960s, Carleton had become a very different institution.

The transition from college to university came suddenly. The college, which had worried each fall about how many students would enrol and, for a decade, had attracted only an average of about five hundred students, suddenly found itself worrying about accommodating the swelling numbers. By 1970 the full-time enrolment exceeded seven thousand students. By then Carleton was divided into four faculties – arts, science, engineering, and graduate studies – and had a number of specialized programs at the undergraduate and graduate levels. It became more and more difficult to speak of the history of the institution, because each faculty and each school operated as independently as possible and had its own subhistory. Carleton had become a university, a complex institution of many parts and diverse interests.

The changes were not unique to Carleton. The 1960s was a decade in which all institutions changed and in which universities, more than most institutions, changed dramatically. The history of Carleton in those years is in part the history of higher education. Universities were responding to changes in the society which supported them and which they served. Sociologists talked of the gradual shift from an industrial to postindustrial society, to a society characterized by technology and innovation. This new society depended on research, which was expected to reveal more and more of the mysteries of the material world. This knowledge would in turn be used to produce new materials, new drugs, new techniques, and would expand our control over the world in which we lived. It was an optimistic and even naive view of the future, but it was not completely unfounded. Jet airplanes, antibiotics, and the contraceptive pill were evidence of how research and technology could transform ordinary lives, and if men could be landed on the moon there seemed few limits to what could be achieved if scientists were given the resources.

Universities were directly affected because they were seen as the central institutions of this postindustrial society. They were expected to train and certify the professionals and technicians whom this society needed. They were also expected to be research centres where the secrets of the material world could be unveiled. Their third crucial function was the training of young researchers who would, in their turn, unfold more mysteries of nature for the benefit of humankind. Universities were expected to adapt, and they did adapt, in order to play this expanded social role.

The most obvious impact on universities was the pressure to expand. During the 1960s, university enrolment in Ontario rose from 32,000 to 120,000. Some of this increase can be attributed to the baby boom after the war; in the 1960s these babies reached university age. More important was the growing awareness of parents and young people that a university degree was becoming an admission ticket to a more interesting and better-paid career. Within the universities, the spiralling demand for admission included a shift towards higher enrolment in the professional programs, which were seen as preparation for more rewarding careers in a more complex society. There were special circumstances for each institution. For example, there was less demographic pressure in eastern Ontario because, although Ottawa grew rapidly, the region did not have the same population explosion as the southern part of the province. For new universities, there were also constraints on how they could respond to the growing demands for professional credentials. Carleton expanded its offerings in engineering, journalism, and commerce, and added social work and architecture, but it could not offer medicine or law, because these had already been pre-empted by the University of Ottawa. On the other hand, Carleton had the advantage of more space for buildings to accommodate students than downtown universities such as Ottawa and Queen's, where residential land would have to be expropriated. Every university in Ontario, however, was marked by extraordinary increases in enrolment.

At Carleton, as at other universities,[1] the external pressures affected different sectors of the university in different ways. The administration, which had had so much difficulty finding the money needed to provide the requirements of a small college, now found that money was available for professors and buildings if Carleton could convince the government that this money would be used to provide more places for more students. All these developments affected the faculty. Increased enrolment meant competition among universities for qualified professors, so professors at Carleton and elsewhere could negotiate higher salaries and better working conditions. Their status was also enhanced by the increased importance given to research. Professors who had been respected employees in the college years – but nonetheless employees – now found that their research skills gave them a prestige that changed their status within the university. By the end of the decade they controlled the Senate and had representatives on the Board of Governors. The status of the students also changed. In academic terms, the common cultural experience – the exposure to English literature, to a second language, to an introduction to science – was eroded by increasing specialization. A university degree now promised some expertise, but it no longer implied that a university graduate had acquired a certain cultural sophistication. At the same time, the students were questioning and even challenging the traditional authority of the administration and their professors. They were not sure what their new status should be or what "rights" they should claim, but they were sure that the status quo was unacceptable.

None of this was unique to Carleton. The times were changing, and Carleton, like other universities, had to change with the times. Again like other universities, Carleton responded to the external social pressures in its own way because of its special circumstances and because of the individuals who influenced its decisions. The history of Carleton University in the 1960s, like the history of Carleton College in the previous decade, is the story of the administration, the faculty, and the students, and how these parts of the university tried to resolve their sometimes conflicting ambitions in an era of social change.

CHAPTER SIX

Carleton Becomes a Provincial University

The dramatic developments on the new campus began at Queen's Park. Early in the 1960s the provincial government adopted a new approach to its financial support for higher education. Instead of giving grants grudgingly to support higher education, it abruptly decided early in the 1960s to stimulate university expansion by generous grants to defray the construction and operating costs. The new policy transformed the existing universities and created new ones.

Carleton University changed more dramatically than most of the older institutions. It had the advantage of a new campus, where expansion was relatively easy. Just as important, however, was the new president, Davidson Dunton, who took advantage of the opportunity and transformed Carleton from a small college into a mid-sized university. The fortuitous combination of a new policy at Queen's Park and an ambitious president at Carleton meant almost a new beginning.

The expansion had some unpredicted consequences. In 1960 Carleton was still in many ways a private institution. Forty per cent of its income came from student fees. It is true that half of its operating revenue came from public funds, with just over 30 per cent from the Ontario government and 20 per cent from the federal government, but the politicians showed no great interest in how the money had been spent or how Carleton planned to spend its money in future. Governments might complain about the financial burden of higher education, but they did not try to substitute an agenda of their own. In general they assumed that universities were doing what was necessary and doing it competently, and they accepted a limited financial responsibility to enable the universities to con-

A. Davidson Dunton (1912–87), president and
vice-chancellor of Carleton University, 1958–72

tinue to function as they had in the past. They saw no need to interfere
with admissions policies or academic programs.

This changed in the 1960s because higher education became an important
aspect of public policy. By the end of the decade Carleton University, like
other universities in Ontario, was clearly a public institution. The provincial
government grant by then paid for almost 80 per cent of the universities' operating costs and, in addition, the government determined the size of the student fees the universities could collect. At the same time, it was generously
funding the extraordinary building programs which the higher enrolments required. No universities objected to the infusion of provincial funds – except
to complain that it too often fell short of what was needed. Most universities,
including Carleton, were delighted to be able to build more buildings, hire
more professors, and introduce new programs. As long as the aims of the
government and the universities seemed congruent, the paymaster felt no
need to call the tune and the universities felt no threat to their autonomy.

I

What accounts for the generosity of the provincial government in the 1960s? To understand this we must shift attention briefly from the Carleton University campus to Queen's Park. This is not a digression. The decisions at Queen's Park and the responses of the heads of the universities in Ontario created the context in which Carleton developed. To understand the history of Carleton in this decade, we must understand what was happening to higher education all across Ontario.[1]

The provincial government took the initiative because it was becoming more and more unhappy with its reactive approach to university support. Since the 1950s, the government had relied on an advisory committee of senior public servants to scan the budgets of the nonsectarian universities of the province and to recommend the size of the grant for each institution. There was no coordinated planning. In effect, the university administrators were almost encouraged to be extravagant, because the larger their projected deficit, the better were their chances of getting more money from the government. Each year the committee questioned the amounts requested and reluctantly recommended increases, which nevertheless fell short of what the universities had asked for. Nobody was pleased and nobody could plan for the future with any confidence.

The change came when the government realized that it faced a political danger that outweighed its reluctance to spend money. In the past, the government had not given the universities a high priority. Some politicians knew that scientific research could have important consequences,[2] but they had more pressing concerns. In the early 1960s, however, the estimates, which projected a tripling of university enrolment over the next decade, began to register.[3] What if the universities could not accommodate the applicants and had to turn many of them away? Irate parents – who might become irate voters – would ask why the government had allowed it to happen. Suddenly university expansion became a high priority, and instead of trying to limit university expenditures, the government decided to encourage university expansion. Higher education in Ontario would never be the same again.

The shift in government policy began in 1961, when the Advisory Committee on University Affairs was expanded to include some prominent businessmen and the retired premier Leslie Frost. Frost, affectionately known as Old Man Ontario, had been in the legislature for twenty-four years and been premier of the province for twelve of those years, and he still had more political influence than most cabinet ministers. For the next decade he was a key figure in the shaping of government policy for higher education in Ontario.

Leslie Frost, premier of Ontario, laying the cornerstone of the Tory Building in 1957. *Seated, left to right:* Hart Massey, the architect; James Coyne, chairman of the board; Claude Bissell, president; and Rev. A. Ian Burnett (Capital Press Service)

Leslie Frost was a traditional Ontario conservative. He believed in working through the existing institutions in preference to direct government intervention. Instead of telling the university presidents what they should do, he convoked them to a meeting in Toronto in March 1962, told them of the government's concern about the expected influx of students, and asked them how they could help to accommodate these numbers. What was new, he explained, was that the government was ready to loosen its purse strings. If the universities could produce a plan for expansion, the government would provide the necessary funds. In Frost's words, "Your greatest sugar-daddy will be the Province of Ontario."[4] Frost was right. Over the next few years this sugar daddy financed the most remarkable expansion of postsecondary education in the history of the province.

The university presidents were eager to take advantage of the province's generosity. For each of them it meant the chance of getting more money. But there was more than money involved. Frost had made it clear that if they could not propose a plan for university expansion, the government would impose one. The presidents had always acted as rivals in the past, competing for government funds. The challenge now was to see if they could cooperate and preserve some degree of autonomy. The immediate response was impressive. They quickly organized themselves as the Committee of the Presidents of the Universities of Ontario and asked J.J. Deutsch, the vice-principal at Queen's University to prepare a study on the future of postsecondary education in Ontario. No time was wasted. By May 1962, Deutsch had submitted his report, the Committee of the Presidents had adopted it and had submitted it to Frost and his Advisory Committee.

The existing universities, the report stated, were prepared "to stretch their enrolment to the utmost ... if the financial resources were available." Each university had been asked to estimate a feasible enrolment target for 1970–71. The sum of these targets, it was estimated, would accommodate about half of the expected increase. The report went on to recommend new undergraduate institutions, two in Toronto and one in St Catharines, to cope with the students who would not be able to find places at the existing universities.[5]

The report did not stop there. If the students came, somebody would have to teach them. The universities now had 2,500 professors. Within ten years they would need 8,300, preferably with PHDs. Some of these might be found in other countries, but the competition would be great because universities everywhere were expanding; most of the professors would have to be trained at home. In the previous year only 305 doctorates had been awarded in all of Canada, so a crash program would be needed to double graduate enrolment in Ontario within the next few years. To make its point more forcefully the report said, in its only italicized sentence: " *We regard this as the first and most essential action of all those that must be taken to meet the approaching emergency.*"[6] It suggested a major program of provincially funded graduate fellowships.

It was not easy to put a price on the proposed expansion. So much would depend on whether the enrolment projections were reliable and whether the funds would be available. Nor would it be wise to try; the estimated costs for the next ten years might vary considerably, but even the most conservative estimates were staggering. It was less controversial to limit the estimates to the next three years, because they were more reliable and would be less frightening. Even then, the costs were intimidating. The report projected capital costs for this three-year period at $150 million or more, with annual operating costs rising from $23 million to almost $50 million, and the fellowship program which would reach $12 million by the third year. Frost suspected that the estimates were inflated; his comment to the Advisory Committee was that the presidents saw "a God-given opportunity and you can't blame them for asking."[7] But the government was committed to expansion, and it accepted the recommendations of the presidents' report in principle. It promptly initiated the program of provincial fellowships for graduate students, and the Advisory Committee discussed with each university the capital and operating grants it would need over the next few years to reach its target. The sugar daddy was opening his wallet.

Sugar daddies, however, have their own agenda, and the provincial government was no exception. Government spokesmen continued to pay lip service to the autonomy of the publicly supported universities of Ontario, but increased government funding came with some strings attached. Early in 1966 William Davis, the minister of education and now also the minister of the newly created Department of University Affairs, pointedly reminded the universities of what was expected of them. In a widely reported speech he referred as usual to the exceptional degree of autonomy enjoyed by the Ontario universities and added, "We should undoubtedly be better off if they were allowed to operate with such autonomy." But Davis went on to say that this autonomy was contingent on the universities meeting certain obligations:

If, for example, large numbers of able students must be turned away because the university is not prepared to accept them ... or if costly duplication of effort is evident, I cannot imagine that any society, especially one bearing large expenses for higher education, will want to stand idly by. For there will inevitably be a demand – there have been indications of this in other jurisdictions – that government move in and take over.[8]

In other words, the universities were expected to provide enough places to meet student demand, and at the same time they were not to take advantage of the situation by offering expensive programs that were already available elsewhere. If they failed, the government would step in.

Did Davis think that the universities were likely to be extravagant? He did not say so directly, but he did say that many people "have suggested to me that there is little evidence that our universities have tightened their proverbial belt to any significant extent." And he warned the universities that if they initiated new programs without government approval, the government might not fund them. Should the universities avoid wasteful competition by cooperating? For Davis the answer was obvious. The more significant question, he pointed out, was whether the universities would have the wisdom to prevent unnecessary duplication. He hoped for the best. In his experience, he said, university administrators and professors were wise men, and he believed they would be realistic. He was sure they would behave sensibly and do what was necessary to retain their autonomy.[9]

The university presidents recognized that Davis's warning should be taken seriously. As J.A. Corry, principal of Queen's, put it, "If the universities don't get together and do the job themselves the Government will step in and do it for them."[10] For the next few years the Committee of the Presidents of the Universities of Ontario tried to plan a system of university education that would respect the government's concern for the expenditure of public funds and at the same time would preserve the principle of university autonomy.

The Deutsch Report – with its plan for cooperation among the universities to cope with the expected influx of students, and its proposals for graduate studies – was only the beginning. Another major achievement was the development of a formula for distributing the provincial operating grants to the individual universities. The existing system, based on the line-by-line assessment of university budgets, was frustrating for both the universities and the government. The solution, devised by a committee appointed jointly by the Committee of the Presidents and the government's Advisory Committee on University Affairs, was a formula based on enrolment. Each year the government would establish the dollar value of what was called the basic income unit (BIU). Each university would receive a grant calculated by multiplying the BIU by its "weighted" enrolment. One BIU would be given for each arts undergraduate; students enrolled in more expensive programs would be allocated more units, with six BIUs for doctoral students.

The formula had obvious advantages for both the government and the universities. For the government there would no longer be any need to respond to the annual requests of sixteen universities. The crucial decision each year would be the size of the BIU. Once the government had made that decision, the formula would determine the size of the provincial grant to each institution. To protect against universities trying to maximize their income by increasing student fees (and so frustrating the government's policy of encouraging university enrolment), the university's fee income would be deducted from the amount based on the formula to determine that actual grant. The result was that the universities could not increase their income by raising student fees. For the universities there were obvious benefits. Their annual income would now be based on enrolment figures instead of depending on the arbitrary response of the government to their annual requests. It was also important that the money came with no strings attached. The university administrations could spend the money in ways that seemed best for the institution, thus maintaining a significant degree of university autonomy.

The formula, for all its apparent advantages, was not a magic wand. There was no guarantee, for example, that it would produce adequate operating grants. In 1967–68, the first year of formula financing, the government set the value of the BIU at $1,320, an amount which the Committee of the Presidents protested was far too low. The presidents could only try to persuade the government to be more generous in future. But this was not the fault of the formula. Ultimately the public cost of university education had to be decided by political factors. The formula would only determine the distribution of public funds among the universities. It would not determine how much money would be provided.

However, the formula did have steering effects that were not obvious at the time. Each university was different, but the formula was inflexible. Instead of encouraging the universities to build on their own individual strengths, the formula tended to encourage conformity. The inability of any university to increase its income by raising its fees also limited diversity. As long as the formula determined university income, universities had to respond in similar ways in order to maximize their revenue. For the moment, that meant admitting more students, especially at the graduate level, where the formula weighting was advantageous. In the 1960s, however, this was not seen as a problem, because both the government and the individual universities shared the common objective of increasing enrolment. Whatever its limitations, the formula was clearly an improvement on the earlier system of allocating operating grants.

The importance of formula funding became even more apparent when, in 1967, the federal government changed the form of its support for universities. The federal government had recognized the economic importance of higher education and as early as 1951 had initiated federal grants to Canadian universities. In the 1960s, however, the provincial governments asserted their constitutional jurisdiction over education. The federal government did not withdraw from the field, but it did back away. It replaced its direct subsidies to universities by subsidies to provincial governments to reimburse them for half of their operating grants for postsecondary education. From the perspective of the universities, there was now only one source of public funds to help defray their operating expenses.

Operating costs were not the only costs. Increased enrolments meant that every university needed public funds for classrooms and residences, for faculty offices and administration buildings, for gymnasiums and parking lots. How much should the government spend and how should it distribute its largesse? Initially the universities applied to the Advisory Committee on University Affairs for grants to cover the cost of construction of the buildings they needed. If the committee approved the application, the government usually provided a grant to cover 85 per cent of the cost of academic buildings such as classrooms and laboratories, but only 50 per cent of the cost of buildings to house student or administrative services. The universities had to find private donors to make up the balance. This had the advantage for the government of shifting some of the financial burden to the private sector and, at the same time, providing a brake on capital expenditures because private funds were limited.

Experience soon showed that the brake was too effective. Universities could not build some needed buildings because they could not raise the required private funds. Eventually the government eased this difficulty by paying 95 per cent of the cost of academic buildings and 85 per cent for other buildings. But this still had a steering effect. The private funds collected were more likely to be used for classrooms and laboratories, where the private dollars went further, than for buildings for athletics or other extracurricular activities that were not considered academic. For the students, especially at the newer universities, this could limit their university experience.

How could the Advisory Committee on University Affairs determine how much money was needed for university buildings and how the money should be distributed? Could a space formula be devised that would be equivalent to the formula for enrolment? A formula was developed that began with an estimate of the square feet of space required for full-time students in various programs. The need for new space could then be calculated on the basis of a university's existing space and its enrolment. The capital grant would then be the space entitlement multiplied by the average cost per square foot of construction. However, this formula was never entirely satisfactory, because the space in older buildings could not always be used efficiently and because the space requirements and the costs varied widely among different programs. So although the government used the formula as a factor in allocating capital grants, it was never applied rigidly; special consideration had to be given to the space requirements of each university.

In addition, plans were needed to coordinate the development of graduate studies in the province – to decide what new programs should be authorized and where they should be located. In 1965 the Committee of the Presidents and the government's Advisory Committee (now known as the Committee on University Affairs) appointed a commission to study the development of graduate program in Ontario. The commission, chaired by J.W.T. Spinks, president of the University of Saskatchewan, reported late in 1966. Its blunt conclusion was that to have sixteen separate universities in Ontario was a recipe for anarchy, and it stated: "The most striking characteristic of higher – not only graduate – education in Ontario is the complete absence of a master plan, of an educational policy, and of a co-ordinating authority for the provincially-supported institutions." The commission therefore recommended "in the strongest terms" that these universities be integrated into a provincial University of Ontario.[11]

This was not what the university presidents wanted to hear. Each of them had a primary responsibility for his own institution, and each saw enticing opportunities for his university in this period of rapid expansion. The opportunities might be lost if his university was integrated into a provincial system. The presidents preferred a system of voluntary cooperation, which seemed to promise more local autonomy. The government wanted a coordinated system that would eliminate costly duplication butit it was reluctant to impose a centralized system that would provoke criticism from university cities across the province. If the Committee of the Presidents could coordinate the development of graduate programs in the province the government was not interested in a University of Ontario.

How could the presidents respect the autonomy of the individual universities yet plan a system of graduate programs for the province that would avoid duplication? The response of the Committee of the Presidents was to establish a procedure for appraising any proposals for new graduate programs. These proposals would have to meet high academic requirements, based on admission standards, the curriculum, the qualifications of the professors in the program, and the facilities provided by the library or laboratories. If an application met the required standards, the university could then offer the program and would receive the provincial grants for the students who enrolled. Individual universities could still offer the program even if it was not approved, but there was a high price to pay for this autonomy: there would be no provincial funding for the students. Eventually this appraisal system was extended to include periodic appraisals of established graduate programs.

This appraisal procedure did not impose a master plan for graduate education in Ontario. In a period of rapid expansion, this was probably one of its strengths, because it made it possible for smaller institutions to offer graduate programs if they met recognized academic criteria. One criticism was that the procedures did not assess the demand for graduates. Should new doctoral programs be approved in history or physics, for example, if the existing programs could graduate enough students to satisfy the demand? Or should all academically acceptable programs be allowed to compete for students and leave it to the individual students to assess the future demand? These would not be easy questions to resolve; but for the time being, the demand for graduates exceeded the supply in almost every field, so these questions did not have to be answered.

By the end of the decade, therefore, higher education had been dramatically transformed. The provincial government had responded to the increasing demand for admission to universities by financing the expansion of established institutions and the founding of new ones. At the same time the government and the universities had collaborated to maintain a delicate balance between the responsible administration of public funds and the autonomy of the individual institutions. The procedures that were devised relied on the cooperation of competing universities and their respect for the objectives of the provincial government, which was paying the bills. What is remarkable is how successfully the system functioned in these years of expansion. By 1970 there were three times as many students at university as there had been ten years earlier, yet the buildings and professors and programs were in place to accommodate them.

II

How did Carleton University fit into the new structures and new procedures that were shaping higher education in Ontario in the 1960s? The history of Carleton's evolving relations with the provincial government and with the other universities in Ontario is marked by the leadership of A. Davidson Dunton, president of Carleton from 1958 to 1972. Dunton could only react to the social and political forces of the era, but he guided Carleton's responses. The new and different Carleton that emerged was marked by his influence. If Henry Marshall Tory can be called the founder of Carleton College, Dunton can be seen as the founder of Carleton University.

Claude Bissell's resignation in 1958 had meant another selection committee. C.J. Mackenzie, the chancellor, chaired it, joined by Brooke Claxton and E.W.R. Steacie from the Board of Governors. The faculty were not directly represented, but this time two members of the Senate were included: Frank Underhill, the eminent political commentator and intellectual, and Kaye Lamb, the national librarian; they were appointed to the committee "because of their knowledge of university matters and because they would serve as representatives of the university staff."[12] The faculty objected to being excluded, but the board ignored their protests.[13]

The priorities of the board had not changed since the last appointment. Carleton was still expected to develop as a liberal arts college, with its arts-oriented schools of journalism, public administration, and engineering, and it was assumed that the necessary academic structures were already in place. What the university needed was a president who would get Carleton established on its new campus. The construction of the first phase of the new campus was underway, but money was still needed for this and for the next phase. The selection committee again wanted somebody who had some familiarity with the corridors of power. James Gibson, the dean of arts and science, who had been acting president for a year after MacOdrum's death and was acting president again after Bissell's departure, was the most obvious internal candidate, but apparently he was thought to be too identified with the academic side of the university.[14]

Tradition has it that the choice was made one day when C.J. Mackenzie was lunching with the chairman of the Canadian Broadcasting Corporation, Davidson Dunton, and learned that he might be available. Dunton was not an obvious choice – he had studied at universities in Canada, England, France, and Germany, though he had never stayed long enough in

President Davidson Dunton (*left*) and Chancellor C.J. Mackenzie awarding Frank Underhill an honorary degree in 1959, with James Gibson, dean of arts, putting on the hood (Newton)

any one of them to earn a degree – but he did have the qualification that interested Mackenzie: he had experience in dealing with the public and with governments. Dunton had been editor of the Montreal *Standard* and general manager of the Wartime Information Board before becoming chairman of the CBC at the precocious age of thirty-three. Now, thirteen years later, with the television network in place and a less sympathetic federal government in office under John Diefenbaker, he was interested in other opportunities. Mackenzie apparently convinced the selection committee, and then the Board of Governors, that there was no need to look any further. In July 1958, Arnold Davidson Dunton became Carleton's fourth president. He presided over the university for the next fourteen years.

Dunton had a very personal style of leadership. Carleton was a small college when he became president, and in many ways he continued to think of it in these terms long after it had outgrown its college days. In his early years he even acted as adviser to six first-year students, just like other members of the faculty.[15] In later years he still made a point of having his office door open to student leaders. Dunton knew the name of every professor and most of the support staff; expansion must have made this a challenge, but he had the advantage of a phenomenal memory. His attention to detail was also in the tradition of small and intimate college life. Even when the university was spending millions of dollars, he wanted to know from the deans how their lecture and travel funds were being spent.[16] The administrative structures remained those of a small institution. Although science, engineering, and graduate studies became separate faculties with their own deans, there were no vice-presidents, and even with the deans Dunton tended to share rather than delegate authority. This may not be the approved model for administering an institution which, by the end of the decade, grew to have 400 full-time faculty and more than 1,300 employees. It worked only because Dunton had an exceptional memory for facts and people.

Dunton's own version of his role as president gave great importance to the faculty. He once told a committee on university government "that his role was to keep balance and fairness in the allocation of scarce resources within the university; to carry out the wishes or conclusions of the academic body of the university, taking into account the needs of the students; and to clothe these wishes or conclusions of the academic community with the executive action to carry them out." This left a limited role for the Board of Governors. Its function, he went on to explain, was "to review or audit the recommendations made by the President."[17]

In many ways his behaviour was consistent with this image. He was a good listener, whether he was presiding over meetings of the Senate or discussing current events or academic questions at Spring Conference or at whatever table he joined for lunch in the Faculty Club. Meetings at which he presided were likely to be long because he respected the right of all committee members to have their say. His patience must have been sorely tested on the many occasions when professors exercised their highly developed debating skills to argue about commas or when they propounded some high principle to challenge a minor detail. On such occasions Dunton seemed to have "an infinite capacity for boredom," as one of his colleagues put it;[18] he rarely declared any intervention out of order. If Carleton was a relatively happy community, even in those tumultuous years, it was not unrelated to the confidence of faculty and even students that their opinions were heard and were respected.

To accept Dunton's version of his role without any qualifications would be to underestimate the man. The professors at Carleton were not a com-

A senate meeting, with the customary piles of documents and varying degrees of interest. President Dunton (*fourth from right*) is giving his full attention to the text as usual (*Raven 70*).

munity of scholars; their opinions could be inconsistent and contradictory, and their wishes had to be interpreted before they could be carried out. Dunton could influence decisions by his choice of committee members and by strategic delays when he disagreed with a decision. His allocation of scarce resources may have been balanced and fair, but he had his own criteria for balance and fairness. He may have known "where he stood and what he stood for," but he was not a man to reveal himself even to his friends.[19] His personal influence on Carleton in these formative years was clearly important, even though it was not always clear how his influence was being exercised.

Dunton's role is difficult to assess because he had no blueprint for the university; it was not always clear to him, much less to others, where he wanted to go. He was to some extent an opportunist, pragmatically responding to shifting pressures, whether they came from Queen's Park, the Board of Governors or the faculty. But his pragmatism was guided by an implicit philosophy of higher education. Dunton was a liberal, with a liberal's faith in reason and the potential for human betterment. His theme in his inaugural address was the freedom that knowledge can bring and the social benefits of providing easier access to this knowledge.[20] Fourteen years later, in his last convocation address, he showed that he had become more circumspect. Universities, he now warned, were concerned with the intellect and thus were not suitable for everybody; even so, his emphasis was still on the benefits of the intellectual development of an individual, whereby "a young person can come to a better understanding of himself and his relations with the world and society."[21] It was a faith in liberal education without the exclusiveness of the traditional liberal arts college, and it was a faith that fitted easily into an era of university expansion.

Dunton believed that Carleton could and should expand. It could expand because this was one of those rare eras when governments were prepared to finance university expansion. Not to expand would mean that Carleton would lose a magnificent opportunity. Dunton knew that the established universities would have difficulty absorbing the expected flood of applicants. Some universities might choose to remain small, but as he explained to other university presidents in 1967, "It had become more and more apparent that a very large part of the load in the foreseeable future will have to be taken up by another kind of small university; a group that are now small, some very small, but that will have to grow with extreme rapidity."[22]

Why did Dunton believe that Carleton should be one of the small universities to choose rapid growth as its option? He never put it into words, and indeed he may never have formulated the reasons even to himself. Because of his faith in the benefits of education for most people, he would be reluctant to turn away students. More positively, he could see that Carleton would benefit from expansion. It was more than a platitude when he said that it was the "teachers and scholars who make the quality of the university."[23] He also recognized that in a period of expansion, the competition for the best professors would be fierce. Special incentives would be needed to attract them. Competitive salaries would be important, but ambitious highly qualified professors would also want graduate students and research opportunities. Graduate programs are linked to large undergraduate enrolments, because large undergraduate classes bring in revenue that sustains the laboratories and libraries needed by graduate students; those students in turn can gain teaching experience and supplement their income by acting as teaching assistants in undergraduate course. So if Carleton wanted to attract outstanding professors, it would have to expand.

III

How did Carleton under Dunton fare in its relations with the Committee of the Presidents and the Advisory Committee on University Affairs? Carleton was a small and little-known university at the beginning of the decade, remote from Queen's Park and not included in any informal networks of the older and well-established universities. It never did become a major player in the province. During the decade, however, Dunton took advantage of the opportunities presented. Carleton's ranking improved among Ontario universities, both in terms of size and academic reputation.

The Committee of the Presidents, as we have seen, played an important role in the planning of higher education in Ontario in those years. Dunton was not a forceful member of the committee, partly because the secretariat was in Toronto but also because he was busier than most men. Not only was he preoccupied with the problems of Carleton in a period of rapid growth, but he was also co-chairman of the Royal Commission on Bilingualism and Biculturalism. Among the university presidents, Dunton was a well-known and respected figure – Claude Bissell, who was then president of the University of Toronto, recalls that the Committee of Presidents regularly sought Dunton's advice.[24] The respect of his colleagues led to him being chosen as the third incumbent of the rotating chairmanship of the committee, succeeding Claude Bissell and J.A. Corry, even though the university he represented lacked the prestige of many others. The minutes of the committee meetings also show that Dunton did on occasion intervene effectively to defend Carleton's interests. For example, he objected forcefully when in July 1962 a subcommittee of the Committee of the Presidents suggested that the lion's share of provincial funding for graduate work should go to the five universities that already had graduate programs. While Dunton conceded that this would produce results more quickly, he argued that more than five graduate schools would be needed in Ontario to meet the demand and the money should be more widely distributed. The committee agreed that in future the ambitions of the newer universities would be given more consideration, and a subsequent letter from Bissell to Dunton shows that his objection was taken seriously.[25]

Dunton's response to the Deutsch Committee in 1962 provides a more striking example of his role in Carleton's development. This committtee had asked each university president how many students his institution could enrol by 1970. In 1962 Carleton had an enrolment of 1,300 undergraduates and 30 graduate students. Dunton boldly proposed 6,000 undergraduates and 500 graduate students as Carleton's target for 1970. In effect, he was suggesting that in less than ten years Carleton should leap from being a small college to one of the province's middle-sized universities.

These targets were not completely arbitrary, but neither were they the result of extensive consultation or detailed calculations. The anticipated enrolment on the new campus for the year 2000 had been 6,000 students; Dunton apparently decided that if the student demand was there and if the government was ready to pay for the buildings, 6,000 would be a feasible target for 1970. He did not consult or even seek formal approval in advance from either the Senate or the Board of Governors. The Senate had already advocated rapid growth as a prerequisite for an institution committed to high academic standards. In December 1961 the Senate minutes commented: "It is difficult to maintain a high level of undergraduate and graduate work while remaining small." In February 1962 it again emphasized the link between size and academic goals when it stressed the importance of honours and graduate work and linked this to the suggestion that Carleton should plan for an increase of 400 to 500 students each year.[26] In May, then, Dunton felt confident when he informed the Senate of the enrolment targets he had proposed, even though, as he admitted, the target of 6,000 students "represents a growth rate somewhat above the upper figure ... previously adopted by the Senate." He offered no apologies, and the Senate raised no objections.[27] The Board of Governors had not discussed enrolment projections, but it would have been out of character for Dunton not to have discussed the issue with some of the leading members of the board. In any case, he informed the board of his enrolment proposals at its June meeting and the board, "after some discussion," gave its approval to the targets.[28]

Dunton's target of 500 graduate students was more daring. For a university with only 30 full-time graduate students in 1962, it implied a significant change in the character of the institution. It was commitment to something more than a liberal arts college. It stemmed from Dunton's view that bright young scholars would only be attracted to Carleton if the university offered opportunities to work with graduate students. The majority on the Senate clearly shared this point of view, and it is revealing that nobody on the faculty or on the Board of Governors objected openly. While the consequences of the proposed expansion at the graduate level may not have been clear to everybody, the priority to be given to graduate studies had now been officially approved.

Dunton's relations with the government's Advisory Committee on University Affairs were also important for Carleton. When Dunton took office he was probably less well known to provincial politicians than to the other university presidents, but he quickly established a reputation for competence and reliability. After 1962 each university submitted its proposed budget to the new Committee on University Affairs and asked the committee to cover the anticipated deficit. Carleton did well under this system because Frost and his colleagues on the committee were impressed with the restraint of Carleton's estimates. In 1963, for example, the Committee on University Affairs' assessor responsible for the Carleton file noted that Carleton had not been favoured by the government in the past. "For several years prior to 1961–62," he commented, "provincial maintenance grants to Carleton were insufficient to meet its requirements. Not only did Carleton suffer 'real' deficits in its operations but it was also compelled to run down its reserves, obtain bank loans and take other special measures to finance its operations."[29] He noted with approval that Carleton's forecasts of expenditures had "proved to be reasonably realistic." Two years later the minutes of the government committee reported that a committee member "spoke in favour of Carleton. Never hear from them – adjust accordingly. Have run economical show."[30] Carleton did not get everything it asked for, but at least the Committee on University Affairs treated its submissions with less skepticism than it showed for the submissions of some of the other universities.

Carleton was less favoured after 1967 when the funding formula was applied. The formula may seem objective, but its impact depended on the weight given to different programs. Carleton was at a disadvantage compared to older universities in the province because it had relatively fewer honours students among its undergraduates and because a smaller proportion of its student body was in professional or graduate programs. As a younger institution, Carleton also had special costs, because it had fewer endowments for scholarships than the more established universities and it needed to build up its library and build athletic and recreational facilities for its students. On the other hand, Carleton had too many students to qualify for the special funding for the small "emergent universities" that could not benefit from economies of scale.[31]

The capital grants also depended on an annual submission to the Committee on University Affairs. In 1963, when the committee first visited Carleton and met with Dunton and David Golden – the deputy minister of industry, who was chairman of Carleton's Building Committee – Frost expressed concern at Carleton's request for a building program of $14 million for the next four years and with more to come. He conceded that the students would have to have places, and money would be needed, but suggested that expenses might be reduced. He recognized, he said, that "temporary" was "a nasty word with academics," but asked if Dunton had thought of temporary buildings. Dunton assured Frost that he shared his concern but pointed out that the money was for science and engineering, whose special requirements would make provisional accommodation more expensive in the long run; and while he conceded that the requirements for the humanities were simpler, he pointed out that the arts building at

Carleton had cost only twenty dollars per square foot and temporary accommodation would have been almost as expensive. David Golden then explained that Carleton was planning another fundraising campaign, but he pointed out that Ottawa had few industries and the money collected would be needed for residences. Frost then asked when Carleton could start if it was given the funds. Dunton said he was prepared to let the contracts the next day. What if he did not get all he asked for? Again Dunton was ready. He would go ahead with the engineering building and postpone the chemistry building.[32]

Frost and his committee were favourably impressed. Frost, who was proverbially close-fisted, even suggested that Dunton's reference to construction at twenty dollars per square foot should be used to judge submissions from other universities.[33] Carleton did not get everything it wanted. The committee recommended a grant of $3 million for the next year instead of the $4 million requested, but only because it did not think that all the money could be spent in one year. There was the implicit promise of more to follow.

The regulations affecting capital grants complicated the building program at Carleton. It was not easy to find the private funds required to supplement the government grants, and the construction of one building would have been delayed but for an unexpected donation from the Loeb Family Foundation.[34] The building formula, based on the average footage per student, also worked to Carleton's disadvantage after the acquisition of St Patrick's College.[35] This college housed a high school when it was acquired. When the high school moved away, the building had more room than St Patrick's College needed, so the justification for more space on the main campus was negated by this unused space. But the overall theme was one of extraordinary expansion. The book value of Carleton's physical plant had been less than $8 million in 1960; by 1970 it was $74 million. Most of this money had come from the provincial treasury in one way or another. The provincial government had indeed become the university's sugar daddy.

By 1970 the years of physical expansion were coming to an end. In 1970–71 Carleton exceeded the enrolment targets that Dunton had proposed eight years earlier; in that year it enrolled more than 7,000 undergraduates and more than 700 graduate students. Enrolment would continue to rise but the baby boom crisis was over. Possibly more important, the government had now decided that the political threat had been averted and was shifting its attention to other priorities. In the years that followed, operating grants increased at less than the rate of inflation and capital grants were frozen. The years of plenty had come to an end.

The changes, however, would never be reversed. The small city college was by then a university, with a growing emphasis on graduate studies and research. It was also a provincial institution with a wider geographic base for its student population. It had not been integrated into a hierarchical provincial university system, but it had clearly become a public university, almost completely dependent on the provincial government for its operating revenue and capital expenditures. The university that was now established on the new campus bore little resemblance to the old college on First Avenue.

CHAPTER SEVEN

The New Campus Takes Shape

In 1961 the new campus had three academic buildings: the Maxwell MacOdrum Library, the Henry Marshall Tory Building for the Sciences, and Norman Paterson Hall for the arts and social sciences. Enrolment would increase each year for the next decade but each year, with some judicious juggling of space, there would be enough classrooms and laboratories to accommodate the influx. There were crises and compromises and many frustrations, but no students were turned away and no students lost their year because essential courses could not be offered. And because a university is more than classrooms and laboratories, the construction program also included offices for the professors and administrators, residences for students, athletic facilities, and even a parking garage. By 1973, at the end of this sustained burst of activity, there were twenty-five buildings on the campus, with plans for an art gallery and a major extension to the library. Although a freeze on government funding drove the cranes from the campus for the next decade, by then space had been provided for some eight thousand students, and the broad outlines of the modern campus had been established. It was no mean achievement.

The pivotal figure in this expansion was Ross Love, the chairman of Carleton's Building Advisory Committee which, as we have seen, had become the planning agency for the physical development of the new campus.[1] The crucial decision at any time was which building would be next. This depended on academic priorities – on what space would be most needed in one or two years' time when the new students arrived on campus. It also depended on financial factors – on what private and public funds would be available. Love would first assemble the relevant information to guide the president and the Board of Governors in their discussion of which building should come next. Once the decision was made, the location of the building would be chosen, guided by the master plan but influenced by the building's impact on roads, sewers, and steam pipes. Then Love's real work began. He had to find out from the prospective users of the building what they wanted and to convey this information to the architect. After many exchanges between the users and the architect, with Love as intermediary, the building would be designed and tenders called for. If the tenders exceeded the amount budgeted by the board, as they often did, it was then up to Love to discuss possible modifications with the users and the architect, and to explain the financial and academic consequences of the various options to the board. Nor did it end there. Even after the decision was made, the contract signed, and construction begun, there were always some last-minute modifications to be considered. By then Love would be working on the design of the next building and involved in preliminary discussions of which building would follow it.

This approach to planning was effective because Love had a talent for appreciating the concerns of users, architects, builders, and board members, and for explaining these concerns to others. It helped that he was a man of great civility and infinite patience. The potential for conflict was always there because there was never enough money to provide everything the professors wanted. Love was careful to keep the Senate informed and even encouraged it to take a more direct role in planning.[2] At the same time, he established good working relations with the members of the board's Building Committee, who gained confidence that Love and Fred Turner (the bursar, who was also on the Building Advisory Committee) could be trusted to avoid any unnecessary frills or extravagances. For more than a decade, Ross Love served two masters, the Senate and the Board of Governors, with remarkable harmony.

I

The move to the new campus in 1959 had been a significant event in Carleton's history, but within a distressingly short time the university needed more accommodation than its three buildings could provide. As President Dunton explained in his annual report in 1961, enrolment was going up each year and these buildings would soon be inadequate. "The University as a whole," he noted, "seemed to have become well settled in the quarters which had seemed so strange the year before" and "for a change, no construction was going on." The bad news, however, was that "the buildings on the new campus were used just about to their full capacity."[3] The need for space had become so urgent that even before Frost's crucial offer to finance university expansion, Carleton began a second phase of construction on the new campus. In the summer of 1961 several contracts were signed: for an extension to Paterson Hall; for a new classroom building, which would become Southam Hall; for two student residences; and for a gymnasium across the tracks, which would also serve as a temporary centre for student activities.

In this second phase of construction the design of the buildings still incorporated some assumptions that were already out of date. For example, when the extension to Paterson Hall was designed, it was still assumed that the more junior professors would have to share an office.[4] But by the time the extension was completed, the status of professors had improved to the extent that sharing an office no longer seemed acceptable. The fortunate professors who moved into the new wing found themselves alone in much larger offices than their colleagues in other buildings.

The students were less fortunate. The board and most of the faculty talked of the importance of athletic facilities and a students' centre, and although this was more than rhetoric, other priorities intervened. Financial factors played an important role. At this stage the provincial government was only prepared to finance buildings that would serve academic purposes, and its definition of academic activities did not include athletics or students' clubs. The Carleton administration had a broader view of academic life, but it was short of private funds. What private money it had was spent on student residences, which also fitted into the administration's view of college life, as well as meeting the need to provide some accommodation for out-of-town students. The available funds were invested in Lanark House and Renfrew House, with the balance covered by a long-term mortgage.

The original master plan had given the students' centre a prominent place on the fourth side of the central quadrangle. In the meantime, the students were promised space, first in the Tory Building, then in the library, and then in Paterson Hall; but in each case, classrooms and office space took precedence over space for the students' extracurricular activities. The students volunteered a fee increase of ten dollars per year as a contribution to the cost of a Students' Union building, but without government funds and with private funds going to the residences, a separate building for the students was still in the future. For the time being, the students had to be satisfied with space in the gymnasium across the railway tracks.

Two decisions associated with this second phase of construction were measures for which all future generations of students would be grateful. The first was to install air-conditioning. Many public institutions in Ottawa, following the lead of the federal government, had refused to recognize that the city could be unpleasantly hot and humid in the summer. The new MacOdrum Library, with inadequate insulation and poor air circulation,

In 1960 the new library was described in the *Raven* as "one of
the most modern libraries in eastern Canada." One feature
was that all of its holdings were accessible to the students in
open stacks, though it might mean sitting on the floor to see
the titles on the bottom shelf (Malak). The smoking lounge
(*bottom*) was an innovation that did not survive the
combination of shortage of space and antismoking
campaigns.

and without the protection of the great elms of the Glebe, quickly drew attention to this reality; Hilda Gifford, the librarian, recalls that many of the offices were unbearable on sunny days.[5] Fortunately, Ross Love had proposed large ventilation ducts, with the possibility of air-conditioning in mind, and it was installed when the additions were made. The second decision was to link all the buildings by tunnels. It had been decided from the beginning that heating and other services would go underground to make the campus more attractive. The maintenance of the service lines would require a crawl space, and it was Love who suggested enlarging this crawl space to create pedestrian tunnels.[6] The board approved. Thus, one of the distinctive – and, on blustery winter days, most popular – features of the campus was introduced.

One troubling question was where the money would come from to pay for this spurt of construction. The board was not sure. The contracts totalled over $3 million, and with furniture and equipment the costs would come to more than $4.5 million. A public appeal for funds had raised a million dollars, the provincial government had produced another million, and a mortgage from Central Mortgage and Housing would cover the cost of the residences. That left a balance of $1.5 million to be taken care of, with an extension to the library and a new engineering building still needed.[7]

The capital costs – the costs of buildings under construction and those that would soon be needed – were only part of the problem for the Board of Governors. It was also concerned about operating deficits. Annual operating expenses had exceeded annual operating revenues for the first three years on the new campus. The shortfalls were not large, but they were worrisome because each year the deficit had to be added to the accumulated debt. Even balancing the budget, much less paying off the debt, would not be easy.

The board found it had few options. Fred Turner, the bursar, ran a tight ship, and the costs of administration and plant maintenance could not easily be reduced. The amount spent on scholarships and bursaries and on library acquisitions was low when compared with other universities. The major expenditure, almost half of the total, went on faculty salaries. Some savings were made each year when higher than expected enrolments meant larger classes, but these were only temporary economies. Professors accepted the heavier workloads as an emergency measure, but in the long run Carleton could not afford to diverge significantly from the faculty-student ratio of other Ontario universities. Nor were low salaries an acceptable option when Carleton had to compete with other universities for young professors.

It was also difficult to balance the budget by increasing income. Student fees were an important source of income, amounting to $500,000 in a total

Between classes. Why go outside when there is a tunnel?
(*Raven 66*)

income of 1,200,000 in 1960–61. The board raised the fees for the next
years, from $425 to $465 for arts and science students, but raising fees was
a limited option. If the fees at Carleton were higher than at other universities
in Ontario, some students would go elsewhere, taking their fees with them.

This left increases in government grants as the only recourse. The university would only be able to balance its books if the governments increased
their grants each year. In the five years beginning in 1958–59 Carleton's total revenues did increase, from just over $1 million to more than $2.5 million. In each of these years, close to one-half of this annual income came
from the combined grants of the federal and provincial governments, with
the federal government providing about 20 per cent and the provincial government about 30 per cent.[8]

However, the pattern was far from clear at the time. There was never any
advance assurance that the government grants would be increased. Each
year the university had to make commitments about classroom space and

the hiring of new professors without knowing how much government money would be provided. In 1962, for example, Dunton complained that "financial suspense hung over all the planning that had to be done for the following year."[9] Enrolment was expected to go up again in the fall of that year, which meant that decisions aboout new appointments had to be made before the amount of the government grants was known. Carleton's financial problems were shared to some degree by all the universities in Ontario. Expanding enrolments and higher costs meant that they all relied on government grants to bring revenues and expenditures into balance.

The breakthrough came in 1962, as we have seen, when Leslie Frost and the Advisory Committee on University Affairs decided to finance university expansion. From then on, Carleton could submit its capital budget in advance with the reasonable expectation that the money would be available. Decisions about new appointments still had to be made before the operating grants from the two governments were announced, but at least the pattern of increasing grants each year gave some reassurance. The introduction of formula financing in 1967 was an inprovement because the decisions were less subjective, though the universities still had to estimate what their enrolment figures would be and what the basic income unit would be. Needless to say, Carleton, like the other universities, never got as much money for buildings or operating costs as it felt it deserved, but in comparison with earlier – and later – years, it was generously treated.

In the meantime, Carleton was still a construction site. In 1962 the building extensions and the new buildings were all scheduled to be completed by September. Not one of them was finished on schedule. Dunton, who was not given to expressing his feelings openly, did comment wryly in his annual report that although "universities are not usually regarded by industry as shining examples of efficiency," they did at least respect timetables, whereas the building industry appeared to be "one to which undertakings about dates and the importance of time seems to be of little account."[10] The irony is understandable; the confusion and inconvenience during that fall term was long remembered by the survivors. One student recalls wearing an overcoat and gloves to lectures in Southam Hall because the windows were not installed until November.[11] Even the satisfaction of an official opening of five buildings on the same day by Minister of Education William Davis was marred by last-minute efforts to tidy up the site. The ceremony was seen as an exceptional occasion to draw attention to the dramatic growth of the new university. Unfortunately, as Dunton and the minister approached the campus, they saw smoke billowing out of the top storey of the library. A fire had started in the debris in one of the ducts. It was quickly under control with no serious damage done, but it limited the success of the public relations exercise.[12]

By 1962 the MacOdrum Library and Paterson Hall had been enlarged, and Southam Hall, Lanark House, and Renfrew House had been added.

The smoke from a fire in the MacOdrum Library was an embarrassing sight when the minister of education arrived for the opening of the library and four other buildings (*Raven 63*).

11

The decision of the provincial government in 1962 to finance university expansion in Ontario gave Carleton an opportunity to look beyond its ad hoc efforts to accommodate the rapidly increasing number of students. With the assurance of some financial assistance, it could now consider what kind of university Carleton should become. Dunton's proposal to accommodate 6,000 undergraduates and 500 graduate students by 1970 did not define Carleton's pedagogical or academic goals. The importance of planning Carleton's growth was raised in the Senate. Dunton responded by appointing a Senate Committee on Enrolment. Ross Love was the obvious choice to chair the committee.

The committee, which reported late in 1962, was concerned about the impact of large enrolments on "the future academic character of the university."[13] It had no misgivings about the expansion of graduate studies. Indeed, it saw the possibility of as many as 1,200 graduate students by 1970 "because of Ottawa's special attractions for graduate studies and because of Carleton's growing reputation," and it clearly favoured vertiginous expansion at this level, but it was concerned about expansion at the undergraduate level.[14]

The difficulty was that the ideal undergraduate experience did not seem compatible with large numbers. A survey of the faculty showed that most professors wanted a university large enough to offer diversified degree programs but not so large as to limit the contact between students in different programs. The faculty ideal was an academic community in which professors would still know their students and in which the formal education of the students would still be supplemented by extracurricular activities and informal contacts. The committee shared these traditional views of undergraduate life. It did not envisage any major changes in the programs already offered at Carleton. (The predicted new programs in architecture, fine arts, and law as a social science would only be logical extensions of the existing programs.) Consequently, the committee regarded 6,000 as the upper limit at the undergraduate level. Even this would mean about 1,500 students enrolled in the first-year English course; any enrolment beyond that would be dangerously cumbersome and impersonal.

The impact on the campus was also important. The committee believed that Carleton could accommodate 10,000 students without resorting to high-rise buildings, but it considered that this "may be higher than is compatible with efficient operation of the University and a pleasant layout of buildings."[15] Again, 6,000 seemed a reasonable compromise. What would happen when undergraduate enrolment reached this upper limit? The committee recommended the development of a second campus in the western part of the city to accommodate the surplus. With a provincial

government eager to find places for students, it would presumably be prepared to finance the new campus.

The report was well received. For the next few years planning was based
on the assumption that the Rideau River campus would serve only 6,000
undergraduate students. What hardly anyone realized at the time was that
the undergraduate experience would be affected by more than size. The addition of a relatively large graduate school would dramatically change the
academic environment. An emphasis on graduate work meant professors recruited for their commitment to research, a commitment which would often
compete with their teaching responsibilities at the undergraduate level and
would almost certainly limit their involvement in the students' extracurricular activities. It was also significant that these professors were likely to stress
the importance of more specialized undergraduate programs to prepare the
better students to go on to graduate work, at the expense of a more well-
rounded academic experience. To this was added the presence of graduate
students who needed to gain teaching experience and the pressure on the
university to use graduate students as teaching assistants. Graduate studies
at Carleton, as elsewhere, would mean that the undergraduate experience
would bear little resemblance to the traditional ideal of an earlier era.

The concerns about an overcrowded campus required no immediate action. In the meantime, the provincial support for capital construction would
make it possible to accommodate more students each year. The first new
buildings approved by the Committee on University Affairs were the engineering building, named after the chancellor, C.J. Mackenzie, the chemistry
building, named after E.W.R. Steacie (who succeeded Mackenzie at the National Research Council and served as chairman of the Board of Governors),
and the physics building, named after Gerhard Herzberg, a distinguished research professor who would later become chancellor. These buildings, along
with Southam Hall, were seen as a second stage in the development of the
master plan; they were sited around the buildings of the central quadrangle
and were distinguished from them by their more modest brick facing. But
any ordinary brick would not do; the architects insisted on a special ceramic-
finished brick from Pennsylvania whose colour, in their view, was what these
buildings required. The board was not easily convinced: surely there must be
some Canadian bricks that would be quite satisfactory and much cheaper.[16]
But the architects and their aesthetic arguments won the day.

The Loeb Building, the next major construction on the campus, was designed to house the social sciences. Ten years earlier none of the faculty at
Carleton would have thought of the social sciences as a group of disciplines
clearly distinguishable from the humanities. Since the war, however, social
scientists had been much influenced by the astonishing breakthroughs of
the natural sciences and had become more concerned with methodology,

with an emphasis on statistical data. The emphasis on the rigorous testing of hypotheses and the objective of creating new knowledge distanced them from their colleagues in the humanities. In some universities, the traditionalists and the new behaviourists fought bitterly for control over appointments and curriculum changes, but at Carleton the rivalry was muted by the youth of the faculty and the shared adventure of creating a new institution. By the 1960s, Scott Gordon and John Porter and many of the professors who had fought for higher academic standards at Carleton were more narrowly concerned with the appropriate curriculum for the social sciences.[17] The opportunity to have their own building came with the open-purse years in Ontario and gave them a chance to design a building specifically for their needs as social scientists.

The users' committee for the Loeb Building outlined its requirements in the spring of 1964. The emphasis was on the links between teaching and research, and on closer and more informal contacts between professors and students. The natural sciences were the obvious model, with their close collaboration of professor and students on research projects, and this was reinforced in the 1960s by the emerging youth culture and the questioning of traditional authority. Most of the classrooms were to be seminar rooms, with only two auditoriums that could seat more than a hundred students. Each large department was to occupy one floor, with offices, seminar rooms, and common rooms close together to encourage informal contacts between faculty and students. The design of the building reflected the assumption that, in future, much of the advanced research in the social sciences would be done in research institutes and that Ottawa, as the national capital, was the logical site for such institutes. Space was to be available on each floor to be leased to these institutes. Carleton, it was believed, would benefit financially and, more important, would benefit intellectually from the association with cutting-edge research. The building was to have its own library and even its own cafeteria, in recognition of "the effectiveness of food consumption, or even simply coffee, as a catalyst of discussion."[18]

The architects were faced with the challenge of incorporating these requirements on a difficult site. For the convenience of students, the building would have to be close to other classrooms and to the main library. Since the space around the central court was now largely occupied, it was decided to build along the cliff over the Rideau River. The solution was a sequence of four connected towers. The design, which included offices and seminars on each floor, meant that corridors and passageways took up much of the internal space. The Department of University Affairs raised questions about the extravagance of the ambitious project but was not prepared to challenge the academic arguments used to justify the design; it gave its approval to the plans late in 1965.[19]

There were still more hurdles. When the tenders were opened, the lowest was for $7 million – $1.5 million more than expected. The government was now paying 85 per cent of the costs of academic buildings, but would it pay its share of this amount? The Department of University Affairs conceded the urgent need for space at Carleton, and it agreed to produce the money on condition that some other items on Carleton's building program were postponed for a year.[20] But could the university find the million dollars to cover its share of the cost? This would have been a serious problem, but fortunately it had just received an unexpected windfall of half a million dollars. Bertram Loeb had offered this sum to Ottawa Civic Hospital for a research centre, but when Charlotte Whitton stridently objected to the gift on the grounds that the centre would eventually cost the city money, Loeb withdrew his offer and gave the money to Carleton.[21] So the contract was let, and the building – named after the donor – was completed by the fall of 1967. And the possibility of having to restrict enrolment for lack of space was once again averted.[22] But the expected research institutes, for which the building had been planned, never materialized. The departments concerned, however, benefited from the mistake. As enrolment rose, they were able to use the unoccupied space for offices and classrooms instead of having to find space elsewhere on the campus.

The University Centre was another building that showed how Carleton was adapting to change. The shortage of space for student clubs and student entertainment had became increasingly obvious. By the mid-1960s the new campus provided proportionately less space for student activities than the First Avenue campus had done. The crux of the problem was that the provincial government would pay only half the cost of a students' centre, and Carleton needed all the private funds it could raise to pay for its share of the cost of the academic buildings and residences. The voluntary student fee of ten dollars for a students' centre had been a good example, but it did not bring in the sums that were needed. By 1965 the Board of Governors was so conscious of the need that it decided to plan the building even if there was no money in sight. A committee of nine, including four students, was appointed.[23] Fortunately, other universities were also pressing the government to be more generous, and the financial problem was eased when the government agreed to increase its share of the costs of students' centres from 50 to 95 per cent. The remaining 5 per cent was covered by equal contributions from the students and the university.

The University Centre is, to a remarkable degree, a monument to the idealism and optimism of the 1960s. Even the name reflects the aspirations for an egalitarian community, where not only students but all sectors of the university community would mingle. In the words of a consultant, the building was to be a "laboratory of citizenship."[24] A scenic site overlooking the river

was rejected in favour of a central location in an area that had once been reserved for the sciences; the master plan was modified in order to place the
new centre at what was intended to become the intersection of academic and
residential life. The concept of the University Centre as a crossroads was
highlighted by the planning committee in its brief to the architect. "The
physical layout," the committee explained, "is to force all users of the building to go through some common areas before reaching areas of specialized
interests. We must encourage all members of the University to use this building in order that a sense of community be achieved."[25] A striking example
of this community ideal was the unusual inclusion of the Faculty Club in a
building in which the students would be the principal users.

The emphasis on unstructured social encounters explains why the University Centre had no main entrance. Instead, users could choose a number
of entrances on each of three different levels. This accessibility reflected the
rejection of formal structure, a characteristic aspect of the 1960s, but it had
its drawbacks. It encouraged vandalism and theft. As the architect put it,
much of the furniture "walked out of the building" in the early years.[26] But
this, too, was typical of the 1960s.

Inside the building the most distinctive feature was a large electronic mural on one side of the central stairs. The mural, the gift of an anonymous
donor, had thousands of coloured bulbs, which produced kaleidoscopic
patterns when sensors were initiated by people walking past it. With its
combination of technology and individualism, it was a striking metaphor
for the times. It also became a metaphor for the less admirable aspects of
the individualism of the 1960s, because the sensors were constantly being
broken or stolen. By the end of the decade, the maintenance staff had given
up and the mural no longer lit up as the students passed by.

The University Centre also reflected the shifting attitude towards alcohol.
In an earlier era, the university and municipal authorities had cooperated to
try to control the students' consumption of alcohol. Drinking on campus
was forbidden and in Ottawa, as in most Canadian communities, the municipal officials kept bars away from the campus by refusing to grant liquor
licences near the university. Despite this, students still managed to drink at
university functions, but they did so in defiance of the university authorities.
By the 1960s, students wanted to be treated as adults and this included the
right to drink. The government responded to the pressure by lowering the
drinking age from twenty-one to eighteen, which meant that most university
students could now drink in public. There was no resistance from the university authorities. Alcohol, which had been seen as a dangerous drug for
the young, was now seen as a desirable stimulant for social exchanges. The
decision to allow liquor to be served in the University Centre was made with
almost no discussion and provoked no strong objections.[27]

The first sod was turned in 1968 and the building was completed in 1970. The initial administrative arrangements were unusually liberal by most university standards. The Students' Council would name a majority of the members of the management committee in charge of the operations of the University Centre. The university would rent space for health and food services and for the Faculty Club, but the rest of the building would be run by the students for the students. The salaried director, named by the committee, would run the student enterprises and take his instructions from the executive of the Students' Council.[28] The maintenance costs would be covered by the continuation of the special student levy, the rent from the university, and any profits from the pub and other commercial enterprises in the building. The autonomy conceded to the student services is illustrated by an incident at the pub on the opening day, when off-duty police were at the door to check the age of the customers. President Dunton, who attended the event, asked Vic Valentine, the dean of students, if he thought everybody was over seventeen. Valentine assured him that everything was under control, but Dunton was not convinced; he could see one of his daughters among the students, so he knew that at least one of them was under the drinking age. But neither Dunton nor Valentine raised any objection to this breach of the law.

III

In the midst of the hectic construction on the Rideau campus, Carleton University acquired a second campus. In 1967 St Patrick's College abruptly ended its association with the University of Ottawa to become part of Carleton University. It was an extraordinary development for both St Patrick's and Carleton. The college had been a Roman Catholic institution, owned by a Catholic order and associated from the beginning with the Catholic University of Ottawa. Nobody would have predicted that it would ask to be part of Carleton, just as nobody would have predicted that Carleton – which prided itself on being nondenominational and which had been founded to serve non-Catholic students in the Ottawa area – would welcome the acquisition.

St Patrick's College had been founded after the First World War because of a feud between the Irish and French Catholics in Ottawa.[29] The University of Ottawa, which had begun as an English-language institution, had become bilingual by the turn of the century, despite objections from the Irish Catholic leaders in the community. The bitterness between the French- and English-speaking Catholics was further exacerbated during the First World War by the debates over Regulation 17, which attempted to impose English as the language of instruction in the Catholic separate schools of

St Patrick's College campus on Echo Drive

Ontario. The Oblates sought a truce by creating a separate English-speaking province for its order in Canada. St Patrick's College was a product of this truce. This English-language college was administered by the English-speaking Oblates and was financially autonomous, though it was affiliated with the University of Ottawa, which granted the degrees.

The new college did not have a prosperous beginning. The first phase of construction coincided with the onset of the Depression, and neither the English Oblates nor the Irish Catholic community had the material resources to complete their ambitious plans. However, over the next few decades St Patrick's developed a style that seemed well suited to its students. The college offered a three-year program with specialization in arts, science, or the social sciences. Its intellectual horizons may have been narrow, judging by its small library, but the students had the advantages of small classes and devoted teachers. The college prided itself on its humane values and its emphasis on service in the community. Over the years it became a close-knit institution, with priests, parents, and students sharing the conservative values of a double minority, united in opposition to the Protestantism or secularism of the wider community and the dominance of the French Oblates at the University of Ottawa.

By the end of the 1950s, St Patrick's was entering its golden age. Enrolment was expanding. The ever-increasing federal grant to colleges and universities meant that the college felt financially secure for the first time. The academic program became more diversified; undergraduates now had a commerce option, and the School of Social Welfare offered a professional degree at the graduate level for social workers. Already, however, the shared values of this tightly knit community was under siege. The Oblates, like most religious orders, were attracting fewer recruits, and more of the teaching had to be done by lay professors, both men and women. Even within the church, Vatican II had shown that many of the traditional Catholic values were being questioned.

St Patrick's was given no time to adapt to these changes. In 1967 the federal government changed the way in which it provided financial support for postsecondary education. Instead of granting funds directly to colleges and universities, it decided to reimburse the provincial governments for half of their expenditures at this level. In Ontario, where the provincial government had a long-standing policy of not supporting denominational colleges, this threatened to bankrupt Catholic institutions. The University of Ottawa reluctantly decided to become a nonsectarian institution in order to receive the provincial grant in full. It would no longer be Catholic, but it would emphasize its bilingualism to give itself a distinctive role. This left St Patrick's College in a quandary. There seemed no place for it as an English-language college in a university that was bilingual; and it could not survive on its own, even as a nonsectarian institution, because the provincial government was not prepared to authorize a third degree-granting institution in Ottawa.[30] At the last minute, in March 1967, the desperate college administration approached Carleton.

Carleton University was interested. Expansion was the order of the day, and St Patrick's would bring some eight hundred students, complete with buildings and professors. An element of rivalry with the now nondenominational University of Ottawa may have been a factor. If Carleton did not admit these students, they might go to the University of Ottawa. The acquisition could also be justified because Carleton was already considering a second campus, which was expected to include a number of small undergraduate colleges, and St Patrick's might become one of these colleges. The most attractive feature of the proposed affiliation, however, seems to have been the college's School of Social Welfare. Carleton would be acquiring an established professional school at the graduate level.[31]

The radical proposal in March left little time to negotiate an agreement before the beginning of the next academic year. The Department of University Affairs was involved in the financial discussions because it would have to provide the funds for Carleton to buy the property from the Oblates. The administration at St Patrick's wanted to ensure job security for its professors and for their pensions on retirement, and to obtain as much autonomy as possible for the college after its affiliation. There were also problems for Carleton. The anti-Catholic sentiments of its founders had not completely faded, and some members of the board argued vehemently that the affiliation of St Patrick's and the hiring of ordained priests would be a violation of Carleton's nonsectarian principles. Dunton had to convene a special meeting of the board to override these misgivings.[32] There was also opposition from within the Carleton faculty. Here the misgivings were expressed in academic terms, with reservations about the academic reputation of the college and the academic qualifications of the professors at St Patrick's – though unstated religious prejudices may have provoked these objections.

The final agreement, signed in July 1967, met most of these concerns. St Patrick's would become a separate division within Carleton's Faculty of Arts, with the rector, Father Kelly, as the first dean. The tenured professors at the college would retain their tenure at Carleton and would receive pension coverage for their years at St Patrick's. Carleton, however, would decide the fate of the untenured professors and would exercise academic control in future by requiring that decisions on appointments, tenure, promotion, and salaries would require the consent of Carleton's dean of arts, who would consult the chairman of the relevant departments at Carleton.

For some disciplines, the curriculum for the affiliated college proved to be as controversial as personnel matters. Now that St Patrick's was to be nondenominational, it was readily agreed that there could be no obligatory courses in theology or religion. But what of St Patrick's compulsory courses in philosophy in the first two years of its arts program? The Philosophy Department at Carleton, doubtless suspicious of the prominence given in these courses to the ideas of St Thomas Aquinas, insisted that the courses be dropped and that the first-year students at St Patrick's be enrolled in sections of the first-year course in philosophy that was already being offered on the Rideau River campus. For the future, any changes in the college curriculum would have to be submitted to the Carleton Senate and would require the prior approval of the relevant department on the main campus.[33] Although St Patrick's College would be a separate faculty, its autonomy was clearly circumscribed. Carleton would determine its future.

One thing missing from the records is any discussion of what this future should be. Would the links with the Irish Catholic community on Ottawa survive? The administration at Carleton does not seem to have asked the question. It seems to have taken it for granted that somehow St Patrick's would become part of the proposed second campus when that materialized. In the meantime, the aim was to disturb the existing institution as little as possible. Father Kelly was more definite. He explained that times had changed and that the college had been forced to adjust, but "the Oblate Fathers wanted the college to continue to serve the community it has served for thirty-five years."[34] Nobody seems to have asked what community St Patrick's could serve when the compulsory religion and philosophy courses were eliminated, when the curriculum was controlled by the main campus and the professors' careers were dependent on the evaluation of departments on the main campus. Two institutions with different traditions and different objectives had been joined together, and the future of the college was far from clear.

Over the next few years St Patrick's was a college in search of a role. The clerical influence in its management quickly declined. There were eighteen priests on its faculty in 1967, but four years later there were only ten; the others had retired, resigned, or left the order. Enrolment patterns also changed. The college needed a full-time student body of more than a thousand to be financially self-sustaining. Registration increased from 800 students at the time of affiliation to 950 by 1969–70, but this was the peak enrolment, and by 1971–72 it was down to 850, of which it was estimated that only about half came from Catholic high schools.[35] The college was losing its connection with the Irish Catholic community without having established another base.

One option might have been the development of a distinctive liberal arts program in contrast to the Rideau River campus, where freer choices were undermining the traditional arts degree. The college did introduce a Unified Liberal Arts Program, an integrated program over three years with a number of credits based on lectures, tutorials, and discussion groups on a special theme. But there were not enough interested students to solve the college's enrolment needs. Another proposal, which showed how far the college was prepared to move from its roots, was a bilingual program with the first year entirely in French. The appointment of Derek Sida, a mathematician from the main campus, to succeed Father Kelly as dean in 1971 was part of the search for a new role. Sida favoured a rigorous liberal arts program as well as a number of multidisciplinary programs. The college that had attracted a conservative Irish Catholic student body was now trying to attract the more restless youth who wanted courses on "relevant" topics, such as ecology and the Third World.

It was not a propitious time for such an experiment. The decline in enrolment might be only temporary, but it meant that there was unused space at the college at a time of overcrowding on the main campus. This situation became even less acceptable when the provincial government imposed the new formula for building funds, linking space entitlement to enrolment. Unused space at St Patrick's meant that Carleton did not qualify for more space on the Rideau campus. This difficulty was resolved when Algonquin

College, the new college of arts and applied technology, wanted to take over the St Patrick's College buildings. The provincial government made the transfer possible by agreeing to pay for a new building for the college on the main campus.

Could St Patrick's College maintain a distinct identity after the move? The change in its location further weakened the links with its Irish Catholic beginnings. A group of Irish Catholic students vociferously objected to the move; but the faculty of the college, most of whom had been appointed since the affiliation with Carleton, were not impressed by what they described as "irrational sentimentality." Some of them welcomed closer links with their colleagues on the main campus; others, with stronger commitments to a small college, may have convinced themselves that St Patrick's could still survive with a separate building and a separate residence.[36]

An effort was made to meet these demands. The new building was located far from the other academic buildings, to the north of the student residences. It was specially designed for St Patrick's College, with library, theatre, faculty offices, and small classrooms. The funds from the province could not be stretched to build a separate residence, but two floors of Renfrew House were set aside for St Patrick's students. In physical terms the college would have the separate existence it needed. Whether this would be enough for it to develop a distinctive identity was still far from clear.

The transfer of the School of Social Welfare was less controversial. Under Father Swithun Bowers the school had emphasized treatment – "the restoration, maintenance and enhancement of social functioning," in the words of a 1969 Self-Study Report[37] – and had established a high reputation for supervised training based on placements at social agencies. The school, now named the School of Social Work, saw the need to broaden its curriculum to give more attention to the development of social policy and to research; it was agreed that this was to be achieved by two new academic appointments.[38] Future graduates would receive their degrees from Carleton rather than from the University of Ottawa, but otherwise the school was expected to continue much as before.

IV

In the years after the acquisition of St Patrick's College, construction had continued on the main campus with no respite. Growth had become a way of life with no end in sight. The campus was still busy in the evenings with part-time students, but more and more the focus was on full-time students and the professors who would teach them. In the fall of 1965, 3,000 full-time students enrolled, and 40 new professors were added that year. Undergraduate enrolment was still expected to reach 6,000 by 1970, and graduate studies were expected to continue to expand after that date. Plans were already underway for the buildings that would be needed, at an estimated cost of $23 million. A few years earlier the university's portion of this amount would have seemed unattainable. Dunton still did not know where the money would come from, but expansion now seemed so inevitable that he saw "no alternative but to proceed with the program in the expectation that the funds would be forthcoming."[39] The editor of the *Carleton* put it even more bluntly, stating that the future of the country depended on higher education: "The universities must have the money and it's up to the province to get it for them."[40]

The mood at Queen's Park, however, was changing. The provincial government had encouraged the expansion of universities and the creation of new ones at great expense. It could hardly be blamed for worrying about costs. Carleton was now one of fourteen universities in the province, and all of them had ambitious plans. The government was looking for a way to turn off the tap. It was now feeling less sense of urgency, because university places were being provided for the baby boomers.

The provincial purse strings were tightened gradually. As Ross Love told the Senate early in 1969, the Ontario universities "seem to be moving from an era in which, in retrospect, it was relatively easy to make decisions on new programs, new space and new facilities into one in which such decisions can sensibly be made only after a searching and realistic appraisal of alternatives."[41] The careful scrutiny of each project by the Department of University Affairs, however necessary, was frustrating for university planners because there were no satisfactory guidelines. Buildings had to be planned years in advance, but it was difficult to predict which of the many university proposals the government would approve. In 1969 the department tried to resolve the problem by a formula for capital grants equivalent to the formula for operating grants. Buildings already under construction would be completed, but future buildings would be eligible for provincial grants only if the floor space at the university fell below 120 square feet per student. This formula was admittedly arbitrary, but it at least had the advantage from the government's point of view that it would eliminate some projects. At Carleton, for example, it meant that the university would be overbuilt when the buildings already under construction were completed, and the university would have to wait four or five years until increased enrolment entitled it to more space. Half of the universities in the province were in the same position, but the government was adamant.[42] The university building boom was coming to an end.

At Carleton the proposed satellite campus was one of the first victims of the shifting financial climate. Academic planning for the new campus had been relatively uncontroversial. The traditional preference for small classes had been reinforced by the student protests of the 1960s against the impersonal and authoritarian pattern at large institutions, so the planners had envisaged a number of small undergraduate colleges on the new site.[43] The Department of University Affairs had originally approved of the idea, but it showed no interest in providing the money. By 1968, with not even a site selected, it was clear that there would be no satellite campus by 1970.

The university administrators were not taken completely by surprise. As early as 1966 the university had sponsored a study of the impact on Carleton if no satellite campus was built and if enrolment reached a predicted 15,000 students by 1980. The consultant saw no insuperable difficulties. He projected a number of additional academic buildings close to the main quadrangle, most of them still four or five storeys high, though some might have to rise to ten storeys. Parking received more attention because there would be more cars, and some of the existing parking lots would be occupied by the new buildings. His solution was a parking garage. The significant conclusion was that in physical terms at least, the campus could cope with this expansion.[44]

The consultant's concern for parking was well founded. Municipal transportation carried public servants to and from work with commendable efficiency, but the Carleton campus was not as well served. Initially, the new site had been isolated from the settled areas of the city, and for the first year or two the university had to pay for any bus service to the campus. In any case, public transportation, even with a subsidy, would not be enough. It was the age of the car; professors and an increasing number of students preferred to drive and wanted places to park. Car parks were already taking up more land than university buildings. Carleton was more fortunate than many older universities because it had vacant space, but parking was also a matter of convenience and status; some professors felt they should be able to park under their office windows. The Ottawa winters also meant that snow would have to be removed and that electrical outlets would have to be provided for the block heaters of the more privileged.

Carleton astutely avoided much of the controversy. The President's Committee on Parking included faculty and student representatives from the beginning. Fred Turner, the bursar, wisely guided the committee to a policy of avoiding subsidies for parking by setting the fees high enough to cover the full costs. Less affluent employees and students parked their cars in gravelled parking lots south of the library and north of the Tory Building. The most sought-after spaces – those closest to the central buildings – were reserved for those who were prepared to pay premium rents, and the spaces were allocated among this select group on the basis of their rank or prestige. It was a mark of Dunton's sensitivity to the potential friction over status that he personally approved the initial distribution before the parking permits were issued. It also says something about status at Carleton that the president had the most convenient space, with the adjoining spot going to his secretary.

In the early days, policing the parking lots was one of the major responsibilities of the security staff. Students and faculty frequently parked in reserved areas to drop off books at the library and then ignored the tickets issued by the guards. Ignoring the tickets could sometimes lead to trouble. Engineering students soon learned to heed the rules. John Ruptash, dean of engineering and a member of the parking committee, once saw the names of two engineering students on the list of miscreants. He promptly summoned them to his office to tell them that their behaviour was unprofessional and that if they intended to graduate they had better pay their fines.[45] The parking committee was more severe with repeat offenders; it arranged to have the cars towed away to a compound, to be released only after the fine was paid. Even this could sometimes cause embarrassment. "Rusty" Wendt, chair of the Department of Psychology, once got so angered by unauthorized cars in his parking spot that he gave instructions to have any such car impounded immediately. A few weeks later, when he generously lent his space to a senior Soviet diplomat, his instructions were carefully obeyed.[46]

If Carleton was to go beyond six thousand students and was to continue to be a walking campus, with students able to walk from one lecture to the next in ten minutes, the most convenient parking lots would have to be used for building sites. New parking space was provided by a parking garage east of the railway. The parking committee astutely raised fees in advance to build up a surplus, and the balance was amortized, to be paid off by parking revenues. Additional parking garages were considered, but the committee grudgingly accepted peripheral parking lots with longer walks to university buildings; it was less expensive to pave new lots as the demand grew.

The arts tower, later named the Dunton Tower, was the last building to be constructed before the capital grants formula was imposed (with the exception of the St Patrick's Building which was financed by a special arrangement with the new Ministry of Colleges and Universities). The tower was a break from the earlier master plan. If the Carleton campus was to have more than six thousand undergraduates, space would be at a premium, and the idea of fitting Carleton into a sylvan topography was abandoned. The tower was to be a twenty-two-storey building, with classrooms on the first four floors and with faculty and departmental offices on the floors above them. The architects defended the new approach by suggesting a new ideal, that of an academic citadel in sharp contrast to its parkland setting.[47]

By 1972, when the government froze capital grants for university buildings, a middle-sized university had already been constructed on the new campus.

The Dunton Tower would quickly become a landmark, the dominant building on the campus and a recognizable image for the university, though there were some traditionalist critics who felt that an office tower was an inappropriate symbol for a university.

The Ministry of Colleges and Universities insisted on some economies, even though the formula did not apply. Proposed television studios and a small practice theatre were eliminated, and the faculty offices were reduced in size. Only a few years earlier, the Loeb Building had been designed to bring faculty and students closer together. Financial constraints now left no place for this ideal of a community of scholars. Study space for graduate students was restricted to windowless rooms surrounding the elevators, and undergraduates who came to see their professor had to wait in the corridors if the professor was busy. The splendid views of the Experimental Farm or of Vincent Massey Park from the office windows did not fully compensate for the inhospitable atmosphere inside the building.

The Dunton Tower was completed in 1972. It marked the end of an era. The major outlines of the modern campus had been established. Twenty-five buildings had been built to serve some seven thousand students. By then, the government had gone beyond the constraint of a formula and had frozen all capital grants to universities across the province. At Carleton, the plans for a much-needed extension to the library and for an art gallery were put on hold. There would be no more cranes and no more construction on Carleton's campus for more than a decade. The University would have to cope as best it could with the space it had.

CHAPTER EIGHT

Professors at Carleton in the 1960s

The physical changes on the Rideau River campus were only part of the university's story in the 1960s. The role and status of the professors also changed. In part this was because university expansion across North America meant that professors were in short supply and could bargain for more benefits and privileges. Yet supply and demand did not explain all the changes. The nature of the academic profession was being transformed. Research and publications more and more determined the reputation of a professor and of the university to which he or she belonged. Teaching loads were actually reduced at most universities in spite of the increasing enrolments, with graduate students doing more marking and teaching, to allow professors more time for research. Sabbaticals, which had been limited to eminent or promising scholars, were now made available to all faculty members. At Carleton, the practice of sabbatical leave on half salary after six years of teaching was officially confirmed by the Board of Governors in 1965.[1]

The prestige of research altered the relations between the administration and the faculty in subtle ways. The primary responsibility of deans and heads of departments was to make sure that the approved courses in the various programs were offered and that there were professors in the classrooms and laboratories to teach them. Professors had always been on the committees that planned the programs and, once in the classroom, had had a remarkable degree of freedom in deciding what to teach and how, and how to evaluate the students. Nonetheless, there had been a clear sense of hierarchy, with the professors at the base and the president at the top. Now, the enhanced importance of research gave the professors more leverage.

Eminent scholars received research grants from agencies outside the university, and these grants attracted students and prestige to the institution. Successful researchers could therefore negotiate with the administration for quicker promotions and lighter teaching loads. Deans and heads of departments also exercised less authority because they were less able to evaluate this aspect of a professor's work and had to rely more and more on "peer evaluation," which meant relying on the opinions of other researchers in the same area of specialization. Professors were still salaried employees, but they now enjoyed a degree of independence that was exceptional. Many of the institutional changes during the decade would be a recognition of this changing status.

I

This enhanced status of the professoriate would lead to formal changes in the structure of university government, but at the beginning of the decade the faculty at Carleton saw little need for any changes. Carleton was still small. Differences of opinion on academic policy could be attributed to individual disagreements or personality conflicts; the distinction between the professors who taught and the departmental chairman or deans who had administrative as well as teaching responsibilities was blurred by personal contacts and a shared commitment to the institution. Even seniority does not seem to have created any serious divisions within the faculty in these years. Senior professors had a privileged status – they recommended to the president, for example, who was to be promoted – but the more junior members of the faculty seem to have accepted this hierarchical pattern as normal.[2]

The Senate, where academic policies were decided, was initially an august body, including all the full professors and some eminent figures from the local community, presided over by the president. It was expanded in 1963 to include ten faculty members below the rank of full professor, though this was not based on any organized protest by the junior faculty; it was, at least in part, a collegial gesture by the full professors already in the Senate.[3] The collegial atmosphere in the early 1960s is illustrated by the Senate minutes, which sometimes convey the atmosphere of a private club. Instead of being typically dull and matter-of-fact, they show an ironic wit which only a closely-knit community could enjoy. On one occasion, for example, when the Senate amended an examination schedule that a committee of deans had proposed, the minutes rercorded:

Dean Ruptash [dean of engineering] then observed that it would be apparent to all members of Faculty, including members of his own Faculty, that the recommendations of a Committee of Deans had been reviewed and modified by the Senate. The

M.S. Macphail,   A.M. Beattie, English   J. Ruptash, Engineering
Mathematics

G.R. Love, Physics   H.H.J. Nesbitt, Biology   R.A. Wendt, Psychology

These senior professors were both teachers and scholars, but their commitment to
Carleton meant that they also took on administrative responsibilities as departmental chairs, deans, and chairs of the many committees on which university administration depends (*Raven 66*).

Clerk [of the Senate] was constrained to admit that this was so; but he pointed out
that the Committee was a committee of the Senate, that it had submitted its report
to the Senate, and that the Senate was not bound to endorse the views of its committees. Dean Ruptash, however, wished it not to be overlooked that the committee
in question was a committee of deans and one, therefore of which he was a member.
That fact was generally appreciated; but Professor Frumhartz spoke clearly for the
majority when he expressed himself as unconvinced of the infallibility of Deans, either singly or in concert.[4]

This record of the exchange owes a great deal to James Wernham, a philosophy professor who, as clerk of the Senate, wrote the minutes. Wernham
could exercise his sardonic wit because those who read the minutes would
know that John Ruptash could be brash and heavy handed and that Muni
Frumhartz, a sociology professor, enjoyed scoring debating points. Later in

the decade, when the faculty was larger and the minutes were more widely circulated, such an irreverent approach would be out of the question.

The change can be explained in part by the diminishing academic and social contact between the disciplines that had marked the faculty in the First Avenue days. The increased size of the faculty made it easier to form friendships within the larger departments, and it took more effort to know colleagues who worked in other buildings. Academic factors also played a role. Academic research was becoming more specialized and intellectually more isolating. At First Avenue, most of the faculty would have known that John Porter was working on a study of class and power in Canadian society and would have been interested in his progress. By 1964 however, when *The Vertical Mosaic* was published, many of his colleagues in other departments probably knew nothing about it and might be too occupied with their own academic interests to read it. Similarly, only a few in the arts and social sciences would know of Margaret McCully's innovative work on plant structures. For many professors, their work was so specialized that their scholarly exchanges about their research would be with specialists at other universities and not with their colleagues at Carleton.

There were few complaints about the professors' changing status. Colleagues might occasionally deplore the loss of intimacy and talk nostalgically of the good old days, but more often there seems to have been enthusiasm and optimism about the future. Robert McDougall, the first director of the Institute of Canadian Studies, remembers the 1960s as a time when "new buildings sprung up on Carleton's Rideau River campus and departments were staffed on a lavish scale. The atmosphere was feisty. Does somebody have an idea for a new course? Try it."[5] For those absorbed in research, the respect for scholarly activity was some compensation for the lack of interest in what they actually did. Whatever frustrations there were seem to have been transitory or isolated; the records offer no evidence of any grievances for which the administration was blamed or any dissatisfaction with the structure of university government.

Donald Rowat, a professor of political science, had written some articles on university government in the 1950s after the faculty had been affronted at not being consulted on the selection of Carleton's president,[6] but under Dunton neither Rowat nor his colleagues saw any urgent need for change. As president, Dunton presided over Senate meetings with a loose rein; the meetings might be long and some of the discussion barely relevant, but few members were ever ruled out of order. Dunton did appoint the deans, which now included the dean of science and the dean of engineering, but none of the appointments had been controversial, and on one occasion he had even asked the members of faculty for their written preferences.[7] At the departmental level the hand of the president also weighed lightly. At most

Ontario universities the president appointed heads of departments with un-limited tenure; at Carleton, probably because the departmental structure was so recent, the practice was for Dunton to appoint chairs for three-year terms. The crucial figure in all of this was Dunton himself. There was no confrontation between the faculty and the administration largely because of Dunton's respect for faculty opinions on academic matters.

Outside Carleton, however, there were pressures for change in the structure of university governments. Much of the initiative came from the Canadian Association of University Teachers, which was arguing as early as 1960 that professors must somehow exercise ultimate control over all academic decisions. The association had suggested, among other things, that elected faculty members should form a majority on university senates and that these senates should have wider powers. The association also felt that faculty should play some part in the selection of presidents, deans, and departmental chairs, all of whom should have limited terms of office. At the time, it was conceded that these reforms would not come quickly or easily.[8] But the dramatic rise in university enrolment altered the situation sooner than expected. The shortage of qualified university teachers meant that universities were more responsive to faculty pressures. In 1962 the Canadian university presidents, through their National Conference of Canadian Universities and Colleges, agreed to a joint study of university government with the professors' association. Two years later the Duff-Berdahl Report set the terms for the debate within individual universities.

The Duff-Berdahl Commission did not propose a radical restructuring of university governments, but it did see a need to increase the influence of the faculty. The professors, it concluded, should control university senates, where academic decisions were made. The nub of the problem, however, was the link between the Senate and the Board of Governors, where financial decisions were made. The president was the traditional link, but any confrontation between the two bodies left the president in an intolerable position. One of the commission's recommendations was to have senate representatives on the Board of Governors and board representatives on the Senate; better lines of communication between the faculty and the administration would diminish the polarization and give the faculty more influence in university planning. The commission also proposed that the faculty should share in the selection of presidents, deans, and chairs.

The Duff-Berdahl Commission almost overlooked a more controversial issue. In 1964, when the commission was appointed, attention was focused on the complaints of the faculty. Neither professors nor administrators saw much place for students in university government. But by 1966, when the commission reported, the world had changed. Student activists had initiated demonstrations at a number of leading American universities, beginning with Berkeley. The report therefore included a last-minute reference to student concerns and recommended consultation with students on curriculum and teaching. But it saw no useful role for students on boards of governors or senates; students would be better advised to concentrate on their studies.

The Carleton professors still had no grievances. In 1962, for example, the faculty association's committee on promotions concluded its annual report by recording its "satisfaction at the present methods employed by the President in recommending promotions." The committee members especially commended "the President's willingness to consult with members of the Carleton faculty on the subject and to seek the advice of outside referees."[9] Two years later, when the Duff-Berdahl Commission was appointed, the president of Carleton University Academic Staff Association (CUASA) told the *Carleton* that the faculty had no complaints about the governing structures at Carleton.[10] CUASA's brief to the commission was in the same vein; it showed more concern with improving relations with the provincial government than with changes in the way Carleton was governed. The possible role of students in university government was completely ignored.[11]

President Dunton was more alert to the need for change. Even before the commission had reported, he had arranged for the appointment of a Joint Committee on University Governance, with four representatives from the board, four from the faculty, and three from the administration, to prepare recommendations for Carleton as soon as the commission's report appeared. Again, the students were overlooked. This time the Student Council protested and, after some hesitation, three students were added to the committee.[12]

By 1966 change was in the air. The faculty at Carleton may have had no specific grievances, but like professors elsewhere they had become more aware of their importance to the university. If the governing structures were to be changed, they wanted their new status to be recognized. The expanded joint committee had no objections to an increased role for the faculty. From the beginning, there was a consensus that the Senate should be controlled by the academic community; the discussion focused on how faculty members should be elected to the Senate and how to ensure that they would outnumber the various deans, governors, and students who would also be members. It was also agreed that the faculty should be represented at other levels of government, although at Carleton there was no radical talk of "faculty power" or of parity for the professors on the Board of Governors. The joint committee recommended that three senators should be elected to the Board of Governors and three governors to the Senate in order to improve communications. The Senate was also to be represented on presidential search committees, and deans and chairs were to be appointed for limited terms after "the fullest consultation" with the faculty members directly concerned, although it did not seem necessary to spell out the procedures for this consultation. At Carleton the faculty were confident that their wishes would carry weight.

The place of the students in university government was more controversial, but as long as there was no serious talk of "student power" or of student parity with the professors, the faculty had no firm position on student representation. A survey by the CUASA in 1967 suggested that three years of public discussion had "heightened the consciousness" of the faculty (to use an expression much in vogue in the 1960s); it showed that the faculty now believed that they should control the Senate, have elected representatives on the Board of Governors, and participate in the election of chairs, deans and, presidents. To this extent, the report of the joint committee gave the faculty what they wanted. They were less concerned about student representation. Many expressed no opinion on whether students should be on the Senate or the board, and almost half of those who did have an opinion were opposed.[13]

The heightened awareness of their own importance did not mean that the faculty had become militant. When the New University Government (soon known as NUG) was introduced, the first senators elected to the board were Muni Frumhartz from sociology and Ernst Oppenheimer from the German department. Both Frumhartz and Oppenheimer had been active members of CUASA and could be relied on to be articulate expositors of faculty concerns, but neither could be described as radical. Their election was designed more to educate than defy the board. In subsequent years the Senate showed even less interest in challenging the administration; it regularly elected deans or other administrators as its representatives. It is always difficult to interpret the meaning of elections, but this pattern does suggest that the professors were confident that members of the board would listen to academic experts. It also suggests that the faculty still saw the deans as their colleagues. At Carleton, those professors who saw a sharp division between the faculty and the administration were still a small minority.

For the professors, NUG was a recognition of their central role in the university. The discussions, from their perspective, had confirmed their right to be consulted – and, presumably, heeded – on all administrative questions. NUG was a formal recognition that they were something more than salaried employees, but the implications of this special status, and how much influence the professors could or would exercise, was still far from clear.

II

While NUG brought Carleton's professors some welcome recognition of their importance within the university, it had little impact on their daily routine. The met their classes, did their research, and sat on departmental committees as before. The enhanced importance of research had a much greater influence on their role as professors. The curriculum changes during the decade offer a striking example. The central question, as always, was what should be taught. In the 1960s the students' answer was inevitably coloured by the wider revolt against authority, the rejection of patterns and traditions that were seen as outmoded, and the affirmation of individual choice – "doing your own thing" – as the basis for a new moral order. Yet when the dust cleared, the revised curriculum in the arts and social sciences was in some ways even more restrictive and confining than before. Specialized training in a discipline won out over the right of students to choose their own courses. Only the professors were pleased with the results.

The common first year that had been introduced in the Faculty of Arts to give more structure and academic respectability to the degree programs had never been completely satisfactory, because there was no agreement on what should be included. If it was to be a broad introduction to various approaches to knowledge, it would require specially designed courses to introduce students to the fundamental principles of the sciences, the social sciences, and the humanities. On the other hand, each discipline wanted its own introductory course as a prerequisite for its second- and third-year courses. The pressure from the individual disciplines for greater specialization in the first year had led to an expansion of the permitted options, with the result that the "common first year" had become less and less common. Both generalists and specialists found it easy to criticize a first year that seemed to have no apparent rationale, and in 1968 the Senate finally appointed the Commission on Undergraduate Teaching and Learning to recommend reforms.

The commission, chaired by Muni Frumhartz, took its responsibilities seriously. The faculty and student members spent the summer drafting working papers on the role of the university, the theory of general education, and the experience of other universities with experimental programs. Its work was speeded up when David Wolfe – a student activist who, under NUG, had been elected to the board of the Faculty of Arts and then to the Senate – moved in the Senate for the abolition of the common first year. His argument was that students should be treated as adults and allowed to plan their own course of studies based on their own individual interests. It was an argument that students found popular and that professors and administrators in the 1960s were reluctant to challenge. The Senate evaded the issue by asking the commission for its advice.

Jean Loates, Student Awards

Eileen Cox, Residence

Goldie Wilkinson, Engineering

Phyllis Putt, Philosophy

Dolores Neilson, Science

Evelyn Aldridge, Economics

Ruth Deakin, Personnel

These employees of Carleton have been described as invisible because they are so often taken for granted. They came to Carleton when few careers were open to them. The university was slow to appreciate their talents, but as the institution grew and senior administrators came and went, these women provided the continuity and also took on wider responsibilities. Carleton would have been a less personal and less efficient place without them (*Raven* and photos from individuals).

The commission had already decided that the common first year should go. The introductory courses, it had decided, did no more than introduce students to the techniques and skills of the established disciplines. The courses were described as unrelated to each other or to the world in which the students lived; their effect was to blunt the students' enthusiasm for understanding and to impose inappropriate attitudes for the rest of their college life. However, the commission did not believe that interdisciplinary courses would be the answer – it considered such courses more suitable for students in their senior years. Although the commission was not sure what was needed, it was convinced that a free choice in the first year would be better than the existing system. Self-interest would at least reflect the priorities of the young and their concern for "relevance." In a preliminary report, the commission recommended the abolition of the common first year. The Senate agreed, and with almost no debate it adopted an unstructured first year for the fall of 1969.[14]

How are we to account for the Senate's sweeping rejection of the university's responsibility to decide on an appropriate first-year program? Had faint-hearted academics been frightened by a possible confrontation with militant students? Or were they so unsure of what should be done that they could not agree on any alternative?[15] Some may have been pusillanimous, but the student body at Carleton was surely not militant enough to intimidate the majority of the faculty. Nor does it seem fair to write off all the professors as irresponsible. It seems more likely that the majority of the Senate and of the Carleton faculty in general were prepared to accept an unstructured first year because their academic priorities would not be undermined. For professors who focused on their own disciplines, the disappearance of the common first-year did not pose a problem. They would still control the contents of the first year course in their discipline, as well as the departmental requirements for the majors and honours degrees in their disciplines. The faculty had given up the pretence of prescribing a general education at the first-year level, but they had kept control of what seemed important to them. The students had won the right to choose their electives but not the right to plan their program in their field of specialization.

The ideal of a degree that was to be a basic introduction to the major fields of human thought was lost by default. The Commission on Undergraduate Teaching and Learning never submitted a final report. Frumhartz accepted the blame,[16] but it is unlikely that it would have been possible to get a consensus on what should be included in a university degree program. The common first year had assumed that there was a common cultural heritage to transmit to the leaders of the next generation, but by the end of the 1960s individualism and multiculturalism had undermined this assumption. Some universities experimented with liberal arts programs, but few of the experiments survived for long. At Carleton as elsewhere the students now had a relatively free choice of electives, but within their field of specialization the respective departments would largely determine what courses they would take and how much specialization there would be within those courses. Like other universities, Carleton no longer tried to provide its graduates with a common core of general knowledge but did ensure a minimum level of expertise in at least one discipline.

The priority given by many professors to specialization is reflected in the interest in graduate studies. At the beginning of the decade it would have been misleading to talk of graduate programs, apart from the MAs offered in public administration and Canadian studies. Although some departments did admit MA students, their courses of studies were arranged individually, and the time given by professors to graduate training was in addition to their normal course loads. As the director of graduate studies put it in 1961, "The general plan was to allow departments which were already suitably staffed to accept graduate students up to the number which could be given proper direction without reducing the effectiveness of the undergraduate instruction." [17] This approach had the advantage of flexibility. For example, Ivan Fellegi, the chief statistician for Canada, had arrived in Ottawa as a Hungarian refugee with university credentials in mathematics that could not easily be verified. Professor Macphail, who was director of graduate studies and chairman of the Mathematics Department, tested his knowledge and on that basis admitted him to graduate work. Fellegi graduated in 1961 as Carleton's first PHD. He later commented:

Carleton showed incredible flexibility and lack of bureaucracy toward the newly-arrived refugee that I was in 1957. I did not have a formal degree from my home country, but Carleton decided to put more emphasis on knowledge than on papers; it gave me a comprehensive oral examination to ascertain that I did, indeed have the knowledge equivalent to a B.Sc. On that basis it admitted me ... with its own reputation on the line. This literally opened up my subsequent career for me. [18]

Such ad hoc measures needed to be replaced by planned programs as enrolment grew. Carleton was committed to expanding graduate studies, and the province's graduate fellowships financed graduate students. Soon graduate instruction became too demanding for professors to add it to their regular course loads. Formula financing, introduced in 1967, also meant that graduate programs would have to be carefully planned and staffed, because they had to be successfully appraised before students enrolled in them could qualify for basic income units. By the end of the decade the Faculty of Graduate Studies, under John Ruptash. was responsible for more than seven hundred graduate students. For many professors, training graduate students seemed more stimulating and professionally rewarding than teaching undergraduate classes.

In 1961 Ivan Fellegi received the first PH D awarded by Carleton University.
Conferring the degree is Chancellor C.J. Mackenzie, and hooding the
graduand is Professor John Morton, of Chemistry (Capital Press Service).

A different debate, this time on the cultural role of the university, erupted
at the end of the decade. At issue was the hiring of American professors,
though there was also probably a subliminal hostility to specialized research. At the beginning of the decade Canadian graduate schools were not
graduating enough doctoral students to meet the demand for professors.
English Canadian universities looked to Great Britain and even more to the
United States for most of their needs; in some of the less traditional disciplines, such as sociology, almost the only qualified candidates were graduates of American universities. Controversy developed later in the decade
when Canadians were graduating in larger numbers from Canadian graduate schools and it was alleged that some departments, whose senior professors were American, gave preferential treatment to American candidates.
The newly founded universities were especially vulnerable to these allegations, because in many of their departments the majority of the professors
were American citizens. Carleton was less vulnerable, because even in the
social sciences many of its senior professors were Canadians.

However, Carleton was soon at the forefront of the debate, because
Robin Mathews was a member of the English Department. Mathews was a

relentless controversialist who defended his causes with moral fervour and attacked with virulence anybody who did not agree with him. He went beyond the argument that the best candidates were not always hired and argued that foreign professors, whatever their qualifications, were a threat to the cultural role of the university. It was not merely that these professors could not transmit Canadian culture to Canadian students; their more serious fault, especially those from the United States, was that they considered Canadian matters to be parochial and they "suppress the Canadian past and ... prevent the development of a uniquely excellent Canadian future." Mathew's colleague James Steele, another member of the English Department, added a further warning of the American threat to Canadian identity by linking American culture to American imperialism in Vietnam.[19]

Mathews and Steele got little support from their colleagues at Carleton. The practical measures the two men proposed were relatively modest; they argued that Canadians should have a two-thirds majority in every university department, and any department that did not meet this requirement should actively look for Canadian candidates before it considered a non-Canadian. Their intemperate denunciation of Americans, however, was interpreted as a threat to high academic standards, because it seemed to mean denying appointments to American candidates even if they had the best academic qualifications. At a special meeting of the Carleton University Academic Staff Association, the motions submitted by Mathews and Steele were resoundingly rejected.[20]

Mathews was not one to admit defeat, and he continued to fulminate against the "condescending, arrogant, graceless immigrants to whom we unfairly extend the kindness which they do not, for a moment, deserve."[21] He weakened his case by his exaggerations; it was easy for his critics to point to the positive intellectual contributions of many American and American-trained scholars. But there was a problem. Young American sociologists were likely to know more about race relations in the United States than about French-English relations in Canada, and American-trained English professors were not likely to be familiar with Canadian authors. Did universities have an obligation to educate Canadian students about their own society and foster a distinctive Canadian identity? It was a difficult question in a country that was not always sure that it had a distinctive identity. It was also a complex problem, because some American-born professors were better informed about Canadian culture than many native scholars. The faculty at Carleton found it easier to respond to Mathews by ignoring these concerns and relying on the shibboleth of academic freedom.[22]

The decade also saw intriguing changes at the Spring Conferences. The conferences had initially been occasions for the administration to inform the faculty of the state of the university and even to get some feedback. When academics meet, however, academic lectures are soon part of the agenda. As Carleton grew larger, it was logical to use Spring Conference to introduce colleagues from other disciplines. What better way than to have professors lecture about their latest research? The shift from administrative concerns to research activities was yet another example of the increased prestige of research. Another change is less easy to explain. In the 1960s the Spring Conferences often seemed little more than an excuse for many professors to drink to excess. It was not unusual for a few to get drunk in the Faculty Club on Fridays, but the Spring Conferences became so notorious for drunkenness that some of the more sober professors stopped going. The different pattern may have had more to do with personalities than with changing values, but in an earlier era professors would have been less inclined to get drunk on an occasion when the president was present.

Another feature of the 1960s was that the status of women within the faculty changed so little. The evidence for continuing discrimination is circumstantial but convincing. The professional schools remained male strongholds; there were no tenured female professors in engineering, and even in the School of Social Work, where the majority of students were female, all of the tenured professors were men. Some women were hired to teach in departments in the humanities and social sciences, but this is more likely explained by the shortage of male candidates than by an erosion of male chauvinism. Also, it is almost certain that the women professors who were appointed were paid less and promoted more slowly than male colleagues with equivalent qualifications. Direct evidence is lacking because nobody, male or female, protested publicly and no committee was set up to study the question. It is revealing that at Carleton no woman was appointed a dean in the 1960s. Women might be congenial and even respected colleagues, but neither men nor women seemed to think that women could be academic leaders.

III

The goodwill between the faculty and administration even extended to salary decisions. Higher enrolments meant a shortage of qualified professors, with the result that universities across North America were competing for their services. Each year President Dunton had to decide what salary level would be needed to make Carleton competitive. Salaries at Carleton rose sharply during the decade, though they never managed to keep up with the salaries at Toronto. Professors were not consulted individually about their annual salaries. After the Board of Governors had approved the proposed budget, Dunton still had to decide how the money allocated to salaries would be distributed. He consulted with the deans, who in turn might consult with the chairs, but it was he who made the final decisions. There was almost no negotiation. Professors might negotiate their salaries when they were first appointed, and occasionally some told their chair of an offer from another university and threatened to leave if it was not matched. But in most cases, the professors waited passively for the confidential letter from Dunton each spring which informed them of their salary for the next year.

The Carleton University Academic Staff Association (CUASA) became more vocal about salaries as the decade advanced. Formula financing meant that CUASA was more aware of university revenues, and contact with other faculty associations in the province provided information about salary scales elsewhere. By the end of the decade, CUASA's Salary Committee was documenting annual requests to the president, making comparisons with academic salaries elsewhere and also with teachers' salaries and other professional incomes, and asking for specific percentages for increases, catch-up pay, and merit pay. But there was no confrontation. CUASA insisted that it was not negotiating. As the chairman of the Salary Committee explained to Dunton in 1969, the faculty saw him as their spokesman on the Board of Governors and at Queen's Park; their submission was only intended to provide him with ammunition, because "we expect you to fight for us."[23] The same sentiments were expressed the next year when, after a meeting with administration officials, the chairman of the Salary Committee told Dunton, "The two different sides in these discussions seem to me to have met as colleagues, not opponents."[24]

The distinction between discussions and negotiations was not as clear as the chairman suggested. In 1971 Dunton increased the amount he had budgeted for salaries after hearing CUASA's arguments.[25] The next year, Dunton's last year as president, procedures came even closer to formal negotiations. The administration met with the Salary Committee on at least two occasions, though Dunton insisted that the possible salary increases he mentioned were not to be interpreted as offers or counteroffers.[26] This time, however, the faculty were not satisfied with the 8 per cent salary increase which the Board of Governors approved, and the expressed their disappointment in a secret ballot administered by CUASA. Dunton, with the board's consent, then raised the amount by an additional 0.5 per cent.[27] The staff association might deny it was negotiating, but it was clearly becoming more militant.

The shifting outlook of the professors at Carleton over the 1960s was shown even more clearly by discussions late in the decade over the procedures governing tenure and dismissal. At the beginning of the decade, initial appointments were usually probationary for a period of up to five years, though this period might be reduced for professors with previous teaching experience. At the end of the probationary period, the professor could expect to be reappointed with "tenure." Tenure was considered a privilege that was necessary to ensure academic freedom; a tenured professor might be dismissed for incompetence but was not to be dismissed for discussing unpopular or controversial opinions in the classroom. At Carleton, however, the procedures for granting tenure were not always uniform, nor was it clear what protection tenure provided against arbitrary dismissal. In 1960 CUASA asked to have the existing procedures codified.

The request could not be interpreted as a challenge to the authority of the president or of the Senate. CUASA acknowledged that the president had the primary responsibility for initiating a dismissal and it relied on the Senate to protect the academic rights of any threatened professor. But even if the Senate objected to the dismissal, CUASA believed that the president could still recommend it to the Board of Governors. CUASA's aim was to clarify the procedures; it proposed only a minor role for itself. It offered to meet informally with the president and the threatened professor in a mediating role before any formal procedures were initiated, in keeping with "the Association's continued faith in the manifest advantages of informal consultation."[28] However, the Board of Governors apparently still thought of the professors as employees and was not prepared to recognize even this modest role for CUASA.[29] Eventually the board did concede that some formal procedures for dismissal should be established, but discussion was postponed until the Duff-Berdahl Commission presented its report on the broader question of university government.[30]

For the next five years neither the faculty nor the administration took any steps to establish procedures for tenure or dismissal. During these years of expansion, job security was of little concern to professors because they were in such demand; tenure was almost automatic and dismissals were unheard of. In 1969, however, CUASA's president, T.J. Scanlon, a professor of journalism, raised the issue once again. Scanlon was concerned about the implications of a crisis at Sir George Williams University in Montreal, where some students had accused a professor of racial discrimination. The administration there had no established procedures either, and had appointed an ad hoc committee to investigate the charges. When the committee exonerated the professor, the students involved questioned the validity of a committee that had no official status and, according to them, was racially biased. They eventually occupied the computer centre, and when the administration called in the police the students destroyed many of the university records before being arrested.

Scanlon argued that authorized procedures might have averted the crisis and in February he asked the president to appoint a Senate committee to draft a document covering tenure and dismissals, with representation from CUASA on the committee if that seemed desirable. Dunton was slow to reply to the letter, apparently preferring to let sleeping dogs lie, but Scanlon was tenacious. He was a member of the Senate and there, in April, he introduced a motion requiring the president to appoint a committee with representatives from the Senate, the Board of Governors, and CUASA to propose appropriate procedures.[31] Dunton was still in no hurry. The first members of the committee were not appointed until October, and no representative from the board was named until January 1970.[32]

The Committee on Tenure and Dismissal decided at an early stage to deal only with procedures and so avoid the more controversial question of the criteria for granting tenure or justifying dismissal. The first version of the report, however, already suggests that the faculty were less complacent about job security than they had been earlier in the decade. The procedures proposed for tenure were based on guidelines that had been prepared by the Canadian Association of University Teachers. The initial decision on tenure was to be made by a representative departmental committee and was to be reviewed at the faculty level by a committee of departmental representatives. The faculty committee would then send its recommendation to the president, who would submit it to the Board of Governors. If tenure was denied, the unfortunate professor would still be able to appeal the decision to a committee of professors appointed by the Senate.

The report of the Carleton committee paid less attention to dismissal procedures for tenured faculty because, as the committee noted, no tenured professor at Carleton had ever been dismissed. The president would still be responsible for initiating dismissal procedures, but as a safeguard against an arbitrary dismissal, the reasons for dismissal were to be given in writing and the threatened professor was to have the right to appeal to a review board chaired by an academic from outside the university.[33]

There was still no sense of urgency. The committee agreed on its recommendations in the spring of 1970, but there was a delay in drafting the report, and it was not submitted to the president until January 1971. Dunton had no serious objections; his only suggestion was that the decision to dismiss a tenured professor should come from a Senate committee rather than from the president. The committee, in its turn, was reluctant to shift the responsibility to the Senate and compromised by leaving it to the president to make "whatever investigation he may consider necessary."[34] Finally, in 1971, the revised report was submitted to the Senate for its consideration.

At this stage, although the document did not seem controversial, there were already signs of trouble. Some Senate members were uneasy and the Senate spent the first day of debate "discussing how to proceed to discuss" the report.[35] Further discussion was postponed until the faculty members had been surveyed on their reactions to the document. These were generally favourable; when there were objections, it was usually because the report had deviated in some small way from the CAUT guidelines. Thus, some wanted the Committee on Tenure at the faculty level to be elected rather than being appointed by the dean, and others wanted the chair of the Dismissal Review Board to be appointed jointly by the president and the staff association. These were minor points, however. Even CUASA's brief expressed general approval of the report and assumed that any differences could be easily resolved.[36]

The staff association was mistaken. The differences would not be easily resolved because circumstances were changing. The report had proposed procedures for the hypothetical dismissal of incompetent professors, but by 1971 dismissals seemed less hypothetical and might even include competent professors. The provincial government was now talking of financial constraint, and it seemed possible that Carleton might have to reduce its professorial establishment to balance its budget. This context explains why the Senate had five more long and heated debates on the report. Much of the debate was academic, in the worst sense of the word, niggling about the meaning of a word or the proper place for a comma. It is clear that the real fear was about redundancy – the euphemism used to describe the plight of professors associated with programs which a university might decide to close down for financial reasons. Some members of the Senate, and not only those with administrative responsibility, were concerned about the financial stability of the institution, while others were more concerned about job security. These concerns only complicated the discussion of a document which had been drafted to establish procedures for dismissal based on incompetence.[37]

Agreement was finally reached by an Alice-in-Wonderland amendment, which asserted that "where an appointment is terminated because the university has decided that the post in question has become redundant, the faculty member so affected shall not be considered to have been dismissed." Once it was agreed that a dismissal for redundancy was not really a dismissal the Senate was ready to adopt the report and send it on to the Board of Governors. An ominous footnote was added, however, which pointed out that "at the time of the adoption of this document there exists no university definition of redundancy or of procedures for dealing with it." The Senate then appointed a Committee on Redundancy.[38]

The Board of Governors acted with more dispatch. On the question of tenure, Dunton assured the members that similar procedures were already being followed at many Canadian universities, and that faculty members would not award tenure lightly. On the question of dismissal, the board raised only one minor objection; it would not commit itself to paying all the expenses of an appeal against dismissal. If this provision could be dropped, it was ready to approve the report.[39] Since it was now the end of June 1972, this was Dunton's last board meeting as president of Carleton.

Something had been accomplished. At least the procedures were now in place for the dismissal of incompetent tenured professors, if the administration ever decided that a professor was incompetent. But what of the threat to job security from financial stringency? The Board of Governors could not ignore the threat of future deficits because it was ultimately responsible for the financial stability of the university. The professors, through the Senate or CUASA, would surely insist on being involved in decisions about terminating programs for financial reasons if this meant that jobs would disappear. But the implications of financial stringency would be a problem for Dunton's successor.

CHAPTER NINE

Carleton Students in the 1960s

For Carleton students the move to the new campus brought many advantages. Certainly, construction had its inconveniences, especially when buildings had to be occupied before they were completed, but the new buildings were a great improvement over the old college and the renovated houses on First Avenue. The classrooms were bright and airy, the library was less noisy, and there was a feeling of spaciousness around the quadrangle and on the playing fields across the railway tracks. The new college would be a construction site for most of the decade, but nobody questioned the wisdom of moving to the new location.

Student life on the new campus, however, was affected by more than new buildings and a spacious site. The close-knit college atmosphere of First Avenue days could not be sustained in a college in which the full-time enrolment doubled every three years. Such explosive growth would make it difficult in the best of circumstances to adapt established traditions or to maintain any sense of continuity with the past. But these were not normal times. This was the decade of the 1960s in which young people, especially university students across Western Europe and North America, seemed to be rejecting the past and were intent on shaping a new and different future. Carleton may have been remote from the free-speech demonstrations at Berkeley and the sit-ins at Columbia, and even farther from the defiance of political regimes in Paris and Mexico City, but even at Carleton there was the sense that a new world was emerging, a world in which youth was expected to be in the vanguard of change.

This did not transform all university students into radicals. Claude Bissell was surely right when he suggested in 1965 that "the majority of students are not given to speculation of an unsettling nature."[1] But it did mean that students, at Carleton as elsewhere, were more inclined to believe that the world could and should be reformed and that students, because they were young and unfettered by the past, could make a positive contribution. At Carleton the combination of a new campus and a spiralling enrolment in an era of changing social values meant a time when students would debate the forms and aims of student government, participate in the restructuring of the governing institutions of the university, and comment on broader national and international issues.

I

The student leaders adapted slowly to the changing conditions of a new campus, a larger student body, and a new decade. Within a year the *Carleton* was looking back nostalgically to the First Avenue experience and complaining, "We are in danger of losing that personal contact between students and professors which has been Carleton's trademark in the past."[2] The implicit ideal was still a community of scholars in which the students looked to the academic staff for counsel and support.[3] Professors were even invited to broaden the students' horizons by submitting articles of general interest to the *Carleton*.[4] The shift in plans from a students' centre to a university centre can also be seen as an effort to regain the intimacy of a collegial community.

There was apparently no concern that this might limit student autonomy. The student leaders believed, with some reason, that they had more responsibility and more control over student affairs than students at other Canadian universities. The honour system, introduced in 1961, was an unusual example of student self-government. Norman Jamieson, the president of the Students' Council, initiated the experiment, though he clearly had the support of Norman Fenn, who was now the director of student affairs. The system was intended to make students directly responsible for disciplining their unruly colleagues. The underlying principle was that students were expected to report their own infractions of any university regulations and were to accept any penalty or punishment decided on by a judicial committee composed of students. If any student failed to admit his or her misdemeanour, student witnesses were expected "to advise the offender of his duty."[5] The honour system was adopted by a referendum, but not everybody was impressed. The *Carleton* ridiculed it as "idealistic claptrap."[6]

The library provided an early challenge to the system. Increased enrolment brought more demand for library books, and some students took advantage of the open stacks and lax supervision to hide books or take them out without permission. In 1962 the Students' Council, with President

Electronic surveillance eventually proved to be more reliable than student prefects at protecting the library against books being stolen (*Carleton*, 25 Oct. 1965)

Dunton's blessing, established escalating fines for library infractions.[7] Unfortunately, library books continued to disappear and witnesses, it there were any, had little success in reminding offenders of their responsibilities. After two years, Hilda Gifford, the librarian, decided that student prefects would inspect all brief cases at the library exit. The Students' Council was not completely ignored – the prefects were to be chosen from a list submitted to the librarian by the council – but it was clear that the administration had taken over the responsibility for policing the library.

Two other incidents in the next few years tested the honour system severely. Students showed a natural reluctance to confess their crimes, and innocent students were reluctant to accuse others of misbehaving, so the judicial committee was convened only on the rare occasions when unfavourable publicity of student behaviour left little choice. In 1961 and again in 1963 the combination of the Panda game and high-spirited students led to incidents that tested the idealism of the students and the honour system.

In 1961 an inquiry could not be avoided because a brawl after the Panda game involving some inebriated students was witnessed by President Dunton. Only two students admitted being involved, and the sympathetic witnesses put the blame on the University of Ottawa students. The judicial committee let one student off on a technicality and banned the other from attending any more football games that fall.[8] The second incident attracted more attention. On this occasion a group of Carleton students had burned a mock-up of the Quebec flag at centre field at halftime. What had seemed an amusing prank to the Carleton Booster Club was interpreted by the city newspapers as an insult to Quebec. Again, two students honourably identified themselves, but the judicial committee's appeal for others to come forward and for witnesses to identify participants elicited no response. The two students were let off with a warning, and the judicial committee justifiably drew the conclusion that the honour system had broken down.[9] At future Panda games the Students' Council turned to the more traditional off-duty policemen to maintain order. The judicial committee never met again.

Norman Fenn was still prepared to defend the system. In his report that year, as director of student affairs, he acknowledged that the flag burning had been "in extremely poor taste and detrimental to the good name of the university" and that there had been criticism of the handling of the case and of the verdict, but he would not concede that the system had failed. Students, he noted, had been forced "to examine their rules and procedures and to realize the responsibilities which accompanied freedom and authority. It was a learning experience." He admitted the difficulty of maintaining order in a rapidly growing institution but argued: "There is a risk that for expediency's sake aims and objectives of Carleton's way of life might be lost."[10] But Fenn was fighting a losing battle. The editor of the *Carleton* may have been too harsh when he called the honour system idealistic claptrap, but it certainly was too idealistic for a campus where most students knew only a few of their classmates and had little contact with students in other faculties.

The Students' Council in the early sixties showed little interest in Fenn's emphasis on learning self-discipline by conforming to regulations, but it still fell short of challenging the right of the established authorities to make the rules. It protested against the quality of the food in the canteen, the service in the library, and the unprotected railway crossing that led to the playing fields, but there were no suggestions that students should participate in any decisions to improve these services.[11] The Students' Council was aware that students at other universities were concerned about broader issues beyond the university perimeters, and in 1962 it went so far as to say that it was prepared "to support the universal principles of social justice," but it immediately qualified this by explaining that it saw no reason for students to express collective opinions on national or international disputes "which did not actually involve them."[12] The Students' Council was not likely to mobilize student activists with this attitude.

An incident in 1963, however, showed that times were changing, even at Carleton. For some time students had complained that traffic lights were needed at the Bronson Avenue entrance to the campus, and in 1963 Ben Greenhous, the "protest coordinator" for the Students' Council, decided to draw attention to the issue by staging a sit-down demonstration at the intersection. The reaction of the Ottawa chief of police was typically conservative. "No one," he announced, "is going to rule our city by mob violence."[13] Meanwhile, at Carleton, students and even professors were eagerly volunteering to participate. The confrontation was only averted when the City Council and Board of Governors both counselled a peaceful resolution to the problem. The city decided that traffic lights would be installed and that until the lights were operating policemen would be assigned to direct traffic at the intersection. Without a grievance the sit-in was reluctantly cancelled. But the more activist students may have learned from this incident that the threat of an illegal confrontation could be effective.

Whether it was this experience or the example provided by students at other universities, the Carleton students, beginning in 1965, elected a series of activists as president of the Students' Council. Hugh Armstrong, Jackie Larkin, and Bert Painter were distinguished from their predecessors by their conviction that students, privileged as they were by their youth and education, had a responsibility to challenge social privilege and established authority. But it would be misleading to describe them as radicals. They may occasionally have used the rhetoric of the class struggle or of student power, but they were social democrats for whom violence was never a serious option. They were radical only in the context of the socially conservative traditions of university students in Ontario.

Under their leadership the Students' Council found a number of occasions to protest public policies. A teach-in was organized to criticize American intervention in Vietnam; a demonstration was held on Parliament Hill in favour of greater accessibility to university education; and Carleton students were bused to Queen's Park to protest against the inadequacies of the provincial student loan program.[14] The Duff-Berdahl Report, however, gave the Students' Council a more immediate issue. What was to be the students' role in governing Carleton University? Over the next few years the students' presidents largely determined the answer to this question.

The Duff-Berdahl Report, as we have noted,[15] saw no place for students in university government. President Dunton also overlooked the students at first, presumably because they had so far shown no interest in participating. He appointed a Joint Committee on University Governance to study the report, with four members from the Board of Governors, four faculty members, and three from the administration, but no students. It was now 1966, however, and student leaders were no longer so deferential; the Students' Council protested. After some hesitation, Dunton agreed to add three students to the committee, including Hugh Armstrong, the president of the Students' Council.[16]

Armstrong initially treated the Joint Committee like a soapbox. He had a strong personal commitment to social reform, had spent a summer as a volunteer for Operation Crossroads in Africa, and was an active champion of students' rights. In addition to being president of the Students' Council at Carleton, he was concurrently president of the Ontario section of the Canadian Union of Students and would become the national president the next year. Student rhetoric had become more strident by the mid-sixties, and Armstrong startled some of the more conservative members of the Joint Committee by objecting to the idea of mere token representation for students on the Board of Governors, insisting that they "must be one of the power groups on the Board." The minutes of the meeting dryly noted that the proposal "met with little enthusiasm."[17]

But Armstrong was not as radical as he sounded, and the students on the committee eventually settled for much less. The thorny question of student membership on the board was set aside for the moment. A subcommittee of four, including a student, prepared recommendations over the summer on student representation on the Senate. It proposed that two students nominated by the Students' Council should serve on the Senate and that students should also be named to most Senate and presidential committees. With an emphasis on reciprocity, it also recommended that a Senate representative be named to the Students' Council and to most council committees.

When the Joint Committee reconvened early in 1967, it accepted these proposals almost without discussion. The issue of membership on the Board of Governors was more controversial. The board representatives on the committee argued that the students had better things to do than occupy their time with administrative matters. But the faculty members and administrators on the committee were more permissive, and eventually the committee recommended that the Students' Council should appoint two members to the Board of Governors. This could hardly be described as radical; two students was closer to tokenism than to student power. The recommendation, however, still had to have the approval of the board. A letter signed jointly by Hugh Armstrong and Donald Rowat, a professor in political science, defended the proposal but there was no radical rhetoric. Students should be represented on the board, they argued, because the board would benefit from their views. Their answer to the argument that students had better things to do was that it was up to the students to decide for themselves how they wished to spend their time.[18] Some members of the board were still not convinced but it was assumed that the majority would accept the Joint Committee's report. The question seemed to be settled.

The students – or, more specifically, Bert Painter, the incoming president of the Students' Council in 1967 – then disrupted the laboriously negotiated agreement by advocating a new and quite different arrangement. Painter had campaigned as a reformer in the spring election campaign but had had little to say about university government except to express the politically popular sentiment that it ought to be "designed with us, not for us."[19] In the fall of 1967, however, he dropped a bombshell by threatening to resign if the students did not show more interest in educational reform. As he explained it, the administration had responded to his proposals for change with the assertion that the vast majority of students were either satisfied with the present university structures or did not care. "Until there comes a manifestation of some concern," he told the students, "we remain powerless to refute the arguments by the university administration." If the students were not interested, Painter went on, he was not interested in representing them.[20] To test their commitment he called a public meeting. Some six hundred students from a full-time enrolment of some four thousand were concerned enough to show up. Painter was convinced that he could now speak with more authority.

Painter's criticisms reflected the new idealism of the era. Instead of conformity to established rules, his emphasis was on individual development. He objected to the authoritarian approach in the classroom, with professors deciding what to teach and how to teach, and then grading the students on the results. He talked of the possibility of doing away with course requirements, of having seminars instead of lectures, and having optional examinations and self-evaluation.[21] Painter's specific proposals may be questioned, but he was making an important point. What went on in the classroom affected the students much more directly that most discussions in meetings of the Senate or the Board of Governors, but they had no role in the planning of academic programs and no influence on the way in which classes were taught or students evaluated.

Painter began with the recommendation that student representatives should be elected to attend departmental meetings as voting members. This was an appropriate beginning because the individual departments determined course offerings and teaching procedures. Painter was not a radical, however; instead of wanting student parity, he believed the elected students should be in the minority. His timing was good. By 1967, authoritarian structures were not easy to defend, and the idea of consulting students no longer seemed revolutionary and might even be helpful. But there would still be controversial questions, at least from the perspective of the administration and the faculty. For instance, would the elected students take part in decisions affecting the hiring or promotion of their professors? Could they be trusted to deal with questions about student discipline that might require access to other students' files? On other matters, however, most professors would readily concede that students' opinions should be heard.

But Painter did not stop there. His more innovative – and more complicated – proposals dealt with student representation at higher administrative levels. The departments at Carleton were grouped into faculties, each with a faculty board made up of all the professors in the faculty. Every faculty board elected some of its members to the Senate. Painter proposed that the student representatives elected at the departmental level should automatically become members of their respective faculty boards. As members of a faculty board they, like the professors, would be eligible for election to the Senate. Those elected to the Senate would in turn be eligible for election by the Senate to the Board of Governors. There was no question of student power and, indeed, no guarantee that any students would be elected either to the Senate or to the Board of Governors. The scheme was based on an idealistic view of professors and students working together for the good of the university and on the assumption that the professors – who formed the majority both on the faculty boards and on the Senate – would recognize merit and vote for students who deserved their support.

Painter's proposals were adopted by the Students' Council, and this set the agenda for the university discussions that followed. The report of the Joint Committee had not yet been approved by the Senate or the Board of Governors. For most senators the scheme had the advantage that it had student support and virtually conceded ultimate control of academic decisions to the professors. There were misgivings, especially from professors in science and engineering, about students taking on time-consuming administrative responsibilities and neglecting their studies, but this was a permissive era.[22] The board made it even easier for the Senate by increasing the number of senators to be elected to the board from three to four, with the tacit understanding that one would be a student, which meant that the faculty would still have their three representatives. By the fall of 1968 the Senate and the Board of Governors had adopted Painter's proposals.

The students then forced another delay. By 1968 student groups across North America had become more militant and there was much talk of student parity. It was often no more than talk, but there had been some confrontations in Ontario universities, and the disruption at Sir George Williams University created uncertainty about where it was all leading.[23] At Carleton a group of self-professed radicals, calling themselves Students for a Democratic University, protested that the Students' Council had never consulted the students, and they managed to collect seven hundred student signatures on a petition to force a student referendum on the terms of the New University Government (NUG). Student interest was high, with three thousand students voting in the referendum. The vote showed a majority in favour of increasing the student representation at the departmental level, but there was no demand for student parity. A majority also favoured the exclusion of these elected students from any discussion of the appointment or promotion of their professors and from any access to students' files. On the main question, the majority voted to accept NUG without any changes, while leaving open the possibility of amending it later. [24]

NUG attracted a good deal of attention from other university administrations that were facing the same problems of student representation on departmental and university committees. But from the students' point of view, NUG did not dramatically change their role in university government. Whereas faculty control of the Senate and faculty representation on the Board of Governors had been a recognition of the increasing status of the professoriate, the election of students to the departmental committees was not a recognition of student power. The student interest in representation soon faded; by the second year of NUG, more than half of the student places were filled by acclamation. But by this time, many departmental chairs saw the advantage of having designated students whom they could inform and consult, and it became a common practice for chairs to take the initiative to ensure that students were nominated for vacant positions.

The complicated system of student representation at the level of the Senate and the Board of Governors was even less effective. In the first year, the professors were careful to give some recognition to student candidates. Of the thirty-six senators elected by the faculty boards, four were students and one of the four, Robin Findlay, was subsequently elected by the Senate to the board. But what of the utopian view that these students, rather than being spokespersons for the student body, would act in the broader interests of the university? David Wolfe, a self-styled radical who had been elected to the Senate, saw this as co-option; if the students did not fight the system, they would become part of it. On one occasion he deliberately released confidential information which he had received as a senator, on the grounds that he was responsible only to the students. If the faculty found this unacceptable, he explained, it merely showed that "the two-faced liberal façade of the university has gone full turn on the wheel." [25] The mixed metaphor may reflect the frustration of radical students who were finding it more and more difficult to attract attention. None of the students seemed to care. But even the elected students who were committed to the underlying principle of NUG found themselves in a difficult situation. Robin Findlay, for example, was obliged at times to try to represent the interests of the student body because both the students and the members of the board wanted him to play this role.

The system eventually broke down because the professors, who formed the majority on the faculty boards and the Senate, could not be relied on to elect students. A student presence on the Senate was assured in any case because the presidents of the Carleton and St Patrick students' councils were *ex officio* members of the Senate. Robin Findlay, however, was the first and last student elected to the Board of Governors by the Senate; the concern of the professors to make the system of student representation work does not seem to have survived the first election. However, the Board of Governors was now converted to the idea of a student member. As an "interim solution" two students were elected directly by the student body, and this eventually became the established pattern.[26] The principle that there would be no distinction between faculty and students at the level of the Senate and the board was quietly forgotten. At Carleton, what had begun as a unique experiment had given way to a form of representation in university government that resembled the pattern at other Ontario universities.

There would be no return to the brief era in the 1960s when student leaders were seen as reformers who had the support of the student body and were listened to by the professors and the administration. Possibly this was because the student body had grown too large and diverse to pay much attention to the Students' Council. It was also true that the installation of the New University Government meant that if any student leaders wanted to play an academic role at Carleton, it would be through NUG and not through the Students' Council. It was also relevant that the council had become more involved in business activities connected with the University Centre. Less tangible but nonetheless significant was that for Carleton – and for the rest of the world – the high expectations of the 1960s had faded.

II

Student residences also detracted from the role of the Students' Council because they created a distinctive residential life on the campus, with its own set of student leaders. Lanark and Renfrew, the first residences, were opened in the fall of 1962, followed by Grenville and Russell two years later, with Glengarry admitting students in 1969. From the administration's perspective, residences were a necessary part of expansion, because almost 40 per cent of Carleton students were now from out of town, mainly from the Ottawa Valley, and because student housing in Ottawa was at a premium. The residences at Carleton, however, were also associated from the beginning with a philosophy of education that saw them as an opportunity, in Norman Fenn's words, "to foster a sense of individual responsibility in the students and collective responsibility where appropriate."[27] But student autonomy had its limits. The university could not ignore its responsibility for the health and safety of the students, and it could not condone behaviour that would provoke unfavourable publicity for the university. What is remarkable is how rarely university authorities had to intervene directly. Norman Fenn, Eileen Cox, the director of residences, and Professor Rusty Wendt, who succeeded Fenn as dean of students in 1965, supervised with a loose rein.

The emphasis on student autonomy began with the architectural design. Most of the accommodation in Lanark and Renfrew was in double rooms, with four students sharing a bathroom. This had a distinct advantage over communal washrooms on each floor, in that it made the rooms easier to rent to tourists during the summer – an important consideration when the residences were expected to be self-supporting – though the planners emphasized the educational benefits of this form of group living. Two lounges on each floor, across the hall from the rooms, were also intended to enhance the social and educational role of the residences – there was an idealistic image of students informally discussing Aristotle or the meaning of life far into the night. This ideal of student life did not change with the later residences, but financial constraints led to floor plans that used the space more economically.

The supervisory arrangements within the residences followed the traditional college pattern. From the beginning there was a junior professor (or a member of the support staff) as a senior resident in each residence, with a senior student on each floor with the title of residence fellow. The residents and residence fellows had no clearly established disciplinary authority, though their presence was usually enough to ensure a minimum of order and decorum. Most of their time was spent providing advice and emotional support to the minority of students who found it difficult to adapt to leaving home for the first time. A Residence Council, with elected representatives from each floor of each residence, was expected to establish and enforce the rules. Munro Beattie, who had taught at Carleton College during the war and then became a full-time professor of English, become the residence provost in 1965. In this capacity he could veto any Residence Council decision. There was no confrontation, however, because Munro Beattie and his wife Mae were sympathetic and tactful and were respected by the students.

The Beatties, along with the residents and fellows, believed that the residences should supplement academic life by offering cultural and intellectual experiences. They planned concerts, readings, lecture series, and discussion groups. The Residence Council took a more direct responsibility for the students' social activities, but even here the provost and fellows were expected to participate and to act as chaperones at the residence dances.

When the first residences opened there were no traditions and no regulations governing residential behaviour. For the students in a permissive era, there was a natural reluctance to impose restrictions; on the other hand, some students would want to study. When it was suggested that Renfrew, the women's residence, should establish a curfew, the women responded by proposing two o'clock in the morning as a deadline. It was eventually agreed that they would have to sign out after eleven o'clock. [28] Theirs would still be a sheltered life, however, at least in the residence; they were not allowed men or liquor in their rooms. The rules for the men were more liberal than those for the women – and, indeed, those of other universities at the time. They could have women in their rooms on weekends until one o'clock in the morning, and they could have liquor in their rooms, though no drinking was permitted in the lounges. [29] Whether this degree of freedom was a useful educational experience is not clear. From the university's point of view, the concessions to student autonomy seemed justified, and they did not lead to any crises or to any public embarrassments.

One change in the residential pattern in 1969 did raise many eyebrows. Early in that year, a student Commission on the Philosophy and Structure of Residence Life argued that segregation was artificial and that both men and women would benefit socially by learning to live together. The university authorities raised no objections, and in the fall of 1969, without any public debate, Renfrew House admitted both men and women. It was a daring innovation – the idea had been discussed at other universities, but this was reputedly the first co-educational residence in North America. Even so, it attracted little publicity. The students seem to have adapted without much difficulty, showing a combination of pride in being part of a daring experiment and surprise that their lives were not more radically transformed. [30] From the administration's perspective, the experiment was successful; the students in mixed residences posed fewer disciplinary problems than in the other residences. Within a few years the practice was extended to other residences. The only reason why it did not become universal was that some of the women still preferred a segregated environment.

The community life in the residences segregated those students to some extent from other students at Carleton. Each residence – indeed, each residence floor – organized social activities and encouraged the development of "floor spirit." To a columnist on the *Carleton*, this was the breakdown of the Carleton spirit. He was shocked when the "chaps" on the fourth floor of Lanark House announced a dance that excluded non-resident students. Fraternities would surely be the next step! [31] Regrettable or not, the students in residence did become a distinct group within the broader community.

III

Carleton students in the 1960s could therefore make some claims to be distinctive. Their scheme for student representation on the governing bodies of the university was unique, and they were among the first to adopt mixed residences. But this was the 1960s, the era of freedom marches, of student demonstrations and sit-ins, and the so-called counterculture. It is easy to exaggerate the radicalism of the students of the 1960s. Only a minority were involved, and although there was plenty of rhetoric, there was no revolution: there was no significant redistribution of political or economic power. Yet it is also easy to minimize the changes. The 1960s is generally accepted as a decade of cultural change – a transformation of attitudes and values – and this transformation owed much to the student vanguard. [32] It is in this broader context that the radicalism of the Carleton students should be assessed.

For a brief period in the mid-sixties Carleton University had a reputation for student radicalism. Hugh Armstrong, the president of the Students' Council, was even described as a dangerous revolutionary by a columnist in the *Globe and Mail*, who warned that the next step after Armstrong's election as president of the Canadian Union of Students would be violent student demonstrations.[33] But the radicalism at Carleton, was exaggerated. Its student leaders in the mid-sixties had rallied student support for student participation in university government, but it did not rally them for radical confrontation. In the spring of 1968, although the Students for a Democratic University ran a slate of candidates for the student elections on a radical platform, not one member of the slate was elected. Gerry Lampert, the successful presidential candidate, was certainly not a radical; he was described by the *Carleton* as "the politician's politician on the campus" and had run on a platform of working in harmony with the faculty and the administration.[34] In that same year the *Carleton* ended its affiliation with the Canadian University Press, and in a referendum the students voted two to one to withdraw from the Canadian Union of Students – in both cases because these national organizations were now seen as too preoccupied with national and international affairs.[35] By the end of the decade, Carleton students seemed skeptical about student leaders wanting to reform the university or the outside world.

The last radical fling at Carleton came in 1969, when a small group of young people occupied President Dunton's office in an attempt to force him to support the cause of the radicals at Simon Fraser University. According to the *Carleton*, some of the group had been associated with Students for a Democratic University, though only a few of them were still registered as students. It was apparently a chaotic event, with a baby crying and one young man repeatedly accusing Dunton of being "nothing but a part of the fucking capitalist system." According to the *Carleton* reporter, Dunton was "the only one in the room who managed to keep his cool." It was revealing that the *Carleton* made fun of the protesters, and the president of the Students' Council denounced them as "the lunatic left." It was also revealing that the group had no popular support and had so little confidence in what they were doing that after an hour they voluntarily left Dunton's office. [36]

The Panda game also suggests that, even in an era of change, older traditions survived. The annual football game against the University of Ottawa was exceptional to the extent that in the 1960s it could still be described as a major university-wide extracurricular occasion. It was in part a mimicking of the tradition of older universities, fostering a rivalry with the other Ottawa university, with the panda as a focus for a weekend of hijinks. The student newspapers at both institutions stimulated the rivalry in the mid-sixties by encouraging "hate week." In 1966 the administration linked the event to the first homecoming weekend. The football game sometimes seemed almost coincidental. Certainly, neither university had a strong football tradition or fielded teams with a national ranking, and neither the Carleton nor the Ottawa team attracted many spectators to their other games. For most of the students who attended the Panda game, the drinking and vandalism seem to have had precedence over the game itself, even if, by then end of the decade, the administration and the student leaders felt that matters had gone too far. [37]

It is also surprising that for a decade associated with emancipation and equality, there are few hints of women's liberation in any of the student records. The constant search for a variety of beauty queens throughout the decade, duly recorded by the *Carleton*, suggests that the male perspective on women had not been much modified; the passive response of the women suggests that they either accepted or condoned the emphasis on physical beauty or they lacked the confidence to protest.

The evidence for change, however, was unmistakable. Most students were not radicals, the residences were orderly, and there were still drinking parties and beauty contests, but it was not the same. The lifestyle had changed. The more formal social events of the university, such as the Christmas Dance and Spring Prom, disappeared from the Students' Council calendar during the 1960s. It was a decade when ballroom music was giving way to rock and when formal attire and corsages seemed out of place in a world that was challenging the traditions of an earlier generations. Although social functions were still being organized, they were more likely to be specialized events organized by students grouped by residence, faculty, or department. The Hleodor Society was dissolved in 1963, suggesting that women were distancing themselves from the tea-party tradition. It is true that the student body was larger and more fragmented, but it was not only a question of numbers. Topics verging on the improper received wider coverage. In 1964 there was a debate in the *Carleton* on premarital sex, and a few years later there was a frank article on birth control.[38] The *Carleton* also broadened its vocabulary; its articles included words that had formerly been confined to locker rooms and still did not appear in the city newspapers. The students were deliberately challenging the prevailing prudery of the wider community.

Dunton's analysis of the situation was perceptive and also revealing. In 1968 he warned the Board of Governors that there was a small minority of students at Carleton who favoured "drastic actions" and that some other students questioned the values of the university and the broader society but did "not seem to be prepared to adopt violence." The majority of students were not looking for trouble, he said. The real danger was that the radicals might win the support of a majority of students on some specific issue. His aim was to work with the Senate to avoid this; he would turn to the police to maintain order only as a last resort.[39] Dunton's comments are a reminder that it was not only the students whose attitudes were changing. University authorities, like authorities beyond the university, were no longer confident about what behaviour was acceptable and where the lines should be drawn. Students were no longer *in statu pupillari*, even if the implications of their new status were not clear.

A more telling response to the changes in student attitudes came at the end of the decade with the resignation of Fred Turner, the bursar. Turner had come to Carleton to teach accounting and had been appointed bursar in 1948. He had handled the financial affairs of the university through good times and bad, and had earned a well-deserved reputation for efficiency and frugality. He was devoted to Carleton, but his image was of a university that offered cultural and economic opportunities to deserving students who might not otherwise continue their education. While he could accept the casual dress and informal manners of the decade, he could not endure the incivility and disdain for authority. In his final report as bursar, he objected to being considered "a tame tool of the Establishment, brainwashing the younger generation into unthinking cogs in some giant machine." His time at Carleton, he affirmed, had been "a rewarding adventure," but he was now resigning because of his "regret that the changes in relationship with the students, and to some extent with faculty, have reduced these psychic rewards recently and prospectively to such an extent that I no longer want to have a direct part in the University's future."[40] Stu-

dents were now claiming to participate in making the rules, and many ob-
servers had come to see this participation as desirable, but Fred Turner's
reaction is a reminder that these students sometimes showed little respect or
understanding for the motives of an older generation.

Norman Fenn also had difficulty with the changing attitudes of students.
In a more stable era most students had found that Fenn's emphasis on character building had given them a cherished degree of control over their
extracurricular activities. Now, however, some student leaders objected to
what they interpreted as a paternalistic assumption by Fenn that he knew
what they should do and how they should behave. In 1963 the *Carleton* reported a formal debate in the residence over "Fennism," with its "world of
harmony and tolerance" in which "the function of the university is to produce well-rounded 'good citizens.' " One critic conceded that this sense of
responsibility to the community might be a noble vision but argued that it
left little place for individualism. The debaters did not agree on what
should replace it. One stressed the need for more authoritarian administration of the residences so that students who wanted to could study, while another thought that individuals should be subordinated to the community.
But nobody supported Fennism.[41] Fenn's resignation as director of student
affairs the next year was never linked publicly to changes in student attitudes, but these changes were surely a factor.[42]

This evidence of changing attitudes and values may be convincing, but it
leaves many questions unresolved. What accounts for the change? Most an-
alysts would stress the generation gap, arguing that the postwar generation
– the students of the 1960s – had grown up in the postwar years of
economic growth and were distinguished from – and sometimes alienated
from – parents who had been marked by the insecurity and instability of
the Depression and the war. This explanation may seem convincing, but the
records at Carleton provide no evidence either for or against. Nor does the
evidence tell us whether Carleton students were more – or less – affected by
shifting values than students elsewhere. There were no violent confrontations at Carleton. We may attribute this to the conservatism of the Ottawa
community or to Dunton's responsiveness to student demands for a place
in the sun, but we must also remember that there was very little violence
at any Canadian universities in this decade. What is striking is that at Carleton, as elsewhere, many of the consequences of the changing attitudes
would only emerge later. The students of the 1960s had challenged the traditional view of the status of students, but it was only in the 1970s that
new behavioural patterns reflected the changed attitudes and values, and
confirmed a new and different status.

The tunnel walls became the battlefield where the feminists challenged sexist images and where some men (including some third-floor Russell residents) challenged the women's right to act as censors (*Charlatan*, 23 Sept. 1977, 27 Jan. 1978)

Epilogue

The changes of the 1960s meant that Carleton, like other universities, would never be the same again. For the next decade the administration, the faculty, and the students tried to come to terms with what had happened. How would Carleton adjust to being a publicly funded university, financially dependent on a provincial government that no longer saw university education as a high priority? How would professors adjust to a society that had become more ambivalent about the consequences of research and to an era in which there were no university openings for many of the newly graduated PHDs? How would students, with their modified lifestyles, respond to the traditional authority of administrators and professors? And how would administrators, faculty, and students adapt to the changing status of women? The responses to these questions would change Carleton and would be, in part, the history of Carleton for the decade of the 1970s.

This qualification is important. Carleton University, as always, was exposed to many influences. By the 1970s it was a medium-sized university, a multiversity, in which different faculties and schools had their own histories, responding to their internal leadership and to the wider society in quite different ways. The computer, for example, revolutionized design in the School of Architecture. The growth of high technology in the Ottawa region led to new and innovative programs in engineering and computer science. Even the break-up of the Soviet Union was mirrored at Carleton when the Institute of Soviet and East European Studies became part of the wider Institute of European and Russian Studies. The history of Carleton, therefore, is the story of a university that is always evolving. It has a beginning but no end.

This epilogue is therefore only part of the story. It focuses on the responses of the administration, faculty, and students to the changes of the 1960s. It does not attempt to deal with the other ways in which sectors of the university were changing. It is not a history of Carleton University in the 1970s but an epilogue to the 1960s. It marks the end of an era in the story of Carleton without attempting to discuss continuities or new beginnings. The responses at Carleton were unique, though the broader pattern was remarkably similar to what was happening at other universities. The story, therefore, is also a case study of a period of transformation for all Canadian universities.

I

By the end of the 1960s the universities in Ontario were vulnerable. The provincial government controlled some 90 per cent of their annual revenue and provided an even higher proportion of the money spent on buildings. Every year Carleton, like other universities, hoped to admit more students and expected the government to give it more money per student. It was obvious that this escalation, which had gone on for ten exciting years, could not go on forever. Higher education now absorbed over 10 per cent of the provincial budget, and its share was still rising. Late in 1969 William Davis, the minister of education, talked of "the feeling that we have reached the end of the line; that we cannot afford to increase to any significant degree the amounts being directed to universities in future years."[1] The universities' years of affluence would have to come to an end.

The change came abruptly early in the 1970s. The decade began with high rates of inflation and unemployment. The government responded to declining revenues and higher welfare costs by looking for ways to save money. At the same time, the political and economic benefits of university expansion were being questioned. The baby boomers had been accommodated. It was also relevant that university graduates could no longer be sure of finding jobs, and even a PHD might be looking for work. Why should governments pay universities to graduate an increasing number of students when they were not needed?

The government wanted to limit its commitment to higher education, but it was not sure how to proceed. It had promised that every high school graduate who wanted to go to university would find a place. Although money might be saved by raising admission standards and so restricting first-year enrolment, there would be a political price to pay. Politicians would naturally be reluctant to face the outcry if some students who had completed grade 13 found themselves ineligible for a university education. In any case the demographic pattern suggested that such draconian

In the 1970s student demonstrations had shifted from international causes to more immediate student concerns. Here the Carleton delegation is protesting at Queen's Park against inadequate government support for universities (*Charlatan*, 23 Nov. 1978)

measures would not be needed. The high schools had fewer students and so fewer graduates. On the other hand, a higher proportion of these graduates wanted to go to university. Nobody knew whether the interplay of demographic and social forces meant there would be more or fewer university applicants over the next few years. The government decided not to touch the thorny issue of entrance requirements.

What could be done? Graduate programs were the most vulnerable. The provincial government had agreed to support these programs because of the need for university professors, but surely some of them could be eliminated now that there was no shortage of professors? But how could the government persuade reluctant universities to reduce the member of graduate programs? If the government was to avoid criticism for encroaching on academic freedom or university autonomy, it would need to proceed cautiously. It began in 1969 by appointing the Commission on Post-Secondary Education in Ontario. The commission's preliminary report in 1972 argued that drastic measures were needed. It proposed a centralized structure of university education in which a board appointed by the government would coordinate the provincial universities by deciding what programs they could offer. The board would also decide how the provincial funds for the universities should be distributed.

The reaction to this preliminary report was not what the government had hoped. The university presidents did not want an appointed board telling them what to do, and they interpreted the proposals as trying "to remove from the universities all the functions essential to the very idea of a university."[2] It was significant that the presidents received widespread public support. The commission chose to avoid confrontation; in its final report it tamely suggested that the board should have only advisory powers.[3] The lesson drawn by the commission and the provincial government was that direct intervention would be very unpopular.

The government did get advice from the university presidents and its own advisory committee, but it was not the advice it was looking for. The Council of University Presidents had responded to the anti-establishment sentiments of the 1960s by adding faculty representatives from each university. The newly formed Council of Ontario Universities, however, was as convinced as ever of the benefits of higher education and research, and it consistently recommended even higher levels of funding than the government was providing. The Committee on University Affairs was also broadened to include academic representatives, but the new Ontario Council on University Affairs was no more helpful. It too argued that the government should invest more money in higher education.

The government would not change its mind. It was still determined to limit its expenditures on higher education. In 1972, after the preliminary report of the commission and the outcry over the threat of direct intervention, it took an unprecedented step. It abruptly raised student fees, without any consultation or warning. This met the government's immediate objective because any increase in fee income for the universities reduced the government's share of the basic income unit. It also sent a blunt message to the universities: the government was serious about retrenchment even if it meant making it more difficult for some young people to go to university. In the words of the annual report of the Council of Ontario Universities, "to say that the universities were shocked is an understatement."[4] The government made no apology. Next year it froze capital grants to universities. For the rest of the decade it regularly increased the annual basic income unit at less than the rate of inflation. Ontario's support for higher education on a per-student basis dropped from close to the provincial average to the lowest among the Canadian provinces.

The year 1972 can thus be seen as a turning point. Ten years earlier Leslie Frost had initiated a decade of government support for university expansion. Now the government was making it clear that higher education no longer had a high priority. While universities were still important and still expensive, the era of encouraging rapid expansion had come to an end. All the same, the government had backed away from imposing any structural changes – it would not intervene directly in the administration of the universities. But it would keep the purse strings tight. It would be up to the universities to adapt to the new climate.

The Council of Ontario Universities provided almost no leadership. Although it initiated the evaluation of existing graduate programs and made it more difficult to introduce new ones, the number of graduate programs continued to increase. The presidents may have feared that any economies would simply be an excuse for the government to make further cuts. Probably more important, they were primarily responsible for their own institutions and could hardly be expected to sacrifice any of their programs without getting something in return. It was easier to argue the benefits of higher education and protest against the "knife of financial constraint". At the end of the decade the Council of Ontario Universities protested: "The gap between the financial resources that are provided and what are needed has grown unmanageably great. That gap must be closed. If it is not, the integrity and the value of the entire university enterprise is at risk." [5] The Ontario Council on University Affairs agreed. It too saw a "System on the Brink" and could only advise an increase in public funding. [6] Since the government did not intend to spend more money, and ignored their advice, the individual universities were left to deal as best they could with the reality of financial constraint.

At Carleton University this was Michael Oliver's problem. Oliver succeeded Davidson Dunton in 1972. He had been national president of the New Democratic Party and director of research for the Royal Commission on Bilingualism and Biculturalism, but his administrative experience as vice-principal, academic, at McGill during some difficult financial years was probably seen by the search committee as more relevant. Dunton was a difficult man to follow because he had relied on his personal knowledge of most of the people on the campus and had not developed formal administrative structures. Oliver needed to delegate more of the responsibility, and his first major initiative was to create the offices of vice-president, academic, and vice-president, administration. The appointment of Ross Love and A.B. Larose, the bursar, to these positions suggests that Oliver did not plan any dramatic break with the past.

Other administrative changes also showed a difference in administrative style that reflected the changing values of the time. Oliver introduced a more open administrative environment. He initiated weekly meetings with the deans, and he established an Academic Planning Committee of the Senate, which he chaired, which was to advise the administration on academic issues. Another innovation was a Budget Review Committee, with members drawn from the Board of Governors and the Senate, which was to participate in financial planning. This wider consultation was welcomed by the faculty, though the results were not always positive. Oliver listened, but he also participated actively in the discussions, raising hypothetical possibilities and at times acting as devil's advocate. The committee members sometimes interpreted his arguments as statements of a firm position. More significant than the change in the administrative style, however, was the frustration of financial constraint. No president could be popular when expectations nourished during a decade of affluence were being frustrated by years of relative poverty.

Carleton's first reaction to the new policy of constraint was to ask the government for special consideration. The administration at Carleton, Oliver argued, was frugal and efficient; Carleton's salaries were lower and its teaching loads higher than at most universities, and it invested less in its extracurricular activities for students. He pointed out that Carleton was facing a proportionately higher deficit than other Ontario universities because the formula by which government grants were allocated favoured the older universities, on account of their larger number of students in professional and graduate programs. On the other hand, most of the universities that had been founded since Carleton (which, like Carleton, had a higher proportion of undergraduate students in the arts and social sciences) were receiving supplementary grants as "emerging universities." Carleton had been founded too late or had emerged too soon and suffered in consequence.[7] This was apparently a convincing argument, because Carleton received a special grant of a million dollars in 1974 in addition to its formula funds.

Carleton again projected a deficit for the next year and again asked for special treatment, arguing: "If we do not receive a special grant that will enable us to operate without a sizable deficit next year, we will immediately be forced to declare a situation of financial stringency in the university and undertake proceedings for forced terminations of a large number of tenured faculty."[8] The government was again persuaded and came through with a special grant of almost one and a half million dollars. But it made clear that this would be the last supplementary grant.

While the money was welcome, it provided only temporary relief. The permanent solution, as Oliver saw it, was to revise the formula on which the provincial grants were based. Any change in the formula would require the consent of the Council of Ontario Universities, and Oliver, as a newcomer to Ontario and to the council, had little personal leverage. The older universities saw no reason to change a formula that was to their advantage, and the newer universities saw no reason to fight a losing battle. The council preferred to ignore the issue. As Oliver reported to the Board of Governors, "Our efforts to amend the formula have not been universally welcomed by our sister institutions. Some for which the formula is very generous do not want to relinquish their favoured positions, and as a result Carleton's initiatives in this sphere have meant some loss of goodwill from other institutions."[9]

Another option was to take advantage of the existing formula by increasing the enrolment at the graduate level. Potential graduate students regularly applied to more than one university, and their decision often depended on which university responded more quickly and offered the most money. Oliver shifted some funds to the dean of graduate studies, and the dean, with Oliver's support, made offers promptly and made them as attractive as possible by deliberately exceeding his budget, knowing that not all would accept.[10] The results were significant. Full-time graduate enrolment at Carleton rose from less than seven hundred to almost than a thousand by 1975 and stayed at that level for the rest of the decade. Carleton's graduate school was still smaller than those of the older universities but its proportion of the total graduate enrolment in the province rose from 4 per cent to over 5 per cent.

More radical was cooperation with the University of Ottawa at the graduate level. Ottawa and Carleton were natural rivals, competing for students at the undergraduate and graduate levels, but special circumstances could mitigate this rivalry. In 1975 Carleton's doctoral program in economics was in serious danger of being terminated because of its narrow emphasis on economic policy. At the same time, the Economics Department at the University of Ottawa had submitted a proposal for a doctoral program that was likely to be rejected because of its narrow emphasis on development economics. The advantages of a combined program were so obvious that the two departments overcame their reservations about their linguistic and academic differences and made a successful joint proposal. This became a precedent when, shortly afterwards, rumours circulated that four of the senior universities in the province were scheming to have all the graduate work in engineering and science in the province offered on their campuses. The likelihood that this would happen may have been exaggerated, but there was enough smoke to persuade Carleton and Ottawa to combine their graduate programs in engineering and science so that the combined programs would be strong enough to ensure their survival. This collaboration between Carleton and the University of Ottawa was the most noteworthy example of the "rationalization" of graduate programs in the province.

Elsewhere at Carleton the story was more one of attrition than change. The shortage of money coloured almost every decision. Deficits were avoided in Oliver's early years by rigid economies, by the two special provincial grants, and by unexpected increases in enrolment. Nobody enjoyed the economies. The dean of science in his annual report in 1976 complained, "One more slash of the knife, one more thoughtless blow of the hatchet, and an unconscionable and irreparable act of academic vandalism will have been perpetrated."[11] Other deans were less melodramatic in their protests but none of them were happy. And when undergraduate enrolment declined late in the decade, even the rigid economies could not avert annual deficits.

The fate of St Patrick's College gives some insight into the impact of the provincial government's policy of financial restraint. The college had not been able to maintain its connection with the Irish Catholic community after its deconfessionalization and its association with Carleton.[12] It was still widely believed, however, that universities, as they grew larger, were becoming more impersonal and that some of the benefits of traditional college life could be restored by creating smaller units within the larger institutions. At Carleton, St Patrick's College, with its own building on the Rideau River campus, was an obvious focus for those who hoped to create a more intimate atmosphere for some students. There was no shortage of ideas. The planning committee for the college had much to say about "the quest for academic excellence and a concern for moral and social issues ... and innovative development in undergraduate education."[13]

Unfortunately, every proposal seemed to have start-up costs, and the university was not prepared to undertake any new expenditures when it was cutting costs everywhere else. President Oliver favoured a distinctive program for St Patrick's in principle, but he could not ignore the university's financial crisis. In 1974 he even referred to the possibility of eliminating the college to reduce costs.[14] This was too drastic, but the college's Academic Planning Committee did reluctantly recommend that many of the courses offered at St Patrick's should be integrated with similar courses offered by university departments to save money. This meant a much closer integration of the college with the university; for the faculty, it meant becoming members of a university department and being seconded to the college.[15]

For the next few years a handful of committed professors tried to save St Patrick's College. New programs were introduced, including a Canadian studies program at the undergraduate level, and a popular criminology and corrections program. But enrolment at St Patrick's continued to decline, and by 1978 it was down to 350 full-time students. To use the space more efficiently, the administration moved the schools of journalism and social work into the college building, but by then even the most committed champions of the college had lost hope. In January 1979, with flowery expressions of regret, St Patrick's College ceased to exist.[16]

The fate of St Patrick's College should not be attributed to lack of imagination or lack of will. The harsh reality was that Carleton's annual operating revenues were almost entirely controlled by the provincial government, which determined the student fees and the basic income unit per student.

Carleton, like other universities, spent the money as efficiently as it could. That meant larger classes, especially at the undergraduate level, with teaching assistants to help with discussion groups and marking. The programs and academic experience at the undergraduate level became more and more uniform across the province, because the universities could not afford the cost of diversity.

In 1978 the government announced that its policy of fiscal restraint for the universities would continue for the foreseeable future. Carleton's response was to appoint the Committee on Carleton University to 1982, which was to assess the university's prospects for what it called "the new reality." It is revealing that the committee saw no likelihood of the government or the Council of Ontario Universities proposing any structural changes to higher education in the province. Carleton like the other Ontario universities, would have to cope with declining enrolments and declining revenues as best it could. The committee believed that Carleton was and would remain "a mid-sized university with very broad offerings in the humanities and social sciences – the centre of any good university – and a limited range of professional schools."[17]

This left it with few options. Carleton would have to compete with other universities for undergraduate students and would have to do more to retain them. At the graduate level it seemed appropriate to extend the cooperation with the University of Ottawa. The committee was reconciled to the reduction of the staff by attrition. The report referred to the possibility of more financial support from the private sector and more contract research, but did not see these as making a significant difference. In sum, the report accepted Carleton's situation as primarily dependent on public support and accepted the necessity of maximizing its income within the rules established by the government. It saw only a limited scope for initiative or innovation. The most it could hope for was to consolidate the university that had been created in the 1960s. It would be many years before funds from a more generous private sector would create new opportunities.

The committee said nothing about the role of women in the administration of the university. Female professors, as we have seen, had been accepted by most of their male colleagues without obvious discrimination, even to the extent of having their turn as chairs of their departments.[18] The chair however, was expected to act collegially and in any case had little influence on the career patterns of other professors in the department. The position of the dean was different, because a dean's decisions could affect salaries and promotions. The heritage of the 1960s could not be ignored. Gender equality meant that women should be as eligible as men for senior administrative positions. Thus it was hardly revolutionary in 1979 when Naomi Griffiths, an historian, was appointed dean of arts. But it was

exceptional: Griffiths was the first female dean at Carleton and the first female dean of arts in Canada. Even the press interpreted the appointment as
a victory for women. The diminutive Griffiths refused to analyse the motives of the search committee, but she did suggest that her appointment
could as easily be seen as a "triumph for short people." [19]

Not everyody was amused. Some men still found it difficult to accept
the idea of a woman exercising authority over them. Pauline Jewett, who
had become president of Simon Fraser University, warned Griffiths that
she was now a "visible woman" and could expect to become the target of
cranks. Jewett was right. Griffiths received anonymous telephone calls at
night until she had her number privately listed. It was more disturbing
when two male professors in her faculty told her that as a woman she had
no right to make any decision that affected them. The most shocking incident was the delivery of an envelope to her office containing excrement. [20]
But these were isolated incidents. The novelty of a woman as dean soon
faded. The renewal of Griffiths's appointment for a second term and the
appointment of another woman as her successor attracted little attention.
Griffiths's experience, however, is a reminder that it still seemed revolutionary to some men, even in 1979, that a woman should become a university administrator.

II

For university professors the 1970s seemed a stark contrast to the 1960s.
An Ontario study by John Porter and others, published early in 1970, still
reflected the optimism of the earlier decade. "The position of the professor," it stated, "is an attractive one and seems likely to remain so. Professors, like teachers generally, are either reasonably well paid or else well
paid, and the work itself is attractive ... Moreover the conditions of work
are on the whole excellent." [21] Ten years later a study of the academic profession in the United States was equally positive about the 1960s, when
"faculty realized professional gains, social prestige, greater job mobility,
more self-regulation, and greater influence in academic government." But
this same study paints a depressing picture of the profession at the end of
the 1970s: "Faculty gloom seems to result from the dissonance in their lives
between the expectations for their academic careers and their actual career
paths. For most academics, higher education no longer promises the excitement of prestigious careers, rapid advancement, and professional pre-
rogatives that it did in the 1960s." [22] We must allow for some exaggeration
– there were frustrated professors in the 1960s and there were professors in
the 1970 who still enjoyed their teaching and their research – but the mood
of the professoriate had certainly changed.

The story of the faculty at Carleton in the 1970s is consistent with this picture of gloom. Here, as elsewhere, the 1960s had led to unrealistic expectations, based on an inflated view of the prestige of academics in a postindustrial society. The harsh reality was that by the 1970s the governments and the wider public no longer assumed that investing in research would automatically provide all the answers, and professors could no longer rely on getting more time or more money for their favourite research projects. At Carleton, as elsewhere, unrealistic expectations led to disillusionment. Special circumstances at Carleton, however, meant that the professors responded in a way that would have been unimaginable only a few years earlier. They formed a union.

Salaries were not the major issue. Although the salaries at Carleton had not kept up with those at the older universities, the professors did not blame Dunton or Oliver. While they wanted more money, they were prepared to believe the presidents when they said that Carleton could not afford higher salaries. The fault, they felt, lay not with the administration at Carleton but with an intransigent provincial government and its policy of financial constraint. The divisive issue within the university was not money but job security.[23] Retrenchment seemed inevitable, in the administration's view, because it faced the prospect of declining enrolments and the refusal of the government to match grant increases to inflation rates. Since salaries were the major university expenditure, any significant savings depended on reducing the number of employees. At Carleton the insecurity created by this situation was exacerbated by two special factors. A prolonged debate over procedures for dismissal had alerted even the tenured professors to the possibility that they could lose their jobs, and President Oliver's frank discussion of the options open to the administration only made the faculty more nervous. Some defensive action seem urgent.

As described earlier, the extended discussions over tenure and dismissal had established formal procedures for dismissing tenured professors who were incompetent. The question now was whether the administration could use financial stringency to justify the dismissal of tenured faculty even if they were competent. The Senate Committee on Redundancy conceded that the Board of Governors could do so if the alternative was bankruptcy for the university. To protect the faculty against arbitrary action. however, the committee recommended that nobody should be dismissed until the Senate, with its faculty majority, agreed that there was a financial crisis.

Some younger academics were still worried; they suspected that some of their more senior Senate colleagues would side with the administration and, as a result, even the Senate would not be an adequate shield against dismissal. They insisted that if any professors were dismissed they should have a right to appeal the decision to an unbiased committee.[24] The heritage of the 1960s, with its emphasis on the rights of the individual, meant that few would question the right to appeal against dismissal, and in the spring of 1973 the Senate approved the amended report. The Board of Governors did not object in principle, but it did want to be sure that the wording was consistent with its legal responsibility to ensure the financial stability of the university, and a joint committee of the Senate and the Board of Governors was appointed to revise the document. To an insecure faculty, the prolonged discussions gave the impression that the document had become something more than a discussion of a hypothetical possibility.

The final wording of the document on tenure and dismissal was still being negotiated in the fall of 1974, when the administration produced a preliminary budget for 1975–76. The Budget Review Committee was told of a projected deficit of more than $4 million. This disturbing news could not be kept secret for long in a university environment. Oliver tried to reassure the faculty by calling a special meeting to present the facts and outline the options. The crisis atmosphere meant that five hundred professors attended the meeting. Oliver explained that major economies would be necessary and mentioned staff reduction as one of the possible options, but he insisted that there were no plans to dismiss any professors.

Some of the professors were skeptical. That same day they called for a special meeting of the Carleton University Academic Staff Association (CUASA) "to initiate the establishment of collective bargaining." For most professors, union membership had once seemed incompatible with their professional status, but times were changing. Job insecurity had led to the formation of unions in some universities in the United States, and recently the faculties at the University of Manitoba and at St Mary's in Halifax had opted for collective bargaining; unionization was also being considered at some Ontario universities. At Carleton this still seemed an improbable option. Only a hundred professors attended the special meeting, and only sixty of them voted in favour of consulting the faculty on certification. The next CUASA newsletter headlined its reported with an equivocal "CUASA Takes a Leap???" Even the president of the staff association, who was openly suspicious of Oliver's motives, commented on the faculty's apparent lack of interest.[25]

The attitude of the faculty may have been affected by the final version of the "Report on the Release of Teaching Staff in Times of Financial Stringency," which was submitted to the Senate in December. During the Senate discussion of the document, Oliver asked hypothetically whether the Senate could act quickly enough if the Board of Governors declared financial stringency. Or would he be obliged to act unilaterally to save the institution?[26] This was a legitimate question, but it was not one that the Senate could answer, and it might have been wiser not to raise the issue. The leaders of

CUASA concluded that the president could not be trusted to champion their cause before the Board of Governors. But they were still cautious. The two-day session they organized to discuss unionization included a panel that presented both the pros and cons. While the leaders did stress the protection that a collective contract could provide, there were no denunciations of the president and no clarion calls to join in the class struggle. The opposition to the association leaders, mainly economists and engineers, stressed academic freedom and the primary responsibility of professors to their students. By this time, however, a union at least seemed an option worth considering. It was agreed overwhelmingly to ask the membership to vote by secret ballot on the issue of collective bargaining.[27] Those who voted supported the idea.

This expression of opinion had no legal force, however. The significant vote would be the formal vote on collective bargaining conducted by the Labour Relations Board. There was still enough collegial tradition to ensure that the campaign would avoid any bitter confrontation. The Board of Governors announced that it had no intention at this time of declaring a state of financial stringency.[28] President Oliver used a special edition of the university newsletter to question whether collective bargaining was consistent with the collegial traditions of a university, but he did not question the sincerity of those who disagreed with him.[29] Similarly, the leaders of the faculty association were careful to avoid personal attacks on the administration. It is not easy to know what influenced the voters. Some may have seen their vote as a vote for job security. Even those who felt that their jobs were secure may have wanted to show their support for their less fortunate colleagues. Whatever the reasons, the result was sweeping support for collective bargaining, with 292 in favour and 44 against.

This settled the issue. From then on, both the faculty leaders and the administration behaved as if the union was a foregone conclusion. In every department a canvasser solicited signatures in support of CUASA as the bargaining agent. Even many of the doubters opted to go along with the majority. By mid-March an astonishing 80 per cent of the eligible professors and librarians had been signed up. Even the certification proceeded relatively smoothly. Collective bargaining, which only a year before would have seemed unthinkable to most of the faculty, was now seen as an appropriate option.

Why did the majority of the faculty at Carleton opt for a union? The prolonged debate over tenure and dismissal, the financial problems of the university, and the widespread impression that the administration saw dismissals as a probable option were certainly significant. But other factors may also have been important. Most faculty associations within the province at least toyed with the possibility of forming a union at this time, but it is surely more than a coincidence that the more recently established universities in the province opted for collective bargaining while the older provincial institutions

The official notice of the vote that would certify the Carleton University Academic Staff
Association as the bargaining agent for the
teaching staff and the librarians (*This Week
Times Two*, 8 Apr. 1975)

continued to rely on informal bargaining. What accounts for the difference?
If job security was the crucial issue, why did the professors at the older institutions feel less threatened? Did they assume that their universities, with their
larger endowments and wealthier alumni, could more easily weather the financial constraint? Or did even the younger professors at the more senior institutions feel more confident about their status in the academic profession
and feel less inclined to consider the less dignified status of membership in a
trade union? Whatever the explanation, the professors and librarians at Carleton were now committed to collective bargaining.

Within the faculty, at Carleton as elsewhere, the changing perspective of
the 1960s on gender relations raised questions that were even more complex than the question of a union. Female professors were in the minority
at all Ontario universities in the 1970s,[30] but it was hard to know how to
increase their numbers. A quota system seemed inappropriate, because in
many disciplines there were no qualified female candidates. On the other
hand, when there were female candidates, they might be passed over because men were likely to be in the majority on the search committees and
they might well have an unconscious bias against women. There was much
discussion but not much positive action. As late as 1979 a report to the
Board of Governors was still suggesting that each search committee should
include at least one woman and that the committee should report on the
number of female applicants when it submitted its recommendations.[31] At
that rate it would be some time before Carleton significantly improved the
balance between genders among its faculty.

There was also statistical evidence of discrimination against the women
who were appointed; comparisons with comparable male professors
showed that women's salaries were often lower and that promotions
came more slowly. This problem received a good deal of attention at Carleton in the 1970s. The faculty union raised the issue of the anomalies in
salaries and promotions, and the administration was sympathetic. But
apart from increasing the awareness of injustices, nothing was accomplished until the 1980s.

Both male and female professors, also had to introduce changes in the
classroom. One of the characteristics of the 1970s was that the traditional
approaches of some disciplines were under attack. There was a demand for
greater relevance, and this frequently took the form of a demand for more
attention to the role of women in literature, history, and the social sciences.
Professors had to broaden the scope of the courses they taught, and introduce new courses that dealt specifically with women. At Carleton, graduate
work in women's studies was introduced under the umbrella of the Institute
of Canadian Studies. There were rumblings from the more traditional academics that scholarly standards were being undermined, and certainly not
all of the generalizations of the feminist scholars could be rigorously supported by evidence. Even so, it was a change for the better. In many disciplines the most innovative and most dynamic scholarship of the 1970s was
in the field of women's studies.

The changes of the 1960s also modified the relations of the faculty with
the students. When students had been *in statu pupillari*, professors had
been expected to behave responsibly to the young people in their charge.
Any social activity, such as dating a student, was frowned on, and any more
intimate relationship was considered unethical. While this did not prevent
some professors from making inappropriate advances, it did make any

harassment less overt. By the 1960s, however, the students wanted to be thought of as adults. At the same time, the egalitarian values of the era encouraged informality in the classroom, as well as more social contacts between professors and students outside the classroom. At Carleton, for example, a young professor openly invited his class to his summer cottage and encouraged nude bathing – and was indignant when some colleagues were critical. The administration and many of the faculty were uneasy about the permissive attitudes, but the old rules no longer applied and there seemed to be no new rules to take their place. If students were now adults, they could be seen as consenting adults. It was still admitted that a professor was in a position of authority – as one who graded the students' essays and final examinations – but the social constraints on sexual harassment had become less effective.

New rules to meet the changing status of the students were slow in coming. They were only codified at Carleton after some women decided to draw public attention to sexual harassment. Three female students in journalism took offence at a professor who seemed to them to be making inappropriate advances to another woman in their class. They went to the dean to protest, probably encouraged by the fact that the dean was now a woman. Dean Griffiths was prepared to believe them – the professor had a reputation as a womanizer – but because there were no formal procedures to follow, she persuaded them to let her handle the matter informally. She then summoned the professor to tell him of the "rumours" circulating about his behaviour and asked him to sign a statement that he would do nothing in future that might give credence to such rumours.[32] In an earlier era this might have been the end of the story, but it was 1981 and the students were not satisfied. They organized a public rally of students to draw public attention to what they described as widespread sexual harassment in the School of Journalism, "ranging from sexist jokes in class to sexual blackmail."[33] The allegations were never denied. Two professors of journalism, however, took affront at the implication that all professors in the school were harassing their students, and they threatened to sue the women. The case was settled out of court with an apology from the women, but it was clear that the university could no longer ignore the issue. Appeal procedures were put in place, which required the deans to investigate any allegations of sexual harassment in future and to have the accusers confront the accused in a private hearing.

Sexual harassment was later extended to include what became known as a "hostile environment." Locker-room vocabulary and sexual innuendo was common in the classrooms of male-dominated faculties such as engineering, and it was not uncommon in the classrooms of some male professors in other faculties. This had long been resented by women, but it was

not until the 1980s that female students at Carleton felt confident enough
about their rights to protest publicly. Their argument was that derogatory
or sexist remarks by professors at the expense of women created an unsuit-
able learning environment for them. Some professors argued that teachers
had a responsibility to challenge – or provoke – their students to force them
to think, and that to interfere with this pedagogical approach would be an
encroachment on their academic freedom. By the 1980s, however, there
was little sympathy, male or female, for any sexist comments, and carefully
worded regulations were introduced to ban any remarks that could create a
"hostile environment."

III

For students at Carleton the legacy of the 1960s had even more far-
reaching consequences. One of their concerns was defining their relations
with university authorities now that they were no longer *in statu pupillari*.
They also had to redefine their relations with other students now that
women were claiming greater equality. In both cases there were false starts
and misunderstandings as the rules of the game changed. It would be more
than a decade before a new equilibrium emerged, with a new pattern of
relationships and a new understanding of how to behave in the changed
environment.

The broader economic context cannot be ignored. When student leaders
of the 1960s rejected their historic status as pupils, they sometimes linked
their newly claimed maturity to their aspiration to change the world. By the
1970s the interest in international affairs and social reforms were clearly
fading. President Dunton commented in 1971 that Carleton students
seemed to have lost their faith in revolutionary slogans. He observed:
"Most, this year at least ... tend to be quite autonomous people for their
age, with individual concerns, individual questions, and individual interests, and believe very much that people should be left 'to do their own
thing.' "34

This could be interpreted as a selfish turning away from social responsibility. But it could also be interpreted as an awareness that their own economic future was becoming clouded. When the baby boom generation was
at the university, it was privileged because it was riding a wave of economic
growth. Those young people had some assurance that there would be rewarding careers for them after graduation; they could even take time off
and opt out, confident that the career openings would still be there when
they opted in again. The university students of the 1970s faced a different
reality. There were still career opportunities, but the rate of economic

growth was slowing and there were now more graduates competing for the jobs. It was not as easy in the 1970s to dream about reforming the world when your own place in the world seemed a little less secure.[35]

The evolution of the Students' Council over the decade gives some insight into the new patterns that were emerging at Carleton. In 1971, the year of Dunton's comments, elections for the Students' Council were unusual. Richard Labonte had been active in student affairs and editor of the *Carleton*, but his campaign for president showed a disdain for those who took issues too seriously. His slogan was "A coloured-shirt approach to the grey-flannel task of student government." Labonte and his slate never pretended that their campaign was anything more than a student prank, but many of the voters had also lost respect for the more traditional approach to student politics. He won the election, and his slate won a majority on the new council.[36] Next year there were imitators, including the Organized Apathy Party and the Sloth Slate, whose candidates promised to resign if elected. A more orthodox candidate, promising responsible fiscal administration, was elected president that year, though four of the Sloth candidates did get elected and kept their promise to resign.

While all this was irreverent, it was not completely frivolous. The students were more fragmented than ever before, and the Students' Council was becoming less representative. The students' link to academic questions was now through the student representatives in the New University Government. The student residences had their own organization and their own activities. The *Carleton,* renamed the *Charlatan* in 1971, had also distanced itself from the council and had become a self-appointed critic. There were many student organizations but no student body. The frivolous candidates for the Students' Council may best be understood as a recognition of the absurdity of the sweeping promises made by more traditional candidates' to change the world.

This irreverence at election time was a passing phase. Although the Students' Council could no longer claim to be the voice of the students, it had major administrative responsibilities. It distributed its share of the student fees among student clubs and planned some university-wide activities, such as Orientation Week. By the 1970s it was also deeply involved in the administration of the University Centre. Successive Students' Councils looked to profits from the sale of beer to meet their rental payments to the university and were regularly disappointed. Commercial considerations soon overshadowed social objectives. Rooster's, for example, began as an informal meeting place, a cooperative coffee shop in a mezzanine lounge in the University Centre. Two years later it moved to the main lounge on the fourth floor, where it became known to *Charlatan* readers as the Purple Passion Pit; wine and beer were served as well as coffee, and live music was provided for entertainment. The show was still the main attraction, and the bar closed during a performance. But for the Students' Council it was important that Rooster's should make money, and selling beer soon took precedence over conversation or entertainment. The councils seemed more concerned with budgets than with student services. As one caustic editor of the *Charlatan* put it, "Efficiency has become the keynote, expedience the war-cry and bureaucracy the result."[37] By the end of the decade the Students' Association – or CUSA Inc. as the *Charlatan* labelled it – was closer to a business operation, with a budget of over one million dollars and with members of the council paid for their services.

The transformation of the Students' Council is intriguing, but it tells us little about the status of students and their relations with the university administration. An incident associated with the library is more revealing. In 1973 the Senate Judicial Committee, composed mainly of deans, fined a student eighty dollars for defacing a library book. There was nothing remarkable about this; the student had admitted his guilt and a fine was the usual penalty. But in this case the student objected to the fine and asked to have his case reviewed. The Judicial Committee, responsive to criticism of arbitrary behaviour, referred the matter to the Senate.[38] Most of the senators still subscribed to what one of them described as "the happy tradition of accommodation at Carleton, which seemed ... preferable to having recourse to the courts."[39] But since the student was not accommodating and since, by the 1970s, it was difficult to defend arbitrary decisions by what the *Charlatan* described as a "gang of deans,"[40] the Senate agreed to hear the appeal on an ad hoc basis. In the end it upheld the ruling of its Judicial Committee, but in the atmosphere of the 1970s the procedures that had been followed were clearly suspect.

A Senate committee proposed new procedures in 1975. Instructional offences, such as cheating, would first be brought to the attention of the appropriate dean, who would discuss the offence with the student and might then impose an academic penalty, such as a failure in the course. What was new was that the student would still have the right to appeal to an assessment board, composed of two members of faculty and two students, and chaired by a lawyer retained by the Board of Governors. For other offences, ranging from property damage to class disruption, the first hearing would again be conducted by a dean, who could impose some appropriate restriction of privileges or could recommend a reference to the criminal courts. For residence or parking fines there would be an appeal to an assessment board composed of six students chosen by lot and again chaired by a lawyer retained by the board.[41]

The students' proposal for a judicial system in which a board including
representatives from all sectors of the university would hear academic
and nonacademic disputes. The professors successfully resisted the idea
of being judged by students (*Charlatan*, 26 Sept. 1975)

The proposed measures were significant because they introduced appeal
procedures. The university could no longer rely on its quasiparental authority; the students could challenge procedures and decisions before an appeal
tribunal. This had important implications. It would take time to codify the
regulations and procedures, but the students now had defined rights which
the university authorities had to respect.[42] The status of the students no
longer resembled that of adolescents in a family; they were now being
treated as adults who had a contractual relationship with the university.

This new status is also illustrated by the changes in the governance of the residences. When Glengarry residence opened in 1969, the men's and women's residence councils merged. The new council resented any limits on its authority. A student commission it appointed bluntly asserted that the new residence council should be "the *supreme* legislative body of the Residence Community with the Dean of Students and the Provost having only an advisory role."[43] This document was never approved by the administration or the Senate, but neither was it challenged directly. Some may have feared the consequences of confrontation. Norman Fenn, who was now dean of student services, was confident the students would listen to reason, but at least one of the resident fellows actually encouraged the students to assert their autonomy. On the other hand, some of the students in residence found it difficult to study – or even sleep – in what had become almost an anarchic environment. As one student put it, "There was a strong concern for maximum individual freedom but little interest in the mutual responsibility for the promotion of peace, order and good residence."[44] The majority of the resident fellows were so frustrated that they threatened to resign.

The uneasy truce ended with a dramatic incident. Four unidentified men refused to pay for some hashish provided by a resident on the fifth floor of Glengarry House. The vendor grabbed one man, but when other students came to his aid one of the intruders shot a student in the shoulder with a pistol and the four men escaped. President Oliver argued that the students were no longer children and when they broke the law it was a matter for the police.[45] But the university could not ignore the outcry. The issue of authority in the residences was finally resolved by requiring each student to sign a document promising to obey residence regulations, and by the establishment of the Residence-University Management and Policy Board, commonly known as RUMP, to supervise the residences. Here again was the shift was from *in statu pupillari* to a more contractual relationship.

It took some time for the authority of RUMP to be accepted by the students. It was a joint board with five student members, including the president of the residence council, and five administration appointees, including the dean of student services. The students initially saw RUMP as an attempt by the university to suppress student self-government, and some of them occupied President Oliver's office for a few days in protest. The university representatives, on the other hand, were often frustrated by the reluctance of the students to impose any regulations.[46] The board members gradually developed mutual respect; by the end of the decade they could confidently describe themselves as having the "responsibility and power of decision ... over virtually all aspects of Residence and Residence life." Even the president of the residence council admitted that "antagonism between the residence and the administration has declined to minimum levels."[47]

By the end of the 1960s there was little agreement about who should make the rules for the residences or what the rules should be. In 1972 the Commission on the Philosophy and Structure of the Residence proposed that residences offer a choice of "alternate life styles," including one residence that would have hardly any rules (*Charlatan*, 17 Nov. 1972)

This contractual relationship between the students and the administration became the pattern in the new university that was emerging. It would soon be extended to the classroom. Students began to see themselves as clients, paying fees for expected services. Course outlines, which had often been little more than approximate guides to the material which the professor intended to cover, were gradually transformed into quasilegal documents, which committed the professor – and the university – to cover the course content and to follow the outlined marking procedures. This contractual pattern meant that Carleton had become a very different institution from the university of an earlier generation. For the students, it was less personal and more bureaucratic, but it was also less arbitrary and more respectful of their maturity. In a society that had recognized that young people were to be treated like adults, university students would now have more autonomy and more responsibility for planning their own academic experience. This new status at Carleton, as at other universities, was not necessarily better or worse than the status of earlier generations, but it was clearly different.

Another change for the students, no less significant, was the new pattern of relations between men and women. The status of Carleton's women students attracted little attention until the 1970s; the students had focused on other matters. Regardless of their gender, they had united on issues such as racial discrimination and colonialism, and had shown a common front in their campaign for more influence in university government. The Students' Council at Carleton had been primarily masculine, though women had always been eligible for election, and in every decade at least one woman had been elected president of the council. But because the 1960s focused attention on individual rights, women had become more aware that their status was in many ways inferior to that of male students, and by the end of the decade they had begun to argue for gender equality. Of all the revolutions that drew nourishment from the egalitarian faith of the 1960s, the gender revolution was the most effective.

An incident related to daycare facilities illustrates one of the ways in which Carleton tried to come to terms with the new perspectives. The first daycare centre on the campus was established in 1969 on a makeshift basis at Renfrew House, with funding from the Students' Council and the administration. The accommodation was inadequate and the university was under pressure to provide more space. Vic Valentine, who was dean of student services in 1971, saw an opportunity to solve two problems by moving the centre to the Loeb Building. The lower lounge in the Loeb was an embarrassment to the university because it had become a hangout for student hippies, who openly smoked marijuana and slept there. The university would have liked to eject them but, given the mood of the era, was sure that this would provoke student protests. Valentine's solution was to make the space available for daycare services. It was not ideal – there was no convenient place to drop the children off in the morning, and the washroom facilities were on the next floor – but it had the advantage that campus activists could hardly protest. "Kids replace freaks in Loeb lounge" was the *Charlatan* headline,[48] and even what it described the next week as the disruption of "a life style ... which provides a basic social function" could not be put ahead of the daycare needs of young mothers.[49]

The story of the Women's Centre touches even more directly on the gender revolution. In 1975 a number of groups on the campus concerned with women's issues applied to the Students' Council for a women's centre. Their statement of aims included a commitment to "women's liberation," though this seems to have been no more than a curtsy to the inflated jargon of the era. The immediate goal was to provide a meeting place and resource centre for people interested in women's issues.[50] Even this seemed provocative to some members of the Students' Council, who objected to a grant on the grounds that a women's centre would discriminate against men. The organizers, however, were disarmingly moderate; they agreed to admit men to the centre and welcomed male support for their feminist concerns.[51]

The Women's Centre, however modest its initial objectives, was soon involved in bitter controversy. It provided counselling on birth control, sponsored lectures and films, and organized a Feminist-Socialist Study Group and a lesbian drop-in centre. Its most highly publicized activity was its response to some of the paintings on the tunnel walls. Tunnel art had always been a special feature of the Carleton campus. A geology class in the early years had painted a representation of the geological formation on which the campus stood. Students in residence had taken over a nearby section of the tunnels, with each floor offering a pictorial representation of its special claim to distinction. University clubs advertised their existence in colourful ways. Tunnel walkers had imaginative panels to distract them instead of the mindless scribbling or graffiti that deface so many blank walls.

By the 1970s, many of these paintings reflected values that were now outmoded, and volunteers from the Women's Centre began a campaign to obliterate what they saw as sexist messages. As the annual report for 1978 commented, this "spray-paint editorializing brought [the centre] great notoriety and even greater vilification."[52] Male chauvinists responded by doing their own spray painting, with crude comments about feminists. The tunnel walls became a battleground in the war for gender equality. Peace was only restored at the end of the decade when Oliver's successor, William Beckel, had all the tunnel walls painted a drab grey, and any new tunnel paintings had to have the approval of a joint committee, which would make sure that the new status of women would be respected.

It would be some time before student behaviour was consistent with this change in the status of women. An incident in Glengarry residence as late as 1987 is a striking example of how outmoded patterns of behaviour could endure. On Halloween of that year three male students, after a few beers, threw three female students into the showers as a lark. The women were not amused and reported the incident to David Sterritt, the director of housing. The young men were astounded when Sterritt levied fines totalling more than six thousand dollars. They appealed to a residence tribunal and then to the RUMP, but they got little sympathy in view of what the board of the RUMP described as "the serious consequences of the appelants' behaviour." The moral was that male students would have to learn that the rules of the game had changed.[53]

This incident is a necessary reminder that social change can be disruptive. For men as well as women adapting to gender equality was a learning process. At Carleton, since nobody challenged the principle of equality directly, the emphasis was on learning to adapt to the new norms. It proved to be more complicated in connection with gays and lesbians. The importance given to individual rights and liberties was reinforced by the claims to gender equality, and some homosexuals were tempted to demand the acceptance of their sexual orientation. But many students still considered that gays and lesbians were social deviants. The constant references to this issue in the pages of the *Charlatan* and on the tunnel walls are striking evidence of the obsessive concern with establishing what sexual orientation was acceptable and how students should behave in a world in which sexual diversity was becoming more widely acknowledged. There was adaptation at Carleton in the 1970s, but it would be a long time before the attitudes of Carleton students could be described as significantly modified.

IV

Carleton University in the 1970s had some continuity with the past. There were still professors who could remember the years at First Avenue and a few who had taught evening classes in the High School of Commerce. Even the names of the buildings around the quadrangle of the new campus were links with an earlier Carleton – the Tory Building, the MacOdrum Library, the Dunton Tower. But the changes were more striking than any continuity. When professors reminisced at Spring Conference or over lunch at the Faculty Club, they were likely to remember how different Carleton had once been.

The differences were obvious. Professors from the college days could remember when they knew the names of their colleagues – and often the names of their wives and children – as well as the names of many of their students. Students who graduated from the college might also be nostalgic about their experience, of the professors who had shown an interest in their lives beyond the classroom and of the student life which they had shared with others who often took the same classes and joined the same clubs. Nostalgia, however, has a selective memory. The professors might also have recalled that the college had had an inadequate library, little equipment, and an uncertain future, and the students might have forgotten that the college they attended had few recreational or academic resources and offered little protection against professors who could be arbitrary or unfair. By the end of the 1960s Carleton University bore little resemblance to the earlier college. It had a wide range of undergraduate and graduate programs, professors with specialized research interests, and students with individual timetables who could select what they wanted or needed from what the university had to offer.

This revolutionary transformation was more than a matter of size. It was also a response to a wider social revolution. The essential social role of the college had been related to the civic virtues of an earlier age; the college was expected to inculcate the values of self-discipline, the respect for authority, and the obligations of citizenship. Society now expected something different. Leaders in business and government had learned that society would reap enormous benefit from a more sophisticated understanding of the material worlds and of life itself. At the postsecondary level this meant that research would overshadow the stewardship of human knowledge and that intellectual curiosity and critical judgment would be the new civic virtues, challenging the more conservative concern for the heritage of the past. Carleton University had not rejected its concern for traditional values, but its recognition of students as responsible adults and the diversity and specialization of its program can be seen as a response to the new values of the postindustrial society. Carleton was transformed because it was reflecting the profound changes occurring in the society it served.

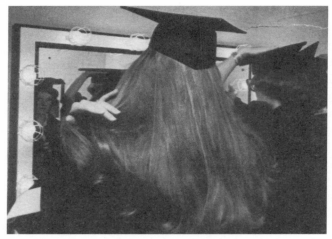

Some things never change. Students at Carleton, whether in the college or university years, faced the ordeal of the final exams before attending the public ceremony which affirmed that they had "successfully completed the requirements" for their degree (*This Weak at Carleton*, 5 May 1977, 10 June 1976).

One thing has not changed. Carleton's major accomplishment, both as a college and as a university, has been to provide the opportunity for thousands of young people to develop intellectually and socially. It is an accomplishment that can never be measured but has been of inestimable benefit to its graduates and to the society into which they graduated. Those who were the creators of Carleton – the administrators, the professors, and the students – could take pride in what they had accomplished.

Appendix

Enrolment at Carleton University, 1942–1982

Year	Undergraduate		Graduate	
	Full time	Part time	Full time	Part time
1942/43	0	660	0	0
1947/48	535	733	0	0
1952/53	442	655	0	0
1957/58	713	812	7	59
1962/63	1851	1371	105	194
1967/68	4677	3185	490	312
1972/73	7532	4998	633	486
1977/78	7797	5751	966	768
1982/83	8499	4536	992	844

Notes

Except where otherwise stated, all archival material is located in Carleton Archives.

CHAPTER ONE

1 This account is based on the article by H.M. Tory, "Phenomenal Beginnings at Carleton College, Ottawa," in *Food for Thought* (a publication of the Canadian Association for Adult Education), Feb. 1943.
2 H.L. Keenleyside in his memoirs makes no reference to this meeting; he merely mentions that Tory was brought into the discussions "somewhat later"; see H.L. Keenleyside, *Memoirs,* vol. 2 (Toronto: McClelland & Stewart, 1982), 135. John Robbins complained about the "myth" that Carleton had its beginning at this chance meeting; see Presidents' files, box 23, "Board of Governors Meetings 1956–57," John E. Robbins to Claude Bissell, 28 Feb. 1957.
3 Ottawa YMCA archives, General Program Development Committee, Minutes, 1 Apr. and 28 June 1938.
4 Keenleyside, *Memoirs,* vol. 1 (Toronto: McClelland & Stewart, 1981), 38. Keenleyside later joined the Unitarian Church.
5 Southam succeeded Tory as chairman of the board in 1947 and became chancellor in 1952. Southam's comment is mentioned in a letter from Edward Sheffield to D.C. McEown, 27 June 1989.
6 In 1939 Arnold Ward, the executive director, was considering a position in Galt; at the time Keenleyside had urged the board to retain his services because he was the "key figure" in the plans for the college (Ottawa YMCA archives, General Program Development Committee, Minutes, 30 Jan. 1939). In

January 1940 Ward left the Ottawa YMCA to assume national responsibilities for the YMCA's war services.

7 For details of Tory's career, see E.A. Corbett, *Henry Marshall Tory: Beloved Canadian* (Toronto: Ryerson, 1954).

8 See Ottawa YMCA archives, College Grade Education Committee, Minutes, 1941–42. The committee met sixteen times between 28 Jan. and 17 June 1942.

9 John A.B. McLeish, *A Canadian for All Seasons: The John E. Robbins Story* (Toronto: Lester & Orpen, 1978), 206.

10 "Notes on the Need for an Undenominational College in Ottawa," attached to College Grade Education Committee, Minutes, 12 Feb. 1942.

11 Ibid. The senior matriculation courses were English, French, Latin, history, algebra, geometry, chemistry, and physics. The second-year courses were English, French, Latin, history, economics, political science, geography, philosophy, mathematics, physics, and accounting.

12 College Grade Education Committee, Minutes, 10 Apr., 13 May 1942.

13 College Grade Education Committee, Minutes, 10 Apr. 1942; Ottawa YMCA archives, Executive Committee, Minutes, 21 Mar. 1942; Board of Directors, Minutes, 2 May 1942. There is a list of donors on page 5 of the first calendar.

14 See College Grade Education Committee, Minutes, 13 May and 4 June 1942 for names and amounts.

15 The proposed articles of association, the constitution, and the bylaws were reviewed and approved by the College Grade Education Committee, 23 May 1942. The letters patent were issued 19 June 1943.

16 Ottawa Association for the Advancement of Learning, Minutes, 18 June 1942.

17 Board of Governors, Minutes, 18 June 1942.

18 A few months later Tory wrote: "After our plans were made it turned out that it would be very difficult to go on unless I took the responsibility for it [the college] as none of the others concerned had any experience in the management of educational institutions ... The result was I found myself launched again in a fairly significant educational activity" (box Pres 83, file HMT personnel correspondence, 1943, H.M. Tory to Abraham Flexner, 3 May 1943).

19 We are grateful to the University of Toronto Archives for access to the Minutes of the Senate Executive and the Senate, including a portion of the Senate Minutes for 13 Nov. 1942, which showed the Senate's opposition but which was superseded by a pasted statement of the Executive Committee's support of Tory's request.

20 See box Pres 83, file HMT personnel correspondence, 1943, H.M. Tory to T.H. Mathews (registrar at McGill), 25 Feb. 1943.

21 Carleton College Committee Meeting, Minutes, 2 June 1942.

22 *Ottawa Citizen*, 28 May 1942. See also College Grade Education Committee, Minutes, 10 Apr., 13 and 28 May 1942.

23 Board of Governors, Minutes, 7 Aug. 1942.

24 Hugh L. Keenleyside, Convocation Address, 18 May 1956.

25 *Ottawa Citizen*, 22 Sept. 1942.

26 Box Pres 83, HMT personnel correspondence, 1943, J.P. Bickell to H.M. Tory, 22 Nov. 1945; H.M. Tory to Rubber Controller, 5 Sept. 1945.

27 Ibid., H.M. Tory to John [Bickell], 22 Mar. 1945; J. P. Bickell to H.M. Tory, 27 Mar. 1945.

28 Board of Governors, Minutes, 15 Sept. 1944.

29 Board of Governors, Minutes, 11 Mar. 1943.

30 The information on the student body is based on the analysis of student questionnaires prepared by John Robbins in 1943 and L.W. Shaw in 1944.

31 Board of Governors, Minutes, 16 Sept. 1943.

32 The first annual yearbook, 1942–43, lists all the courses offered, with the names of the instructors and students. One of the instructors in Japanese was Herbert Norman. Henry Angus, who taught the political science course, did not have a PHD, but he was already a Fellow of the Royal Society of Canada.

33 John E. Robbins, "Analysis of Enrolment in Carleton College 1942–43."

34 See Corbett, *Henry Marshall Tory*, 193, for a summary of Tory's lectures in this course.

35 *Ottawa Citizen*, 22 Sept. 1942.

36 Carleton College Bulletin, 24 Feb. 1943. For an account of the extracurricular activities, see also the yearbooks for 1942–43 and 1944–45.

37 This description of the first faculty meeting is based on Faculty of Carleton College, Minutes, 22 Nov. 1942 and 12 Dec. 1943; and on the recollections of Dana Rouillard in a letter to H. Blair Neatby, 28 Feb. 1982, and of Dorothy Wardle in a letter to H. Blair Neatby, 19 Feb. 1998.

38 Board of Governors, Minutes, 16 Sept. 1943, includes the financial statement. It shows a fee income of about $15,000 and subscriptions of $3,875.

39 Board of Governors, Minutes, 26 June 1945.

40 College Grade Education Committee, Minutes, 23 May 1942. This objective also appears in the letters patent, issued in June 1943.

41 Keenleyside file, "Memorandum on a discussion at the Rideau Club, 9 Feb. 1943."

42 Ottawa YMCA archives, box 41, file 4, "Memorandum on a discussion held at the Rideau Club, 10 March, 1943."

43 Board of Governors, Minutes, 22 Apr. 1943.

44 Board of Governors, Minutes, 23 Oct. 1943.

45 Board of Governors, Minutes, 26 Jan. 1944. For more details on the courses offered, see Institute of Public Administration, calendars for 1944–45 and 1945–46.

46 Board of Governors, Minutes, 26 Jan. 1944.

CHAPTER TWO

1 The last institution of higher learning to be approved by the Ontario legislature was McMaster University in 1887.

2 See Peter Neary and J.L. Granatstein, eds., *The Veterans Charter and Post–World War II Canada* (Montreal: McGill-Queen's University Press, 1998), for details of this program.

3 H.W. Jamieson, Superintendent of Educational Training, Department of Veterans Affairs, to H.M. Tory, recorded in Board of Governors, Minutes, 13 Dec. 1944.

4 Board of Governors, Minutes, 23 Feb. 1945.

5 Board of Governors, Minutes, 21 Sept. 1945.

6 Board of Governors, Minutes, 8 Nov. 1945.

7 Board of Governors, Minutes, 8 Nov. 1945; letter attached.

8 The University of Western Ontario began planning a degree program in journalism in the same year. Carleton can claim that it began its credit courses before Western and that it graduated its first class two years before Western.

9 Kesterton papers, box A198, J.S. Coulter, diary, 22 Oct. 1945.

10 *Ottawa Citizen*, 24 Oct. 1946. Carleton Archives, Special Collections, has a copy of the Convocation Program. The convocation was also reported in the *Ottawa Journal*, 24 Oct. 1946.

11 Board of Governors, Minutes, 8 Nov. 1945.

12 Board of Governors, Minutes, 11 June 1946.

13 E.A. Corbett, *Henry Marshall Tory* (Toronto: Ryerson, 1954), 231.

14 The editorials appeared 17 Feb. 1947.

15 A list of donors was published by each newspaper on 4 Mar. 1947.

16 According to the Treasurer's Report to the Annual Meeting of the Associates, 24 June 1947, 1,527 subscribers had pledged $389,987.84, of which $190,484.77 had been collected. The report of June 1949 showed that $314,017.26 had been received. In the President's Report for 1955–56, the bursar listed the amount as $329,038.25.

17 Ottawa Association for the Advancement of Learning, Report of the President to the Annual Meeting, 22 Sept. 1948.

18 Board of Governors, Minutes, 26 June 1945.

19 Board of Governors Executive Committee, 5 May 1948.

20 Ottawa Association for the Advancement of Learning, Report of President to the Annual Meeting, 22 Sept. 1948.

21 Report of the Library Committee to Faculty, 31 Mar. 1949.

22 Executive Committee of Board of Governors, Minutes, 3 May 1949. The library building had already been discussed at earlier meetings in April 1949.

23 Board of Governors, Minutes, 5 May 1949; Executive Committee, Minutes, 19 May 1949.

24 Ottawa Association for the Advancement of Learning, Report of the Treasurer, 22 Sept. 1948.

25 The documentation for this grant is to be found in Graduate School of Public Administration 1952–53, box "Organization and General files, President's Office," 116.

26 Board of Governors, Minutes, 18 June 1953.

27 In that year the provincial government also made a grant to Hamilton College, the nondenominational science college affiliated with McMaster University.

28 A copy of the campaign flyer is attached to the Faculty Minutes, 5 Dec. 1950.

29 Board of Governors, Minutes, 19 Apr. 1951.

30 President's Report, 1965–66, 47.

31 Faculty Board, Minutes, 6 Mar. 1951.

32 Faculty Board, Minutes, 4 Sept. 1951.

33 Board of Governors, Minutes, 15 May 1952.

34 Board of Governors, Minutes, 19 Apr. 1951.

35 Ottawa Association for the Advancement of Learning, Report of the President, 28 Sept. 1950.

36 This situation is outlined in a letter from Dana Porter, Minister of Education, to M.M. MacOdrum, 24 July 1950; see box BOG 21, file "Correspondence: Transferring Students and Carleton as a Member of the National Conference of Canadian University."

37 Ibid., T.H. Mathews, Secretary of NCCU, to M.M. MacOdrum, 28 May 1950.

38 Ibid., W.J. Dunlop, Minister of Education, "To Whom It May Concern," 4 Nov. 1952.

39 At one stage the Board of Governors had considered a complicated system of election to the new board by the associates and the alumni. Dr Althouse, the deputy minister of education, saw this as overly complicated. Apparently, at the last minute it was decided to leave the board as it was, with the possibility of modifying the procedure for selecting future members by a bylaw.

40 The first associate professors appointed were M.S. Macphail and John Morton; the first members from the community were Kaye Lamb, R.A. Mackay and F.J. Alcock.

41 See, for example, the correspondence between A.E. MacRae and H.S. Southam on this issue (Board of Governors, Minutes, file "Correspondence: MacRea-Southam"). The charter was passed as Private Bill no. 18, 1st Session, 24th Legislature, Ontario, 1952: "An Act Respecting the Ottawa Association for the Advancement of Learning."

CHAPTER THREE

1 National Archives of Canada (NA), Porter Papers, J. Porter to J.A. Gibson, 30 Aug. 1954.

2 Based on interview with Paul Fox, Feb. 1982.

3 Carleton College Academic Staff Association, Executive Committee, Minutes, 24 May 1955.

4 I am indebted to Richard Helmes-Hayes, who allowed me to consult his unpublished manuscript, "John Porter and Canadian Sociology," for the preparation of these paragraphs on Porter's early years at Carleton.

5 Faculty handbook, 1948.

6 Personal correspondence, D.M.L. Farr to H.B. Neatby, 10 Nov. 1999.

7 Interview with H.H.J. Nesbitt, 5 Nov. 1990.

8 Interview with Hilda Gifford, 7 Dec. 1990.

9 The founding members were Munro Beattie, Muni Frumhartz, Pauline Jewett, John Porter, Norman Fenn, and R.A. "Rusty" Wendt.

10 President's Report, 1958–59, 17.

11 Carleton College calendar, 1952.

12 For the experience of another woman, see Michael Hayden, ed., *So Much to Do, So Little Time: The Writings of Hilda Neatby* (Vancouver: University of British Columbia Press, 1983).

13 Interview with H.H.J. Nesbitt, 5 Nov. 1990.

14 Sheffield left Carleton in 1954 and later played an important role as an analyst of higher education. His 1955 forecast was the first to predict spiralling enrolments based on demography and participation rates.

15 Faculty Board, Minutes, 7 Feb. 1949; the report of the committee is an attachment to these minutes.

16 Faculty Board, Minutes, 21 Mar. 1950; the second report of the committee is an attachment to these minutes.

17 Faculty Board, Minutes, 8 Jan. 1952.

18 Faculty Board, Minutes, 21 Mar. 1950.

19 Report to Faculty Board by chairman of Public Administration Committee, 10 Mar. 1949.

20 Faculty Board, Minutes, 31 Mar. 1949.

21 Report to Faculty Board by the Committee on Commerce Studies, 6 Feb. 1951.

22 Faculty Board, Minutes, 1 Nov. 1949.

23 Faculty Board, Minutes, 4 Apr. 1950.

24 Faculty Board, Minutes, 13 July 1950.

25 Personal correspondence, Douglas Hartle to H.B. Neatby, 12 Oct. 1990.

26 Faculty Board, Minutes, 9 and 16 Dec. 1948.

27 Faculty Board, Minutes, 6 Sept. 1949.

28 K. Buckley, "The Declining Status of the University in the Canadian community", *CAUT Bulletin* (mimeo), 1 Dec. 1954.

29 Based on the Carleton University Academic Staff Association files; "CAUT Council Meetings."

30 Faculty Board, Minutes, 6 Mar. 1951; Carleton College Academic Staff Association, (CCASA), Minutes, 8 Apr. 1954.

31 CCASA, Minutes, 6 Apr. 1953.

32 CCASA, Minutes, 30 Mar. 1954.

33 Board of Governors, Minutes, 1 May 1946.

34 Board of Governors, Minutes, 29 Jan. 1948, 20 Sept. 1951; Report to Faculty Board by Committee on Symbols and Ceremonial, 10 Jan. 1950; Faculty Board, Minutes, 7 Feb. 1950. The crest was described in heraldic terms as "On a field

sable; in radiants d'argent, a maple leaf gules charged with an open book; crest – a phoenix propre."

35 Interview with Paul Fox, 12 Feb. 1982.

CHAPTER FOUR

1 "Carleton through the Years: Carleton University History Project, 1990," a re-search report of a journalism seminar under the direction of Professor Alan Frizzell (hereafter cited as "Carleton through the Years").

2 *Carleton*, 4 Mar. 1949.

3 See 88/58. Historical Collection. Administration. Athletics. Publications: "The Ravens, the Cardinals and the Robins," Carleton College Reports, Apr. 1953.

4 The Bytown Inn at the corner of Albert and O'Connor was the most popular off-campus meeting place in the First Avenue years; a survey in 1990 showed that well over half the men who attended Carleton in those years identified the Bytown as their favourite drinking place. See "Carleton through the Years." 30.

5 This paragraph and those that follow are based on T.J. Scanlon, "History of Football at Carleton," 1 Oct. 1966, based on research by a Journalism 220 class; see 86/7, box 4.

6 Arnie Morrison to President MacOdrum, quoted in T.J. Scanlon, "History of Football at Carleton".

7 *Carleton*, 18 Mar. 1949.

8 *Ottawa Journal*, 19 Mar. 1949.

9 *Ottawa Journal*, 21 Mar. 1945.

10 Ibid.

11 *Carleton*, 22 Mar. 1945; interview with Frank McGee, 18 June 1990.

12 *Ottawa Journal*, 22 Mar. 1945.

13 Ibid. Frank McGee, in a telephone interview, 18 June 1990, suggested that the probable explanation for the change in editorial viewpoint is that the Saturday editorial was written by E. Norman Smith while the editor, Grattan O'Leary, was away, and that the subsequent editorials were written by O'Leary.

14 *Carleton*, Apr. 1949 (no day of the month specified).

15 *Carleton*, 28 Feb. 1957. See also 1 Feb. 1951 and 25 Feb. 1954.

16 *Carleton*, 20 Feb. 1948.

17 *Carleton*, 28 Sept. 1956.

18 *Carleton*, 10 Oct. 1955.

19 *Carleton*, 4 Oct. 1956.

20 Daryl Sharp, *Students' Handbook and Directory 1955–56*, 6.

21 Colin Macdonald, *Students' Handbook and Directory 1953–54*, 6.

22 The league operated separately because Queen's, Toronto, Western, and McGill refused to admit other Ontario universities.

23 *Carleton*, 14 Nov. 1955.

24 *Carleton*, 13 Jan. 1957.

25 *Carleton*, 20 Jan. 1955.

26 *Carleton*, 14 Nov. 1955.

27 *Carleton*, 9 Nov. 1954.

28 *Carleton*, 14 Oct. 1956.

29 See, for example, the *Carleton*, 17 Oct. 1958.

30 *Carleton*, 2 Dec. 1958.

31 At McMaster, for example, women only gained the right to be elected to the Students' Council in the 1950s, but even at the end of the decade female council members opposed the idea of a woman running for president (C.M. Johnston and J.C. Weaver, *Students Days* (Hamilton: McMaster University Alumni Assopciation, 1986), 90.

32 This information comes from "Carleton through the Years."

33 *Carleton*, 10 Oct. 1955.

34 "Carleton through the Years."

CHAPTER FIVE

1 Ottawa Association for the Advancement of Learning, Sixth Annual Meeting, Treasurer's Report, 24 June 1947.

2 Board of Governors, Minutes, 15 Apr. 1948; attached memorandum, M.M. MacOdrum to the Governors of the College, 8 Apr. 1948.

3 Ottawa Association for the Advancement of Learning, Seventh Annual Meeting, Treasurer's Report, 22 Sept. 1948.

4 *Ottawa Journal*, June 1953.

5 Board of Governors, Executive Committee, Minutes, 12 Sept. and 28 Nov. 1951. Even this was considerably less than the estimated value when the thirty-nine acres were donated to Carleton.

6 The admiring phrase comes from Claude Bissell in his President's Report, 1957-58, 14.

7 Board of Governors, Minutes, 15 Jan. 1953.

8 Memorandum of J. Coyne to board members, 14 Jan. 1953, attached to Board of Governors, Minutes, 15 Jan. 1953.

9 Board of Governors, Minutes, 15 Jan. 1953.

10 James Coyne, Memorandum, 14 Jan. 1953, attached to Board of Governors, Minutes, 15 Jan. 1953.

11 See John H. Taylor, *Ottawa: An Illustrated History* (Toronto: Lorimer, 1986), 204-6.

12 Presidents' files, Charles Cowan to M.A. MacOdrum, 22 June 1953. Southam's newspaper, the *Citizen*, had been critical of Whitton's opposition to developers.

13 Board of Governors, Minutes, 25 Nov. 1953.

14 City of Ottawa, Council Minutes, 21 Sept. 1959.

15 NA MG30, B122, 4/3/134, C.J. Mackenzie Papers, Mackenzie to Thayer Linds-
    ley, 15 June 1955.

16 Ottawa Association for the Advancement of Learning, Fourteenth Annual Meet-
    ing, Report of the Acting President, 29 Sept. 1955.

17 Board of Governors, Minutes, 15 Jan. 1959.

18 NA, MG30, B122, 4/3/134, C.J. Mackenzie Papers, Mackenzie to Thayer Linds-
    ley, 15 June 1955.

19 NA, MG30, B122, 4/3/182, Mackenzie to A.E. Kerr, 25 Aug. 1955.

20 Ibid., Mackenzie to F.H. Underhill, 8 Sept. 1955.

21 Among those who commented favourably on Bissell were W.A. Macintosh and
    J.A. Corry of Queen's, G.E. Hall of Western, and F.H. Underhill in Ottawa.
    See NA, MG30, B122, 4/4/9, 17 Jan. 1956.

22 Claude Bissell, *Halfway up Parnassus*, (Toronto: University of Toronto Press,
    1974), 17–23.

23 Claude Bissell, typescript of speech given at Carleton, 1 Nov. 1990.

24 Donald C. Rowat, "Comparison of Governing Bodies of Canadian Universi-
    ties," *CAUT Bulletin*, 1955.

25 D.C. Rowat, Personal files, "Committee on Committees," notes on committee
    structures, Sept. 1955.

26 Ibid., "Committee on Committees," Second Report to Faculty Board, 15 Dec.
    1955.

27 Interview with H.H.J. Nesbitt, 5 Nov. 1990, corroborated by interviews with
    Donald Rowat and G.R. Love.

28 Bissell's account of the campaign can be found in *Halfway up Parnassus*, 34–5.

29 Interview with Claude Bissell, 1 Nov. 1990.

30 Claude Bissell, "A Role for Carleton," Installation Address, 13 Nov. 1956.

31 President's Report, 1956–57, 10.

32 Claude Bissell, typescript of speech given at Carleton, 1 Nov. 1990.

33 Senate, Minutes, 23 Apr. 1957; R.L. McDougall, *Totems*, (Ottawa: Tecumseh
    Press, 1990).

34 Presidents' files, "Dow's Lake Development 1953–56," J. Coyne and M. Mac-
    Odrum to chairman and members of Federal District Commission, 9 Nov. 1953.

35 F.J. Turner files, "Rideau River Campus: Miscellaneous," Basis for Planning
    Carleton College Site, 2 June 1954.

36 Presidents' files, box 107, "Building Program 1958–59," C. Hotson to
    A.D. Dunton, 21 August 1958.

37 The associates were Hart Massey, Eric Arthur, Campbell Merritt, and John Bland.

38 *Ottawa Citizen*, 8 Mar. 1956.

39 *The Compass: A Handbook for Students*, 1960–61.

40 *Ottawa Citizen*, 8 Mar. 1956.

41 This façade was later replaced by sheathing, which may have provided better in-
    sulation but was much less attractive.

42 Library Building file, box 21, includes correspondence with a library consultant and the minutes of the planning meeting in January 1956.

43 Board of Governors, Executive Committee, Minutes, 31 July 1957.

44 Presidents' files, "Bissell Vacation Correspondence," Alexandra Irwin to C.T. Bissell, 25 July 1957.

45 Board of Governors, Executive Committee, Minutes, 31 July 1957.

46 Board of Governors, Minutes, 19 Sept. 1957.

47 Board of Governors, Building Committee, Minutes, 7 Jan. 1958. The form of construction would be "lift slab."

48 Presidents' file 1.3, "Provincial Grant 1958–59," A.D. Dunton to W.J. Dunlop, 27 Nov. 1958.

49 President's Report, 1958–59, 5.

50 Bissell, *Halfway up Parnassus*, 36.

51 Ibid., 38.

52 The President's Message, *Raven 57*, 1957.

53 Claude Bissell in *Raven 58*, 1958.

54 *Raven 59*, 1959.

PART TWO

1 See Daniel Bell, *The Coming of Post-Industrial Society* (New York: Basic Books), 1973.

CHAPTER SIX

1 For studies of the changing role of government in these years, see Paul Axelrod, *Scholars and Dollars: Politics, Economics, and the Universities of Ontario* (Toronto: University of Toronto Press, 1982), and David M. Cameron, *"More than an Academic Question": Universities, Governments and Public Policy in Canada* (Ottawa: Institute of Research on Public Policy, 1991).

2 See Axelrod, *Scholars and Dollars*, 80, for Leslie Frost's comments in his 1944 budget speech.

3 Estimates were prepared by Dr R.W.B. Jackson, head of research for the Ontario College of Education. Undergraduate enrolment in Ontario in 1961–62 was 31,800. The Report of the Presidents of the Universities of Ontario to the Advisory Committee on University Affairs, *Post-Secondary Education in Ontario, 1962–1970* (Toronto, May 1962), includes two estimates made by Jackson, of 94,200 and 112,400 respectively, for 1971–72.

4 Provincial Archives of Ontario (PAO), RG32, MCU143, box 42, Advisory Committee on University Affairs (ACUA), Minutes. Frost's reference to the "sugar daddy" is from the minutes of 18 Dec. 1962.

5 Report of the Presidents, *Post-Secondary Education in Ontario 1962–1970*, 4. Enrolment at the existing universities would increase from 26,000 to 74,000.

6 Ibid., 21.

7 PAO, RG32, MCU143, box 42, ACUA, Minutes, 20 Jan. 1963.

8 William G. Davis, "The Government of Ontario and the Universities of the Province," in *Governments and the University* (Toronto: Macmillan, 1966), 34.

9 Ibid., 46.

10 Committee of the Presidents of the Universities of Ontario, *Collective Autonomy: Second Annual Review, 1967–68*, appendix D (Toronto, 1968), 62; Corry's opening address to the General Meeting of Discipline Groups, 11 May 1968.

11 *Report of Commission to Study the Development of Graduate Programmes in Ontario Universities*, submitted to the Committee on University Affairs and the Committee of Presidents of Provincially Assisted Universities (Toronto, 1966), 27.

12 Board of Governors, Minutes, 18 Dec. 1957.

13 Ibid., 28 Jan.1958.

14 Gibson was informed at the time by Frank Underhill that the Search Committee would not give him the appointment (interview with James Gibson, 1 Feb. 1990).

15 Presidents' files, 1963–64, 5.6, "First-Year Advisees"; ibid., A.D. Dunton to Norman Fenn, 6 Sept. 1963.

16 See, for example, Presidents' files, 1964–65, 1.2, "Budget."

17 Joint Committee on the Duff-Berdahl Report, Minutes of the fourth meeting, 7 June 1966.

18 H.H.J. Nesbitt, *The Week That Was*, 29 June 1972.

19 See Gordon Robertson's tribute in the memorial for A. Davidson Dunton, Feb. 1987.

20 A.D. Dunton, "Inaugural Address," 7 Nov. 1958; Presidents' files, "Knowledge and Freedom," box PINFO 47.

21 A.D. Dunton, "Convocation Address," 1972, box PINFO 24.

22 A.D., Dunton, "The Smaller University," National Council of Colleges and Universities of Canada *Proceedings*, 1967.

23 A.D. Dunton, "Inaugural Address," 7 Nov. 1958.

24 Interview with Claude Bissell, Jan. 1991.

25 Archives of the Council of Ontario Universities, Minutes of Meeting of Presidents and Business Officers, 3 July 1962.

26 Senate, Minutes, 8 Dec. 1961, 8 Feb. 1962.

27 Senate, Minutes, 28 May 1962. The Senate's proposal of February would have meant a maximum enrolment of 5,800 by 1970–71.

28 Board of Governors, Minutes, 4 June 1962.

29 PAO, MU5346, Gathercole Papers, Data Book, 1963–64, Carleton University.

30 PAO, RG32, MCU143, box 42, ACUA, Minutes, 7 Dec. 1964.

31 Committee of Presidents, *Collective Autonomy*, 33. The three "emergent universities" were Brock, Laurentian, and Trent.

32 PAO, RG32, MCU143, box 42, Committee on University Affairs, Minutes, 8 Jan. 1963.

33 Ibid, Minutes, 10 Jan. 1963.

34 For details, see chapter 7.

35 For details on this acquisition, see chapter 7.

CHAPTER SEVEN

1 See chapter 5, p. 95.

2 Senate, Minutes, 19 Nov. 1960. See also Senate, Minutes, 23 Jan. 1962 and 7 Apr. 1964.

3 President's Report, 1960–61, 9.

4 General files, 1962–63, 2.A.1, James Gibson to Committee on Enrolment, 12 Nov. 1962.

5 Interview with Hilda Gifford, 7 Dec. 1990.

6 General files, 1964–65, 1.1.2 Building Committee, Memorandum, GRL(ove).

7 President's Report, 10–11.

8 The figures on fees and grants come from the "Report of the Bursar," which is included in each annual President's Report.

9 President's Report, 1961–62, 11.

10 Ibid., 10.

11 Interview with Jill Vickers, Dec. 1992.

12 *Ottawa Journal*, 16 Feb. 1963.

13 Report of the Senate Committee on Enrolment, 31 Dec. 1962, 1.

14 Ibid., 12.

15 Ibid., 4.

16 Board of Governors, Minutes, 3 May 1963 and 19 Mar. 1964; interview with David Golden, 17 Apr. 1990.

17 In February 1959 John Porter had circulated a proposal for distinctive programs in the humanities, social sciences, and natural sciences; see Frumhartz files, "Division II: Other."

18 H.S. Gordon, chairman pro-tem Building Subcommittee, "Size and Composition of New Arts Building," 7 May 1964, box 14, "Loeb Building 1964–67".

19 Building Advisory Committee, Minutes, 15 Dec. 1965.

20 Ibid., 21 Apr. 1966.

21 *Carleton*, 21 Feb. and 6 Mar. 1964.

22 Board of Governors, Minutes, 7 Apr. 1966.

23 Board of Governors, Minutes, 28 Jan. 1965.

24 L.H. Horton, "Planning for the University Union," 9 Dec. 1965.

25 University Union Planning Commitee, Brief to Z.M. Stankiewicz, Apr. 1967.

26 Z.M. Stankiewicz, *Charlatan*, 1 Feb.1979.

27 L.H. Horton, in "Planning for the University Union," 9 Dec. 1965, expresses his satisfaction that "Rusty" Wendt is in favour of a liquor licence for the union.

28 Board of Governors, box 23, University Centre files, D.C. McEown to
   A.B. Larose, 14 May 1970, outlines the terms of the agreement.
29 The best summary of the history of St Patrick's College is H.A. MacDougall,
   "St. Patrick's College 1929–1979: Ethnicity and Liberal Arts in Catholic Education," in Canadian Catholic Historical Association, *Study Sessions* 49 (1982):
   53–71.
30 Provincial Archives of Ontario (PAO), RG32, MCU143, box 43, CUA, Minutes,
   3 May 1965.
31 Discussions with the provincial Committee on University Affairs in June show
   that the University of Ottawa was also more interested in the School of Social
   Welfare than in the undergraduate college. See PAO, RG32, MCU143, box 45,
   Minutes, 22 June 1967.
32 Board of Governors, Minutes, 14 and 19 June 1967.
33 "Agreement between Carleton University and English Oblates of Eastern Canada," 12 July 1967. For the regulations on philosophy courses, see General files,
   1967–68, Academic, St Patrick's Division, D.M.L. Farr to A.D. Dunton et al.,
   26 July 1967.
34 From files of School of Social Work, press release, 8 July 1967.
35 Senate, Minutes, Report of Dean Sida, 12 Apr. 1972.
36 Senate, Minutes, 12 Apr. 1972.
37 General files, 1969–70, School of Social Work, "Self-Study Report," 1969.
38 General files, 1967–68, Academic Graduate Studies, School of Social Work, Faculty Commitee, "Objectives of the School of Social Work of Carleton University
   and Their Planning Implications," 22 Nov. 1967. See also A.D. Dunton to
   Swithun Bowers, 22 Nov. 1967, in which the two new positions are authorized.
39 Board of Governors, Minutes, 27 May 1965.
40 *Carleton*, 14 Feb. 1964.
41 Senate, Minutes, 13 Mar. 1969, appendix B, Report of Building Advisory
   Committee.
42 See Council of Ontario Universities, *Annual Review* (Toronto, 1968–69 to
   1971–72), for reactions to the capital grants formula. A series of studies, entitled
   "Building Blocks," was prepared by task forces for the council. For the impact
   on Carleton, see Building Advisory Committee, Minutes, 6 Mar. 1969 and
   15 Jan. 1970.
43 Report of Senate's New Campus Committee, 31 Jan. 1967.
44 Senate, Minutes, May 1967, appendix, "A Possible Campus Plan for Carleton
   University," Oct. 1966.
45 D.C. McEown was told this story by the students when they came to pay their
   fines.
46 This incident was reported to D.C. McEown by the security chief.
47 Presidents' files, 1968, box 1, Murray and Murray, "Art Campus Extension,"
   1968.

CHAPTER EIGHT

1 Board of Governors, Minutes, 9 Dec. 1965.

2 The Carleton University Academic Staff Association (CUASA) Review Committee, 16 Apr. 1962, saw the need for more formal promotion procedures but approved of the president's consultation with "a representative group of senior members of the faculty."

3 Board of Governors, Minutes, 18 Apr. 1963.

4 Senate, Minutes, 26 Feb. 1964.

5 Robert L. McDougall, *Totems* (Ottawa: Tecumseh Press, 1990), 144.

6 Donald C. Rowat, "Comparison of Governing Bodies of Canadian Universities," *CAUT Bulletin*, 1955; "Faculty Participation in Canadian University Government," *Bulletin of the American Association of University Professors*, Autumn 1957.

7 Joint Committee on Duff-Berdahl Report, Minutes, 24 May 1966, located in Board of Governors, Minutes, "Duff-Berdahl Report, Committee on," 66–7.

8 NA, MG28, I208, vol. 20, CAUT files, "A Statement by the Committee on University Government Presented to the Executive Council of the CAUT as a basis for discussion," 12 June 1960. The interest in university government can be traced back to the dismissal of Professor Harry Crowe by the Board of Regents of United College for his private criticism of the principal. Stewart Reid, who had resigned from United College in protest, had become the executive director of CAUT.

9 CUASA, Minutes, 16 Apr. 1962.

10 *Carleton*, 10 Jan. 1964.

11 NA, MG28, I208, vol. 55, CAUT files, "University Government – Documents, Carleton, 1963." The brief describes the situation at Carleton; vol. 140, "University Government – Carleton," outlines the proposals to be discussed during the commission hearings at Carleton.

12 *Carleton*, 18 Feb. 1966.

13 The results of the questionnaire, administered by the CUASA, are attached to Senate Executive Committee, Minutes, 3 Nov. 1967, appendix F.

14 Senate Commission on Undergraduate Teaching and Learning, Preliminary Report, Mar. 1969, 25–7.

15 See Allan Bloom, *The Closing of the American Mind* (New York: Simon & Schuster, 1987), for a forceful presentation of these views. For an ironic commentary on the decision at Carleton, see Senate, Minutes, 20 Mar. 1969, appendix D, J.C.S. Wernham, "Sock It to 'Em or Scuttle S.C.U.T.L.," and Presidents' files 1968–69, "Frumhartz Commission," J.C.S. Wernham to A.D. Dunton, 7 Apr. 1969.

16 Presidents' files, 1970–71, "Frumhartz Commission," M. Frumhartz to G. Couse, 19 May 1971.

17 M.S. Macphail, Director of School of Graduate Studies, in President's Report 1960–61, 25.

18 This text was submitted by Dr Ivan Fellegi, Oct. 1993, when he was selected as one of Carleton's eminent graduates.

19 Robin Mathews and James Steele, eds., *The Struggle for Canadian Universities* (Toronto: New Press, 1969).

20 Ibid. This collection of documents relating to the controversy includes the motions and the minutes of the CUASA meeting. The vote was 135 to 5 against the motions.

21 *This Week Times Two*, 1 June 1972.

22 Mathews's campaign had some effect. The federal government eventually required Canadian universities to give consideration to Canadian citizens for academic appointments before considering foreign candidates. The controversy subsided with the slow rate of university growth in the 1970s.

23 Presidents' files, 1969–70; general files, CUASA, R. Glover to A.D. Dunton, 31 July 1969.

24 Ibid., 16 Apr. 1970.

25 CUASA Newsletter, Dec. 1970, Feb. 1971.

26 Presidents' files, 1971–72; general files, CUASA, A.D. Dunton to T.R. Robinson, 14 Jan. 1972.

27 CUASA newsletter, Mar. 1972.

28 CUASA files, Minutes, 1960–63, Report of Standing Committee on Academic Freedom and Tenure, 4 Feb. 1960.

29 Board of Governors, Minutes, 2 Feb. and 13 Apr. 1961. The document entitled "Carleton University Proposed Regulations Concerning Tenure and Dismissal" is appended to the minutes of 27 Oct. 1960.

30 Board of Governors, Minutes, 17 Dec. 1964.

31 Senate, Minutes, 8 and 11 Apr. 1969; Scanlon's letter to the president is included in appendix 1, T.J. Scanlon to A.D. Dunton, 19 Feb. 1969.

32 P.J. King, personal files, include the minutes of the committee and the chairman's notes.

33 Senate, Minutes, 24 Sept. 1971, appendix C, "Report of Committee on Tenure and Dismissal."

34 P.J. King files, James C.S. Wernham to A.D. Dunton, 2 June 1971. In a joint interview, 4 Oct. 1989, Professors Wernham and King were not sure who objected to shifting the responsibility to an academic committee but thought it might have been the representative from the Board of Governors.

35 *This Week Times Two*, 28 Sept. 1971.

36 P.J. King files, "Tenure Committee," contains all the replies from the faculty; the most detailed came from D.C. Rowat. The CUASA position was outlined in a submission from N.E.S. Griffiths, Chair, CUASA Executive Committee on Tenure and Dismissal, to Senate (filed with Senate, Minutes, 21 Oct. 1971).

37 Senate, Minutes, 9 and 22 Nov. and 10 Dec. 1971, 25 Jan. and 9 March 1972.

38 Senate, Minutes, 9 Mar. 1972.

39 Board of Governors, Minutes, 27 June 1972.

CHAPTER NINE

1 NA, RG32, MCU42, box 1, "Addresses and Remarks by Claude Bissell, 1963–66," 10 Nov. 1965.
2 *Carleton*, 14 Oct. 1960.
3 *Carleton*, 7 Dec. 1962, 6 Mar. 1964.
4 *Carleton*, 18 Jan. 1963.
5 *Carleton*, 3 Nov. 1961, prints the Students' Association outline of the honour system and honour code; this quotation is from article 6.
6 *Carleton*, 30 Nov. 1962.
7 *Carleton*, 9 Mar. 1962; President's files 5.1, "Students' Council 1961–62," A.D. Dunton to Norman Jamieson, 2 Feb. 1962.
8 *Carleton*, 14 and 21 Nov. 1961, 23 Oct, 1962.
9 *Carleton*, 18 Oct. and 22 Nov. 1963.
10 President's Report, 1963–63, 51.
11 *Carleton*, 6 Nov. 1959, 25 Nov. 1960, 19 Jan. 1962.
12 *Carleton*, 26 Jan. 1962.
13 *Carleton*, 8 Nov. 1963.
14 *Carleton*, 1 and 29 Oct. 1965, 21 Oct. 1966.
15 See above, chapter 8.
16 *Carleton*, 18 Feb 1966.
17 Joint Committee on University Governance, Minutes, 9 May 1966.
18 "Statement in Support of Student Representation on the Board of Governors" is attached as an appendix to the final report of the Joint Committee, 18 Apr. 1967.
19 *Carleton*, 12 Feb. 1967.
20 *Carleton*, 22 Sept. 1966.
21 *Carleton*, 3 Nov. 1967.
22 Board of Governors, Committee on University Government, Minutes, 10 Jan. 1968.
23 Jack Quarter, *The Student Movement of the Sixties* (Toronto: OISE, 1972). The incidents at Sir George Williams cover the period from Dec. 1968 to Feb. 1969.
24 *Carleton*, 8 Nov. 1968.
25 Presidents' files, "New University Government: Senate VI," David Wolfe, "Open Letter to Senate," 20 Mar. 1970.
26 Senate, Minutes, 12 Oct. 1972; Board of Governors, Minutes, 28 Feb. 1973.
27 *Carleton*, 8 Mar. 1963.
28 *Carleton*, 1 Feb. 1963.
29 *Carleton*, 25 Oct. 1968.
30 *Carleton*, 7 Nov. 1969, Supplement. Professor Joe Scanlon, in an interview on 26 Aug, 1980, remembers suggesting in the Senate Executive that this was an academic issue and so should have Senate approval. Dunton, according to Scanlon, preferred to avoid any discussion.

31 *Carleton*, 12 Oct. 1962.

32 For a perceptive study of the changes, see Arthur Marwick, *The Sixties: Cultural Revolution in Britain, France, Italy and the United States, c. 1958–1974* (Oxford: Oxford University Press, 1998).

33 Warren Gerrard, "The New Student Grab for University Power," *Globe Magazine*, 23 Sept. 1967.

34 *Carleton*, 16 Feb. 1968.

35 *Carleton*, 26 Jan. and 29 Nov. 1968.

36 *Carleton*, 10 Oct. 1969.

37 The headline for a front-page edtorial in the *Carleton*, 20 Oct. 1967, was "You Really Blew It."

38 The Reverend G. Paul, the Carleton chaplain, sparked the debate by defending premarital sex in the *Carleton*, 25 Sept. 1964. For birth control, see the *Carleton* 20 Jan. 1967.

39 Minutes, Board of Governors, 25 Sept. 1968.

40 "Report of the Bursar" in the President's Report, 1968–69, 96–7.

41 *Carleton*, 8 Mar. 1963. See also editorial, 1 Mar. 1963.

42 Fenn returned in 1966 as director of counselling and health services and in 1973 became dean of student services. This title, however, contrasts with his earlier title as director of student affairs.

EPILOGUE

1 Ontario Legislative Assembly, *Debates*, 25 Nov. 1969; quoted in Axelrod, *Scholars and Dollars* (Toronto: University of Toronto Press, 1982), 142.

2 Council of Ontario Universities, *Sixth Annual Review 1971–72: Stimulus and Response* (Toronto, 1972), 8.

3 Commission on Post-Secondary Education in Ontario, *The Learning Society* (Toronto, 1972).

4 Council of Ontario Universities, *Sixth Annual Review, 1971–72*, 4.

5 Council of Ontario Universities, *Review 1978–79 to 1981–82: Squeezing the Triangle* (Toronto, 1982), 5.

6 This was the title of the annual report of the Advisory Committee on University Affairs for 1975.

7 Presidents' files, 1973–74: "COU, AUCC and Ministry," A.B. Larose to Michael Oliver, 11 July 1973; D.J. Brown to Michael Oliver, 25 Oct. 1973; R.J. Neill (chairman of the Board of Governors) to the Hon. J. McNie (minister of colleges and universities), 26 Nov. 1973. York University was younger than Carleton yet received no "emerging university" grant, but it could be argued that York received more generous treatment from the government in its early years.

8 Presidents' files, "COU, MCU APC, General"; OCUA file, Michael Oliver to Stefan Dupré, chairman, ACUA, 14 Jan. 1975.

9 EC/140/2 "Financing Carleton University in 1975–76: A Preliminary Examination," 24 June 1974.

10 In 1978 an unexpected number of students accepted the offer and more money had to be found; see Presidents' files 1978–79: general files, Dean of Graduate Studies and Research, Gilles Paquet to Michael Oliver, 10 Nov. 1978.

11 Report to the University 1975–76, 30.

12 See chapter 7, section III.

13 St Patrick's College Planning Committee, Report to the Faculty Board, 4 Apr. 1973.

14 Senate Advisory Committee on St Patrick's College, Minutes, 4 Feb. 1974.

15 Senate Advisory Committee on St Patrick's College, Final Report, is included with the Senate, Minutes, 8 Apr. 1975 as appendix A. For the discussion at the college, see Faculty Board, Minutes, 12 Feb. 1975. A poll of the Faculty Board members showed 19 in faviour and 4 opposed.

16 St Patrick's College Council, Minutes, 2 Mar. 1978; Senate, Minutes, 12 Jan. 1979.

17 Report of Committee on Carleton University to 1982, September 1978, 84.

18 See chapter 3, 49.

19 Ottawa Citizen, 9 Apr. 1975.

20 Naomi Griffiths discussed these events with H. Blair Neatby at the time and confirmed them in an interview, 4 Feb. 2002.

21 John Porter and Claude Bissell, Towards 2000: The Future of Post-Secondary Education in Ontario (Toronto: McClelland & Stewart, 1971), 30.

22 Carol S. Shulman, "Old Expectations, New Realities: The Academic Profession Revisited," in Current Issues in Higher Education (Washington: American Association for Higher Education, 1979), 45–6.

23 For a broader perspective on academic attitudes towards collective bargaining in Canada at this time, see B.L Adell and D.D. Carter, Collective Bargaining for University Faculty in Canada, (Kingston: Industrial Relations Centre, Queen's University, 1972).

24 The Report of the Senate Committee on Redundancy, 17 May 1972, is attached to the Senate Minutes of 10 Oct. 1972. The debate on the report is recorded in the Senate Minutes, 19 Apr. and 8 and 9 May 1973. The appeal committee would be jointly appointed by the president of the university and the president of the faculty association.

25 CUASA News, Dec. 1974.

26 Senate, Minutes, Dec. 1974.

27 The vote was 114 to 1. The details of the negotiations can be found in Debra Mair, "Unionization and the Middle Class: The Case of University Faculty", MA thesis, Carleton University, 1977.

28 Board of Governors, Minutes, 17 Jan. 1975.

29 This Week Times Two, 3 Feb. 1975.

30 See L.C. Payton, "The Status of Women in the Ontario Universities," a study prepared for the Council of Ontario Universities, June 1975.

31 Ross Eaman, "Recommendations Pertaining to the Status of Women at Carleton Univeresity," submitted to the Board of Governors, Nov. 1979; Board of Governors, box 185, "Policy – Sexual Harrasmrent 1979–95."

32 Interview with Naomi Griffiths, 4 Feb. 2002.

33 *Charlatan*, 19 Mar. 1981.

34 *Carleton*, 19 Apr. 1971.

35 See Douglas Owram, *Born at the Right Time: A History of the Baby Boom Generation* (Toronto: University of Toronto Press, 1996).

36 *Carleton*, 12 and 19 Feb. 1971.

37 *Charlatan*, 5 Oct. 1973.

38 Senate Executive Committee, Minutes, 11 Oct. 1973.

39 Senate, Minutes, 17 Oct. 1973.

40 *Charlatan*, 18 Jan. 1974.

41 Senate, Minutes, 13 Jan. 1975, appendix B: Report of Committee to Examine the Senate Judicial Committee.

42 For the debate over the proposals, see Senate, Minutes, 28 May 1975, appendix B. For student proposals, see Senate, Minutes, 30 Sept. 1975, Appendix H, and Senate, Minutes, 2 Mar. 1976.

43 Senate, Minutes, 13 Jan. 1975, quoted in appendix C in a memorandum from R. Brown, Director of Student Housing and Food Services, to Naomi Griffiths, Chair of Senate Committee on Residences, 31 Oct. 1974.

44 Senate, Minutes, 13 Jan. 1975, appendix C: Student brief attached to Report of Senate Committee on University-Residence Relations.

45 *Ottawa Citizen* and *Ottawa Journal*, 23 Jan. 1974. This version of the incident also relies on the *Charlatan*, 25 Jan. 1974.

46 Senate, Minutes, 25 Mar. 1977, appendix B: Second Annual Report of RUMPB.

47 Senate, Minutes, 25 May 1978, appendix: Annual Report of RUMPB.

48 *Charlatan*, 17 Sept. 1971.

49 *Charlatan*, 24 Sept. and 1 Oct. 1971. The Report of the Presidential Advisory Committee on the Status of Women, Dec. 1987, includes a brief historical account of daycare facilities on campus.

50 *Charlatan*, 30 Jan. 1976; Women's Centre files, Minutes of General Meeting, Fall, 1977.

51 *Charlatan*, 22 Oct. 1976.

52 Carleton University Women's Centre, Annual Report, Apr. 1978.

53 *Charlatan*, 26 Nov. 1987; Residence-University Management and Policy Board, Minutes, 12 Feb. 1988; interview with G.F. Goodwin, 11 Jan. 2002.

Acknowledgments

This book began as a study of the development of higher education in Ontario after the Second World War. Time spent at the Provincial Archives of Ontario and the archives of the Council of Ontario Universities gave some insight into the concerns of politicians and senior university administrators, but the story was incomplete because it could say little about the unique concerns of the individual universities and their place in the emerging system. The focus of my research shifted when I decided to begin the story at the periphery, using Carleton University as a case study. The work went slowly, because although I had joined the history department at Carleton in 1964, I had concentrated on my teaching and research and knew little about the rest of the university. I found myself turning regularly to Don McEown for information and advice. He had come to Carleton in 1963 and for more than thirty years was closely involved with the administration of the university; he had also developed a special interest in the early years of the institution. We spent many lunch hours discussing the contributions of individuals or the significance of events, and Don eventually agreed to become co-author. I relied on him to guide me to relevant documents and to debate my theories as I tried to produce a first draft; he then commented on my text and searched out other documents and memoranda which he saw as significant. It was a collaboration which we both enjoyed.

The standard sources for any university history are the minutes of the Board of Governors and of the Senate. These are often dull documents, with the clashes and the confrontations carefully excised. At Carleton they were supplemented by the regular information sheet of the administration, published under titles such as *This Week* and *This Week Times Two* and by the student newspaper the *Carleton* which later became the *Charlatan*. In the early stages of this study two research assistants, Angelika Sauer and Gregory Donaghy, used these sources to produce a narrative of the college years. We are also indebted to Rita Richard, the Special Collections librarian at the MacOdrum Library, and Patti Harper, the university archivist, who have shown a personal interest in the project and have generously searched for documents and illustrations. We would also like to thank Leonard Lackie of the University Archives and Allen Scott of the university's Graphic Services for their assistance in the collection and reproduction of the illustrations.

Unfortunately, the documentary sources were not always adequate. Universities regularly rely on ad hoc committees to study controversial issues and to make policy recommendations, but the files of these committees do not always survive. Carleton is no exception. We sometimes had to rely on the memories of colleagues who were involved in crucial events. Among the people we interviewed were Hugh Armstrong, William Beckel, Claude Bissell, Desmond Bowen, Geoffrey Briggs, Richard Brown, James Downey, Norman Fenn, Peter Findlay, Paul Fox, James Gibson, Hilda Gifford, G.F. Goodwin, Naomi Griffiths, David Golden, Douglas Hartle, Pauline Jewett, Elizabeth Meikle Jones, P.J. King, A.B. Larose, Ross Love, Patrick McGee, Imelda Mulvihill, Bert Nesbitt, Michael Oliver, Dana Rouillard, Donald Rowat, T.J. Scanlon, E.F. Sheffield, Jill Vickers, Dorothy Wardle, and James Wernham. Much of our information, however, came from informal meetings at lunch time in the Faculty Club for which there is no written record. We can only apologize for not giving credit to so many luncheon companions.

We owe a special debt to Mark Phillips and Brian McKillop, who read an earlier version of the manuscript and made constructive suggestions. We are also grateful to Hugh Armstrong and David Farr, who commented on chapters that were of special interest to them. Stuart Adam, Vice-President Academic, encouraged us to complete the manuscript and submit it to McGill-Queen's University Press, which had fallen heir to the Carleton University Press. We were fortunate that Carlotta Lemieux took on the responsibility of editing the manuscript, because her exposure of inconsistencies and her insistence on correct grammar and punctuation have saved us from much embarrassment.

We are also indebted to our wives who allowed the history of Carleton to monopolize our conversation for many years. They will be pleased to see the topic safely between covers.

H. Blair Neatby
Carleton University
May 2002

Index

Page numbers in italics refer to illustrations.